OVER COLD WAR SEAS

OVER COLD WAR SEAS

NATO AND SOVIET MARITIME AIR POWER, 1949–89

MICHAEL NAPIER

OSPREY PUBLISHING
Bloomsbury Publishing Plc
Kemp House, Chawley Park, Cumnor Hill, Oxford OX2 9PH, UK
29 Earlsfort Terrace, Dublin 2, Ireland
1385 Broadway, 5th Floor, New York, NY 10018, USA
E-mail: info@ospreypublishing.com
www.ospreypublishing.com

OSPREY is a trademark of Osprey Publishing Ltd
First published in Great Britain in 2025
© Michael Napier, 2025

Michael Napier has asserted his right under the Copyright, Designs and Patents Act, 1988, to be identified as Author of this work.

For legal purposes the Acknowledgements on p. 320 constitute an extension of this copyright page. All rights reserved. No part of this publication may be: i) reproduced or transmitted in any form, electronic or mechanical, including photocopying, recording or by means of any information storage or retrieval system without prior permission in writing from the publishers; or ii) used or reproduced in any way for the training, development or operation of artificial intelligence (AI) technologies, including generative AI technologies. The rights holders expressly reserve this publication from the text and data mining exception as per Article 4(3) of the Digital Single Market Directive (EU) 2019/790.

A catalogue record for this book is available from the British Library.
ISBN: HB 9781472865526;
eBook 9781472865533;
ePDF 9781472865502;
XML 9781472865519

25 26 27 28 29 10 9 8 7 6 5 4 3 2 1

Originator: Jasper Spencer-Smith
Cover, page design and layout by Stewart Larking
Index by Alan Rutter
Printed by Repro India

FSC MIX Paper FSC® C047271

Osprey Publishing supports the Woodland Trust, the UK's leading woodland conservation charity.

To find out more about our authors and books visit www.ospreypublishing.com. Here you will find extracts, author interviews, details of forthcoming events and the option to sign up for our newsletter.

Image credits:
Pages 2–3: An EKA-3B Skywarrior aircraft is launched from the attack aircraft carrier USS *America* (CV 66), October 1968. (NARA)
Pages 4–5: The Fairey Gannet AEW 3 proved invaluable as an early warning aircraft. (Cooke)

CONTENTS

Introduction		7
CHAPTER 1:	READINESS TO DEFEND OURSELVES – 1949–59	9
CHAPTER 2:	CONTROL OF THE SEAS – 1960–69	67
CHAPTER 3:	THE FLAG OF THE SOVIET NAVY – 1970–79	123
CHAPTER 4:	A COMMON GOAL – 1980–89	177
CHAPTER 5:	THE NEUTRALITY OF A PORT – 1949–89	233
Afterword:	Changing in our Favour	261
Appendix 1:	Abbreviations & Acronyms	290
Appendix 2:	Special Arms Systems	294
Nomenclature of Naval and Maritime Air Units and Systems		
Appendix 3:	A Culture of Innovation and Creativity	300
Complement of the USS *Forrestal* (CV 59) Over Four Decades		
Bibliography		304
Index		311
Acknowledgements		320

INTRODUCTION

'There must be a beginning of any great matter, but the continuing unto the end until it be thoroughly finished yields the true glory.'
Sir Francis Drake, Royal Navy 1587

This book is intended as a companion to *In Cold War Skies*, which records the history of NATO and Soviet land-based air power during the Cold War. Like the previous volume, this book spans the 40 years from the formation of NATO in 1949 to the fall of the Berlin Wall at the end of 1989. This time, the emphasis is on the maritime air power of the period, covering both carrier-borne aircraft and land-based maritime aircraft. I have generally focussed on the activities over the North Atlantic Ocean, and the Norwegian and Mediterranean Seas, rather than the Pacific Ocean, since the efforts of NATO – the North Atlantic Treaty Organisation – were centred on these regions. Specifically, I have not included naval participation in the Korean or Vietnam Wars, which fall outside the scope of this book.

Although this book is chiefly about the aircraft of the period, the subject is closely tied to the evolution of submarines and aircraft carriers during the Cold War. I have therefore included enough detail about these vessels to give context to the development of aircraft, weapons and tactics throughout the period.

In the introduction to *In Cold War Skies* I wrote 'looking back from the comfort of the 21st century, it seems inconceivable that just over 30 years ago the world was never more than a few minutes away from nuclear Armageddon.' Now, only five years later the 'comfort of the 21st century' has been shaken by the Russian war in Ukraine: the security of Europe has been compromised and NATO is on the brink of a new Cold War with a Russia that seeks to revive the 'glory days' of the Soviet Union. Thus, the history of the last Cold War is particularly relevant today. We must not forget the many lessons learned during the four decades that NATO faced the Soviet Union and its allies across the Iron Curtain and in the North Atlantic Ocean.

Michael Napier
Oxfordshire April 2024

OPPOSITE The aircraft carrier USS *Forestal* (CVA 59) In the Atlantic Ocean on 18 September 1962. A-1 Skyraiders, A-3 Skywarriors, A-4 Skyhawks, F-4 Phantoms and F-8 Crusaders can be seen on deck. The evolution of the aircraft complement aboard *Forrestal* during the decades of the Cold War is detailed in Appendix 2. (US Navy)

CHAPTER 1

READINESS TO DEFEND OURSELVES – 1949–59

'That is not to say that we can relax our readiness to defend ourselves. Our armament must be adequate to the needs, but our faith is not primarily in these machines of defense but in ourselves.'

Admiral Chester W. Nimitz, US Navy, 1950.

The end of World War II marked the end of any spirit of co-operation between the Union of Soviet Socialist Republics (USSR) and the western Allies. Perhaps this was inevitable given the ideological gulf between Stalinist communism on one hand and capitalist democracy on the other, but it was also because of the underlying mutual suspicion that each party had aggressive designs on the other. Furthermore, the United States of America (USA) was armed with nuclear weapons whereas the USSR possessed no such arsenal and therefore felt particularly vulnerable to US power. Having lost more than 25 million people killed during the Great Patriotic War (World War II), the Soviet leadership was determined to secure its borders once and for all. Soviet occupation of eastern and central European countries and the establishment of client governments in them also created an effective buffer zone between the West and the territory of the USSR. From the western perspective, the Soviet control of central Europe implied aggressive intentions towards western Europe, so both sides watched each other with suspicion as political and military tension steadily increased.

The tension erupted into a crisis on 1 June 1948 when the western Allies announced the intention to form a new state in West Germany: on

OPPOSITE The Royal Netherlands Navy operated the Hawker Sea Hawk Mk 60 fighter and Grumman TBM-3S and TBM-3W Avenger ASW aircraft from HMNLS *Karel Dooman*, the ex-RN Colossus-class carrier HMS *Venerable*, between 1958 and 1964. (Collection Netherlands Institute of Military History)

ABOVE With a ventrally mounted APS-20 search radar, the TBM-3W Avenger was half of the carrier-borne Anti-Submarine Warfare team. The TBM-3S strike aircraft made up the other half. (US Navy)

23 June, the Soviets responded by closing land access to West Berlin, hoping to discourage the formation of the new state and perhaps in the hope that the western outpost deep within East Germany would capitulate. However, the Soviets had miscalculated the resolve of the western governments who bypassed the blockade by launching a massive airlift that kept the city supplied with food and essentials from 26 June 1948 through to 12 May 1949. The Soviet action also spurred the formation of the North Atlantic Treaty Organization (NATO) the following year. Comprising the original signatories of the 1948 Brussels Treaty – Belgium, Netherlands, Luxembourg, France and the United Kingdom (UK) – along with the USA, Canada, Portugal, Italy, Norway, Denmark and Iceland, NATO was formed as a defensive alliance primarily to protect its members from Soviet expansion into western Europe. Most importantly, NATO was not simply a loose alliance, but an integrated military structure within which the armed forces of each member country were part of a unified command structure.

The formation of NATO on 4 April 1949 emphasized not only the contrast between Western and Eastern ideologies, but also the geographic differences between the two spheres of interest. Whereas the Soviet Union and many of its European satellites were entirely land-based, NATO was, as indicated by its name, centred around a vast tract of sea: the Atlantic

ABOVE The largest single-engine aircraft in the world at the time, this Grumman AF-2S Guardian ASW aircraft is landing on board USS *Badoeng Strait* (CVE 116) on 1 April 1954. The Guardian was intended as a replacement for the TBM Avenger. (US Navy)

Ocean. True, the line of demarcation between the two sides, and the potential battlefield for World War III, lay across mainland Europe, but the NATO forces based there were totally reliant on being reinforced and resupplied from the far side of the ocean.

LEFT Consolidated PB4Y Privateer maritime patrol aircraft, in service with VP-23, flying over Miami Beach, Florida, 4 August 1949. The type was also used extensively for intelligence-gathering missions. (US Navy)

This geographic difference between East and West also influenced the balance of forces on each side. In the late 1940s, the military power of the Soviet Union was concentrated in its huge land armies, while the Soviet Navy of the time comprised only small coastal forces. Conversely, the Atlantic Ocean, so fundamentally important to NATO, was home to the two most powerful navies in the world – the US Navy (USN) and the British Royal Navy (RN). Reflecting the importance of the sea lanes to the alliance, one of the principal NATO commands, the Allied Command Atlantic (ACLANT), was established in 1952, and was responsible for the security of the North Atlantic from the North Pole to the Tropic of Cancer. The post of commander-in-chief (C-in-C) would always be held by a USN admiral with the headquarters located at Norfolk, Virginia. The first Supreme Allied Commander (SACLANT) was Admiral Lynde D. McCormick. In addition to ACLANT, NATO land and sea forces in the Mediterranean came under the control of Allied Forces South (AFSOUTH) which was also commanded by a USN admiral. A subordinate command, Allied Forces Mediterranean (AFMED) was based on Malta with a British commander to control all NATO maritime forces in the Mediterranean. However, the US government declined to place the 6th Fleet under non-US command, and insisted that US naval forces in the Mediterranean came under the command of Strike Force South (STRIKFORSOUTH) that reported directly to the US commander of AFSOUTH (COMAFSOUTH).

Many World War II bomber aircraft were used in early in the Cold War as maritime patrol aircraft, including the Boeing Flying Fortress, which was known as the PB-1W in US Navy service. (US Navy)

Having fought in the Atlantic and the Mediterranean during World War II, the RN and USN still had much experience in theatres where the Soviets had yet to venture. Both navies were well versed both in anti-submarine warfare (ASW) and in aircraft carrier operations. During World War II, aircraft carriers had been used in three roles: firstly, in commanding the sea by neutralizing enemy surface forces, secondly as a strike force to support coastal or amphibious operations and thirdly for ASW. The USN had perfected the first two roles in the Pacific during World War II, where it had fought an enemy that had significant air power but had little submarine strength. As a result, USN doctrine viewed the aircraft carrier primarily as an instrument of power projection and offensive strike. Indeed, the ability of the USN, demonstrated in 1948, to launch nuclear-armed aircraft from its carriers underlined the importance of the type in the nuclear age. The USN also considered that Soviet air power was the most serious threat to NATO in the eastern Atlantic and Mediterranean and that carrier-borne fighters were needed as a counter. Conversely, the RN, in common with the Royal Canadian Navy (RCN), believed that the most important aspect of naval warfare during World War II had been ASW operations against German U-boats the North Atlantic. The British and Canadians therefore saw ASW as being the pre-eminent role for the aircraft carrier.

The Soviet Navy in the Early 1950s

The post-war Soviet Navy, known as the Soviet Maritime Military Fleet (*Sovyetsky Voyenno-Morskoy Flot*), retained its wartime division into four fleets: the Northern Fleet, based at Severomorsk, near Murmansk, the Baltic Fleet based at Kaliningrad, the Black Sea Fleet based at Sevastopol and the Pacific Fleet based at Vladivostok. Despite the impressive number of fleets and its wide geographic dispersal, in 1950 the Soviet Navy had a relatively small number of warships with just one functional battleship and a few cruisers. It did not possess an aircraft carrier, but it did have a significant air arm, the Soviet Naval Aviation (*Aviatsiya Voyenno-Morskogo Flota* – AV-MF), of some 3,000 shore-based aircraft. The navy was essentially a defensive force, covering ports and important coastal installations. In the immediate post-war years, it was envisaged that Soviet naval surface forces would operate within 100 miles of the coast, under air superiority guaranteed by the AV-MF, which would also support the Soviet naval operations with torpedo-strike aircraft. The main threat perceived by the Soviets was an amphibious invasion in either Baltic or Black Sea regions.

ABOVE The Martin P4M Mercator lost out to the Lockheed P2V Neptune as a maritime patrol aircraft and only 19 were built; however, some aircraft were modified to become P4M-1Q electronic intelligence aircraft and served in the role until 1960. (US Navy)

However, the aspiration dating from pre-World War II days for a large ocean-going navy still remained. When Admiral Nikolay G. Kuznetsov returned to be commander-in-chief of the Soviet Navy in 1951, having been removed from office after incurring the displeasure of Stalin four years previously, he initiated a ten-year programme of ship building, with the aim to create such a force. In his vision, the navy was to remain defensive in nature and so the decision was taken not to build aircraft carriers, but Kuznetsov did initiate the construction of a submarine fleet. The Soviets had been impressed with the German wartime U-boat campaign and they considered that a significant submarine force would enable them to interdict the NATO sea lines of communication (SLOC) in the Atlantic, thereby cutting off the European battlefield from transatlantic reinforcements and supplies. Between 1950 and 1957, some 236 Project 613 (Whiskey-class) medium-range submarines were built, as well as 26 Project 611 (Zulu-class) long-range submarines. These torpedo-armed diesel-powered attack boats were intended to interdict the SLOC in the Atlantic, but while the Zulu-class boats could reach into the Atlantic from Murmansk, the Whiskey class could only reach as far as thenorthern waters of the North Sea. Soviet submarines were first detected in the Atlantic Ocean in 1955 (and in the Mediterranean Sea three years later). Subsequently, while the Soviet Navy did represent a very real submarine threat to the NATO SLOC, in the early 1950s, it was not a particularly serious one.

The enlargement of the Soviet Navy also included the re-equipment of its air arm. The 3,000 aircraft that remained in the inventory of the AV-MF by 1950 were mainly short-range types. At that time, most of the attack regiments were still equipped with the Tupolev Tu-2 (Bat) torpedo bomber powered by two piston engines, but these obsolescent types were, from 1951, progressively replaced by Tupolev Tu-14T (Bosun) and Ilyushin Il-28T (Beagle) jet-powered aircraft – the T suffix indicated *Torpedonosets* (torpedo bomber). Both were variants of the tactical bombers that were in service with the Soviet Air Force (*Voenno-Vozdushnye Sily* – VVS) and could be armed with the RAT-52 rocket-propelled torpedo as well as anti-shipping mines, bombs, or other types of torpedoes. In 1951, the Il-28T was first issued to the 943rd Mine Laying and Torpedo Aviation Regiment (*Minno-torpednyy Avia Polk* – MTAP) attached to the Black Sea Fleet and, later in that year, to the 1531st MTAP in the Baltic Fleet. Neither the Tu-14T not the Il-28T had the range to reach far into the Atlantic, but both could cover the eastern Mediterranean, which greatly concerned the commander of the US 6th Fleet. The Il-28T was also deployed to the Northern Fleet in 1953. The modernization of the AV-MF accelerated during the early 1950s as a result of the Korean War, and eventually 22 naval air regiments were re-equipped with jet-powered torpedo bombers.

BELOW The US Navy demonstrated the ability to launch nuclear-armed bombers from the deck of USS *Franklin D. Roosevelt* (CVB 42) in July 1951. The Lockheed P2V Neptune was fitted with JATO rockets to give it sufficient take-off performance. (US Navy)

ABOVE The Martin P5M-2 Marlin flying boat served as an ASW and maritime patrol aircraft from 1954 until 1966. The type operated with a crew of 11 and carried the AS weaponry in a bay located in each elongated engine nacelle. (Jarrett)

RIGHT One of the earliest jet fighters operated by the US Navy was the McDonnell FH-1 Phantom, here at Dow AFB, Bangor, Maine during 1948. The straight-winged fighter, powered by two Westinghouse J30-WE-20 turbojets, entered service in 1947 but was declared to be obsolete in 1949. (US Navy)

At the same time, Soviet naval fighter regiments were being re-equipped with Mikoyan MiG-15 (Fagot) and by the early 1950s nearly half of the naval fighter squadrons were equipped with jet fighters. Some AV-MF regiments also saw action during the Korean War so, just like the USN, the AV-MF could claim to be blooded in jet combat over Korea. For long-range reconnaissance, the AV-MF used both the Tupolev Tu-4 (Bull), a reverse-engineered copy of the Boeing B-29 Superfortress, and the Consolidated PBY Catalina. The latter were an amalgamation of aircraft: some had been supplied by the US under the Lend-Lease Program during World War II whereas others were built under a license (procured in late 1930) in the USSR. In Soviet service the type was known as the 'Transport Seaplane' (*Gidrosamolet transportnii* – GST). From 1951, the aging Catalina was replaced by the Beriev Be-6 (Madge) flying boat. Although the Be-6 had a similar patrol range to its predecessor, it had a cruising speed of 280mph, nearly three times that of the GST, and a better load capacity that enabled it to be armed with two torpedoes. Production ended in 1957 after 123 had been delivered.

US Maritime Aviation in the Early 1950s

The USN of the late 1940s was considerably smaller than it had been at the end of the war, but it still represented a powerful maritime force. It was divided between the 2nd Fleet in the Atlantic Ocean, the 6th Fleet in the Mediterranean Sea and the 7th Fleet in the Pacific Ocean. During World War II, the USN had been the largest operator of aircraft carriers, but from a total of over 100 in 1945, just seven attack carriers plus eight smaller carriers remained on its strength by 1950. The bulk of those forces was based in the Atlantic and Mediterranean: the three Midway-class carriers USS *Midway* (CVB 41), USS *Franklin D. Roosevelt* (CVB 42) and USS *Coral Sea* (CVB 43) were supplemented by the Essex-class USS *Leyte* (CV 32), as well as four light carriers and two escort carriers.

BELOW A Grumman F9F-2 Panther jet fighter on the deck edge elevator of USS *Franklin D. Roosevelt* (CVB-42), circa 1950. The Panther, which saw combat during the Korean War, was used extensively by the US Navy and US Marine Corps and some 437 examples were built. (NARA)

At any time, at least one of the four attack carriers was assigned to the 6th Fleet in the Mediterranean, with the other three ships remaining under control of the 2nd Fleet in the Atlantic. In the Pacific, just three Essex-class carriers, USS *Boxer* (CV 21), USS *Valley Forge* (CV 45) and USS *Philippine Sea* (CV 47), plus two escort carriers were allocated to the 7th Fleet. However, a further four Essex-class ships, USS *Essex* (CV 9), USS *Kearsarge* (CV 33), USS *Oriskany* (CV 34) and USS *Wasp* (CV 18) were undergoing modernization and were due to be delivered back to the navy in the mid-1950s. The remaining wartime carriers were considered to be surplus to requirements and were 'mothballed', but they were still held in reserve and could be recommissioned in an emergency.

Just such an event occurred on 25 June 1950 when the North Korean army invaded South Korea, thereby unintentionally initiating massive rearmament programme in the US. In particular, the four aircraft carriers undergoing modernization were rapidly returned to service: USS *Wasp* was deployed to reinforce the Atlantic Fleet, while USS *Essex*, USS *Kearsarge* and USS *Oriskany* were dispatched to Korean waters along with four 'mothballed' Essex-class carriers: USS *Bon Homme Richard* (CV 31), USS *Antietam* (CV 36), USS *Princeton* (CV 7) and USS *Lake Champlain* (CV 39).

Like the F9F Panther, the McDonnell F2H-3 Banshee flew in combat during the Korean War. Here a pair of Banshees from VF-31 are seen over the Mediterranean Sea on 26 January 1954, at a time when the US Navy colour scheme was changing from blue to grey. (US Navy)

Aircraft carriers continued to be brought out of reserve and by 1955 there were 22 Essex-class ships in service with the USN, along with 17 escort carriers. These latter ships were employed mainly in the ASW role and operated the Grumman TBM Avenger. Two variants of the type were used for anti-submarine missions: a TBM-3W search aircraft, fitted with an APS-20 radar in a ventral housing, and a TBM-3S strike aircraft armed with depth bombs and torpedoes. The aircraft operated in close cooperation as a pair to form a hunter-killer team. The same tactical concept also influenced the design of the Grumman AF Guardian that was intended to replace the ASW Avenger. The Guardian entered service in 1950 and was, at that time, the largest single-engine aircraft in the world. It had a 60ft wingspan and a gross weight of 25,500lb some 4,480lb heavier than the Avenger. Like its predecessor, the Guardian was designed to operate as a hunter-killer pair known to navy personnel as 'Guppy' and 'Scrapper'. The AF-2W was fitted with an APS-20 search radar, and the AF-2S which was armed with bombs, rockets and homing torpedoes, but also had a wing pod-mounted APS-30 radar and a searchlight. An updated variant, the AF-3S, also carried a magnetic anomaly detector (MAD), a sensor that could indicate the presence of a submerged submarine by detecting small disturbances in the earth's magnetic field that it made as it passed by. Unfortunately, the Guardian had very poor handling characteristics, especially at the low speed required for the approach and subsequent landing on an aircraft carrier. In service the aircraft suffered from a high accident rate and as a consequence it never completely replaced the Avenger. The other element of the ASW team, from an aviation perspective, was the land-based patrol aircraft. In 1950, the USN was in the process of standardizing the types that it used in this role. The Consolidated PB4Y-2 Privateer was a development of the wartime PB4Y-1 Liberator, which had proved so effective against German U-boats. The Privateer had a longer fuselage than the Liberator and was also distinguishable from its predecessor by a single tailfin. As well as ASW patrols, Privateers were used for intelligence-gathering flights around the periphery of the USSR. During one such mission on 8 April 1950, a Privateer from the patrol squadron VP-26 was shot down by Soviet fighters over the Baltic Sea, just off Liepaja, Latvia. Apart from anti-submarine weapons, the Privateer could also be armed with the ASM-N-2 Bat, a 1,000lb radar homing glide bomb, to attack surface targets. Surplus examples of another World War II air force bomber, the Boeing B-17 Fortress, were converted to become PB-1s by the fitting of an APS-20 search radar under the fuselage. The Fortress and Privateer were phased out of service in the early 1950s, being replaced by the Martin P4M Mercator and the Lockheed P2V Neptune. In fact, only

ABOVE Only 151 Martin AM-1 Mauler attack aircraft were built, with production terminated when the US Navy chose to standardize with the AD Skyraider instead. This photograph, taken on 31 January 1949, illustrates the impressive weapon load of the Mauler. (NARA)

19 Mercators were built, and the type was only used by VP-21 based at Naval Air Station (NAS) Patuxent River in Maryland: it was withdrawn from the ASW role in 1952, when the USN decided to standardize on just one type and chose the Neptune, but a small number of P4M-1Q electronic intelligence (ELINT) gathering aircraft remained in service into the 1960s. The mainstay of the patrol squadrons in the 1950s, the Neptune was equipped with a wide range of sensors and could carry two torpedoes or 12 depth charges. It mounted a ventral APS-20 search radar and the P2V-5 also carried a tail-mounted AN/ASQ-8 MAD gear. The Neptune was operated by patrol squadrons based along the east and west coasts of North America, stretching as far as north Adak on the western extremity of the Aleutian Islands and Argentia in Newfoundland. Further afield there were also USN air bases on Guam and Midway Atoll in the Pacific and Keflavik in Iceland and Lajes on the Azores in the Atlantic.

US naval aircraft also had a presence in Bermuda, which was a major base for flying boats. These included the Martin PBM Mariner and Martin P5M Marlin, both of which were employed in the ASW role. Originally a pre-war design, the Mariner remained in USN service until 1956, but the Marlin was a more modern design. Entering service with VP-44 in 1952 the Marlin continued to equip front line patrol squadrons until the mid-1960s. The Marlin was equipped with an APS-80 search radar mounted in the nose, as well as the AN/ASQ-8 MAD sensor; its weapon load of torpedoes or depth bombs was carried in the engine nacelles.

While the escort carriers were configured for ASW operations, the attack carriers were equipped to launch fighter and surface attack missions. The typical complement of aircraft for an Essex-class carrier in the early 1950s comprised two jet fighter squadrons (each of 16 aircraft), two propeller-driven attack squadrons (again each of 16 aircraft) and smaller numbers of night fighter, night attack, photo reconnaissance and early warning aircraft, plus at least one helicopter, making a total of some 80 aircraft. The USN had pioneered the use of the jet fighter onboard carriers with the McDonnell FH Phantom I and Vought F6U Pirate in the late 1940s and the decision had been made to equip all fleet fighter squadrons with jet aircraft. By 1950 the most numerous type was the Grumman F9F Panther. This straight-winged, single-seat, single-engine fighter saw action during the Korean War, where it accounted for MiG-15s in combat and was also employed as a fighter-bomber. A contemporary type was the McDonnell F2H Banshee, a development of the twin-engine FH Phantom, which like the Panther was a straight-winged aircraft. The Banshee was also developed into a night fighter, the F2H-2N with a nose-mounted air intercept radar, and a photo-recce variant, the F2H-2P. A carrier air wing would typically include at least two F2H-2P Banshees for tactical photo-reconnaissance. Although both the Panther and Banshee performed well in the Korean conflict, it was clear that straight-

BELOW The long range and excellent load carrying capability of the Douglas AD Skyraider assured that it would remain in front-line service into the early 1970s. Here, an AD-5 taxies forward after landing on USS *Intrepid* (CVA 11), 20 April 1956. (US Navy)

RIGHT Vought F4U-5 Corsairs from USS *Tarawa* (CV 40) fly in formation over the Mediterranean on 15 December 1952. The World War II-vintage Corsair was still in wide service with both the US Navy and US Marine Corps in the early 1950s. (US Navy)

winged designs had reached the limits of their performance and that future high-performance fighters would need to have a swept wing. Nevertheless, both the types remained in front line service until the end of the decade. Another straight-winged type, the Douglas F3D-2 Skyknight, entered service in 1950; the Skyknight was designed from the outset as a carrier-borne night fighter, whereas most previous night fighters had been conversions from established day fighter types. A large aeroplane, the Skyknight was known unofficially as 'Willie the Whale' thanks to its bulbous profile. The US Marine Corps (USMC) unit VMF(N)-513 enjoyed operational success with the Skyknight over Korea, scoring a number of kills, and the type equipped twelve USN and nine USMC night/all-weather fighter squadrons.

Although the fighter arm of the carrier air wing was equipped with jet-powered aircraft, the attack squadrons still flew propeller-driven aircraft, reflecting the better load carrying capacity and range of the contemporary propeller aircraft. In 1950 the main attack aircraft were the Martin AM Mauler and the Douglas AD Skyraider. Both aircraft were similar in size, configuration and performance, but once again, just as the Martin-built Mercator had given way to the Neptune, so the Martin-built Mauler was retired early in favour of the Skyraider for reasons of standardisation. Only 151 Maulers were built, and they were transferred to the reserve in 1950. However, the Skyraider remained in service with the USN into the early 1970s, thanks to the flexibility of its design and its prodigious load carrying capability. During its service, the Skyraider saw extensive action in both Korea and Vietnam. Apart from the attack variants of the Skyraider which could carry a war load of some 8,000lbs, there were also night attack variants (such as the AD-4N), electronic counter measures (ECM) variants (including the AD-2Q) and a three-seat early warning variant (the AD-4W) with a ventral AN/APS-20 search radar. In addition to an attack squadron of AD Skyraiders, each aircraft carrier would also have four AD-4N night attack and four AD-4W early warning aircraft on board. The other mainstay of attack squadrons in 1950 was the World War II vintage Vought F4U Corsair, which gave valuable service during the Korean War. A carrier air wing of the day would typically contain one Corsair fighter-bomber squadron plus four F4U-5N night fighter variants. Corsairs were also operated in Korea by the USMC, along with AD Skyraiders and F9F Panthers; USMC squadrons were often deployed onto both attack and escort carriers to support amphibious tasks. The Corsair was withdrawn from front-line service immediately after the Korean War and the squadrons re-equipped with jet aircraft.

BELOW Designed originally as a carrier-borne nuclear bomber, the North American AJ Savage was later used as an air-to-air refuelling (AAR) tanker. (US Navy)

In 1948, 12 P2V-3C Neptunes had been modified to carry the Mark 1 nuclear bomb, the same weapon as the one that had been dropped on Hiroshima in 1945. The nuclear-armed Neptune was intended to be launched from the Midway-class carriers and because of their size would use Jet Assisted Take Off (JATO) rockets, rather than a catapult, to accelerate them to flying speed. These aircraft were followed from 1951 by the North American AJ Savage strike bomber, which had been designed from the outset as a carrier-borne nuclear strike aircraft. With a 75-ft wingspan the Savage was a little smaller than the Neptune but was nevertheless a comparatively large aeroplane for carrier operations. It was powered by two Pratt & Whitney R-2800-44W radial engines but was also fitted with an Allison J333-A-19 turbojet in the tail to supplement the piston engines during take-off and landing. The USN operated some 140 of these aircraft in the Atlantic and Mediterranean Fleets, and in their later years they were used as air-to-air refuelling (AAR) tanker aircraft. The type was flown by VC-7, VC-8 and VC-9 and was eventually retired from active duty in 1960.

The first swept-wing fighter to reach the USN was the Grumman F9F-6 Cougar, which entered service in 1952. The Cougar, as its designation suggested, was derived from the Panther and essentially it was a Panther fuselage fitted with a swept wing. It had a more powerful engine than the Panther and its maximum speed, at 690mph, was over 100mph faster than that of the Panther. While the swept wing enabled high-speed flight, the practicalities of flying from an aircraft carrier also demanded good handling qualities at the opposite end of the speed scale for the approach and landing phase. In the case of the Cougar, it was equipped with leading edge slots and enlarged tailing edge flaps, as well as spoilers instead of ailerons, in order to ensure its suitability for ship-borne operations. The Cougar was designed and employed as a day fighter, but there was also an attack variant, the F9F-8B, which was optimized for the air-to-surface role. Two years after the Cougar entered service it was joined by the North American FJ-2 and FJ-3 Fury. A development of the straight wing FJ Fury, which had led to the development of the swept wing F-86 Sabre, the

The Grumman F9F-8 Cougar was the first swept-wing fighter aircraft to be operated by the US Navy. The type utilized a slightly modified Panther fuselage, but was fitted with the more powerful Pratt & Whitney J-48-P-8 engine. This aircraft from VF-61 is positioned on the port catapult of USS *Intrepid* (CVA 11), 20 April 1956. (US Navy)

Two Vought F7U-3M Cutlass fighters of VA-86 are readied for launch from USS *Forrestal* (CVA 59) in March 1956. The unconventional Cutlass suffered a high accident rate and was withdrawn from service in the late 1950s. (US Navy)

later Fury squared the circle by being a navalized F-86 Sabre. The FJ-2 was used exclusively by the USMC, but it suffered from problems with its General Electric J47 engine. These problems were solved in the FJ-3 variant of the Fury by fitting the Curtiss-Wright J65, a license-built version of the British Armstrong-Siddeley Sapphire engine, which proved to be more reliable (and powerful). In the FJ-3 Fury, the USN had an aeroplane which could outperform even the F-86. The first unit to be equipped with the FJ-3 Fury was VF-173, based at Jacksonville, Florida and the type eventually equipped 19 USN and four USMC squadrons. The Fury, which continued in front-line service until 1962, was one of the first types to be armed with the Philco AAM-N-7 Sidewinder Infrared seeking Air-to-Air Missile (AAM). Another, rather more unconventionally configured, type which appeared on the inventory in 1954 was the Vought F7U-3 Cutlass. Based on a World War II German tailless design, the twin-engined Cutlass featured swept wings of constant chord with vertical fins halfway along the wings. This ingenious design gave it an impressive performance, including a roll rate of 570 degrees per second, but the type was not a success. The Westinghouse J46-WE-8A engines and the hydraulic system proved very unreliable, and the nose gear was prone to collapsing. In the words of navy test pilot (and later astronaut) Wally Schirra, 'the Cutlass was an accident waiting to happen.' Indeed, the Cutlass suffered from an accident loss rate of 25 per cent, the highest rate amongst USN fighters. Nevertheless, the Cutlass equipped some 13 squadrons before it was withdrawn in 1957.

One perennial problem with aircraft carrier operations was that of managing deck space. If aircraft were to be launched, then the front half of the deck had to be cleared and if aircraft were to be recovered, the rear half of the deck had to be clear of parked aircraft. Thus, it was not practical to carry out simultaneous launching and recovery operations. As a result, aircraft carriers tended to carry out a mass launch of all aircraft, followed by a mass recovery, but this was not tactically efficient or flexible. As is often the case, British ingenuity provided a key to the solution, but American practicality actually solved the problem. The RN had experimented with an angled recovery area, so that landing aircraft did not impinge on launching or parking in the front part of the flight deck. The USN took up this idea and USS *Antietam* (CV 36) was modified in 1952 to become the first aircraft carrier with an angled flight deck. The remaining carriers in the USN were subsequently re-fitted to this configuration which became the standard deck layout for aircraft carriers.

British Maritime Aviation in the Early 1950s

Like the USN, the RN of 1950 was a shadow of its wartime self, but it still consisted of three major commands: the Home Fleet, the Mediterranean Fleet and the Far East Squadron. The prime task of the Home Fleet during wartime was to maintain and defend the North Atlantic SLOC. Given the paucity of Soviet surface ships, it was realized that the threat to the sea lanes in the North Atlantic would most probably come from submarines and ASW was therefore considered to be the most important discipline. In the debate on the Naval Estimates in 1950, the Hon James Callaghan, Parliamentary and Financial Secretary to the Admiralty, stated: 'the highest priority is being given to developing anti-submarine weapons for use by ships and by aircraft… naval aviation researches are at the moment being largely brought to bear on a probable submarine threat'.

In the early 1950s, the RN found itself stretched meeting British worldwide post-war commitments with just six aircraft carriers, for despite its wartime role within NATO, the peacetime priority of RN aircraft carriers was in supporting British interests in the colonies east of Suez. Two Illustrious-class attack carriers were in service, HMS *Illustrious* (R87) and HMS *Indomitable* (R92), with two more, HMS *Implacable* (R86) and HMS *Victorious* (R38) undergoing refit. These larger carriers were supplemented by four smaller Colossus-class light carriers, HMS *Glory* (R62), HMS *Ocean* (R68), HMS *Theseus* (R64)

TOP RIGHT The first British naval jet fighter, the Supermarine Attacker, equipped four squadrons of the Fleet Air Arm between 1951 and 1954, including 800 NAS, seen here aboard HMS *Eagle*. (Jarrett)

BOTTOM RIGHT The optical deck landing system was invented by Commander Nicholas Goodhart of the Royal Navy in 1951 and first installed on the USS *Bennington* (CV 20) two years later. Until then, pilots were guided by the Landing Signal Officer with flags – as seen here – with a Hawker Sea Fury. (US Navy)

ABOVE Perhaps the ultimate single-seat propellor driven fighter aircraft, the Bristol Centaurus-powered Hawker Sea Fury flew combat missions during the Korean War and remained in FAA front-line service until 1954. The type was also flown by the RCN and Dutch navy. (Jarrett)

and HMS *Triumph* (R16), which all saw action during the Korean War. In addition to the ships already in service, two large new carriers were under construction, the first of which, the attack carrier HMS *Eagle* (R05), joined the fleet in 1952. A fifth Colossus-class carrier, HMS *Vengeance* (R71), was also in service until she was transferred to the Royal Australian Navy (RAN) as HMAS *Melbourne* in 1952. While a handful of other former aircraft carriers were still in service at the time, they had been modified to become maintenance vessels or troop carriers and were not available for Fleet Air Arm (FAA) use.

Unlike the USN, the British had been slow to capitalize on the naval application of jet aircraft. The first type used by the FAA, the Supermarine Attacker, entered squadron service in 1951, two years after the USN had transferred its FH Phantom I to the reserve. Like the Phantom, the Attacker had a relatively short front-line career, being phased out of service in 1954. So, instead of jet aircraft, RN aircraft carriers of the early 1950s were mainly equipped with a range of propeller-driven types: the Supermarine Seafire and Hawker Sea Fury were the air-defence fighters while the Fairey Firefly was the mainstay of on-board ASW operations. In fact, all three aircraft types saw action during the Korean

The Fairey Firefly AS6 was a dedicated ASW aircraft. The type was powered by a Rolls Royce Griffon 74 engine and carried the AN/APS-4 air-to-surface vessel (ASV) radar in underwing pods. Cannon armament was not fitted to allow ASW equipment and weaponry to be carried. (Crown Copyright)

ABOVE Just two naval air squadrons were equipped with the uninspiring Blackburn Firebrand torpedo strike fighter. This is a Firebrand TF4, of which 103 were built. (Jarrett)

War during which they were used as fighter-bombers supporting ground troops with rockets or bombs. The FAA acquitted itself well during the Korean War, but the conflict showed that the British aircraft were relatively short ranged in comparison to contemporary USN types. In addition to the Seafire, Sea Fury and Firefly, the FAA operated a smaller number of the Blackburn Firebrand TF4, an unimpressive strike fighter that was poorly suited to carrier operations, and the de Havilland Sea Hornet NF21, a rather more successful twin-engine night fighter. The Firebrand had been described by naval test pilot Capt Eric Brown RN as 'a disaster as a deck-landing aircraft' but it was operated successfully as a carrier-borne torpedo strike aircraft by 813 Naval Air Squadron (NAS) and 827 NAS until it was replaced by the Westland Wyvern in 1953. In contrast to his comment on the Firebrand, Brown was considerably more complimentary to the de Havilland Sea Hornet F20 which had good performance and pleasant handling qualities. Like the single-seat day fighter variant of the Sea Hornet, the two-crew NF21 night fighter equipped just one front-line unit, flying from HMS *Vengeance*, HMS *Indomitable* and HMS *Eagle* until it was superseded by the de Havilland Sea Venom in 1954. From 1951, the FAA also operated some 50 AD-4W Skyraider (known as the Skyraider AEW1), provided by the US under the Mutual Defense Assistance Program (MDAP), in the airborne early warning (AEW) role.

British carriers were smaller than those of the USN ships, so their complement of aircraft was correspondingly smaller; furthermore, the FAA squadrons were around half the size of similar USN units. In the early 1950s an Illustrious-class carrier might typically carry two Attacker squadrons, two Firefly squadrons, one Firebrand squadron, a Sea Hornet squadron; a flight (half squadron) of Skyraider AEW 1 and a Westland Dragonfly helicopter completed the air wing of some 50 aircraft. The smaller Colossus-class ships carried approximately half that number of aeroplanes.

A major re-equipment programme in 1953 introduced a more modern inventory of aircraft, including the next generation of jet fighters. The year saw the first deployments of the single-seat Hawker Sea Hawk day fighter and the two-seat de Havilland Sea Venom all-weather fighter. Both types were also used in the surface attack role. In the same year, 813 NAS traded its Firebrands for the Westland Wyvern turbo-prop strike fighter. Although all three of these new aircraft types represented a large step forward for the FAA, all of them had, to an extent, been overtaken by technology: the Sea Hawk and Sea Venom were both straight-wing types, which were introduced a year after the USN had already started swept wing operations with the Cougar, while the Armstrong-Siddeley Python turbo-prop engine used in the Wyvern proved to be overcomplicated and offered no improvement on other forms of propulsion. Nevertheless, all three types served the FAA successfully through the 1950s and all were involved in combat operations during the Suez Crisis of 1956. The Sea Hawk proved to be a capable ground-attack fighter and was also exported to NATO partners the Netherlands and West Germany, as well as to India. Progressive replacement of the Sea Hawk with the Supermarine Scimitar began in 1958, but the Sea Hawk,

BELOW Cpt Eric 'Winkle' Brown wrote: 'for sheer exhilarating flying enjoyment, no aircraft has ever made a deeper impression on me than did this outstanding filly from the de Havilland stable, the Sea Hornet.' The type was built in two versions – the F20 day fighter (shown) and the NF21 night fighter. (Crown Copyright)

RIGHT When the Douglas Skyraider AEW1 was withdrawn in 1960, it was the last piston-engine powered aircraft to be operated by the FAA in front-line service. Some 45 of the AD-4W were supplied to the FAA in 1951. (Crown Copyright)

BELOW The two-seat de Havilland Sea Venom replaced the Sea Hornet as a carrier-borne all-weather fighter from 1954, although the type was successfully used in the ground-attack role during the Suez Crisis of 1956. (Crown Copyright)

which at its height had equipped 12 front-line squadrons, remained in service until 1960. The Sea Venom FAW22 was also effective in the ground-attack role, although it was designated as an all-weather fighter, for which role it was equipped with a Westinghouse AI 21 radar. From 1958 the type, which equipped eight squadrons, was armed with the de Havilland Firestreak infra-red seeking air-to-air missile (AAM). After overcoming unfortunate problems with the engine fuel feed which occasionally resulted in engine flameout during catapult launches, the Wyvern also provided solid service to four front-line squadrons until it was withdrawn in 1958. Meanwhile the ASW role remained firmly the responsibility of propeller-powered aircraft and in 1953, the US supplied some 180 TBM-3E Avenger (Avenger AS4 in FAA service) to the RN under the MDAP for carrier-based ASW operations.

Unlike the US where maritime patrol aircraft were the responsibility of the USN, in the UK the 'maritime reconnaissance' role was undertaken by Coastal Command of the Royal Air Force (RAF). Like the USN, however, the RAF retained flying boats in service and the Short Sunderland equipped two UK-based squadrons up until 1957. The main type used by RAF Coastal Command was the Avro Lancaster GR3, which like the Boeing PB-1 Fortress was a development of the wartime heavy bomber fitted with an air-to-surface vessel (ASV) radar. From 1951, the Lancaster was progressively replaced by the Avro Shackleton, a development of the Avro Lincoln, which had been designed from the beginning as a maritime patrol aircraft (MPA). Equipped with an ASV Mk13 search radar as well as electronic surveillance systems, and with a range of some 3,500 miles, the Shackleton proved to be a very capable long-range MPA. However, there were delays in the production of the aircraft and in the interim a number of Lockheed P2V-5 Neptunes were supplied to the RAF under the MDAP between 1952 and 1957, until sufficient Shackletons had been delivered.

Canadian and European Maritime Aviation in the Early 1950s

In the same way that the British allocated the maritime mission to the RAF, the Canadians allocated it to the Royal Canadian Air Force (RCAF) Maritime Group. And in similar vein to the RAF, the RCAF operated the Avro Lancaster in this role: three squadrons of Lancasters were formed between 1951 and 1952, with two based at Greenwood, Nova Scotia covering the Atlantic area and one at Comox, British

RIGHT A formation of Hawker Sea Hawk FGA4 fighters of 898 NAS, one of 12 front-line units to operate the type. The Sea Hawk was one of the most successful British naval designs. (Jarrett)

BELOW With its distinctive Armstrong Siddeley Python turbo-prop engine, the Westland Wyvern S4 was an innovative and imaginative design, but it was already obsolete by the time it entered service in 1953, and subsequently withdrawn in 1958. (Jarrett)

ABOVE To bolster British ASW capabilities until the arrival of the Fairey Gannet AS 1 entered service, the FAA received 100 US-built Grumman TBM-3E Avengers in 1953. In service the type was known as the Avenger AS4 and AS5. (Crown Copyright)

Columbia covering the Pacific. Reflecting the increasing importance of ASW as the decade progressed, the Maritime Group was renamed Maritime Air Command in 1953.

In 1948 the RCN had traded the British-built HMCS *Warrior* light carrier for another British-built ship, the HMCS *Magnificent* (CVL 21), which carried a two-squadron air group, made up of one squadron each of the Hawker Sea Fury and Grumman TBM-3E Avenger. The Avengers were configured for ASW and included both MAD equipment and sonobuoy systems. In 1951 the RCN squadrons were renumbered and a year later their titles were altered from the British system to align with USN convention. As a result, 825 Sqn and 826 Sqn operating the Avenger and 803 Sqn and 883 Sqn operating the Sea Fury became VF 880, VF 881, VF 870 and VF 871 respectively. The HMCS *Magnificent* and her aircraft were deployed exclusively in the North Atlantic.

The post-World War II period also saw the re-emergence of the French and Netherlands navies. From the outset, the re-formed Royal Netherlands Navy (*Koninklijke Marine*) concentrated primarily on ASW. It operated an aircraft carrier, the HMNLS *Karel Dooman* (R 81), which was a Colossus-class ship that had formerly been the wartime British carrier HMS *Venerable*. Until 1955 the Royal Netherlands Navy Air Service (*Marine Luchtvaart Dienst* – MLD) flew the Hawker Sea Fury fighter and Fairey Firefly AS4 ASW aircraft from the carrier. For the maritime patrol mission, the US provided 18 Lockheed PV-2 Harpoon to the Netherlands under the MDAP, and these were operated by 320 Sqn at Valkenburg between 1951 and 1955.

If the Dutch were concentrating on ASW in the North Sea and the Atlantic, the focus of French efforts was less obvious. Maritime patrols over the Atlantic and Mediterranean were carried out by the French naval air service (*Aéronavale*) flying the Avro Lancaster. The 10th Naval Air Squadron (*Flottille* 10.F) based at Lann-Bihoué (Lorient), Brittany, was the main Lancaster operator in France covering the Atlantic Ocean, while other units based in Morocco and Algeria were responsible for the Mediterranean area. However, the Consolidated PB4Y-2 Privateer and Lockheed P2V-6 Neptune which were issued to *Aéronavale* in the 1950s were primarily used in the colonial conflicts in Indochina and North Africa. Similarly, the two aircraft carriers *Arromanches* (R95 – formerly HMS *Colossus*) and *La Fayette* (R96 – formerly USS *Langley*) were mainly employed in the Far East. In 1953 they were joined by a third carrier, *Bois de Belleau* (R97 – formerly USS *Belleau Wood*). During this period, the French carriers were equipped with Grumman F6F Hellcat and Curtiss SB2C Helldiver.

In the Baltic region, the Royal Danish Air Force (*Flyvevåbnet* – RDAF) operated a single maritime reconnaissance squadron, 721 Squadron (*Eskadrille* – Esk) which was equipped with the Consolidated PBY-5 Catalina. Further north and despite its proximity to the home port of the Soviet Northern Fleet, little priority was given to maritime aircraft by the Royal Norwegian Air Force (*Luftforsvaret* – RNoAF), and the only maritime patrol unit 333 Squadron (*Skvadron* – Skv) was also equipped with the PBY-5 Catalina flying boat. The unit was based at Sola, near Stavanger in south-western Norway, and flew the Catalina throughout the 1950s.

BELOW Another US aircraft supplied as an interim measure was the Lockheed Neptune P2V-5, which served as the Neptune MR1 in four squadrons of RAF Coastal Command until the arrival of the Avro Shackleton. (US Navy)

The Italian Air Force (*Aeronautica Militare* – ItAF) acquired Douglas SB2C-5 Helldiver in 1950 for the ASW role, which were operated by the 86th Anti-Submarine Squadron (86° *Gruppo Antisom*) at Grottaglie in southern Italy. Two years later, the Italian Navy air arm (*Aviazione Navale*) procured two more Helldivers, but since only the air force was permitted to operate fixed wing aircraft, these were quickly taken over by the ItAF. By this time a second squadron, 87° *Gruppo Antisom*, based at Catania in Sicily had been formed. From 1953 the Helldivers were replaced by the Lockheed PV-2 Harpoon. Another PV-2 Harpoon operator was 61 Sqn (*Escuadra* 61) of the Portuguese Air Force (*Força Aérea Portuguesa* – FAP) which was based at Montijo and patrolled the Iberian Atlantic.

NATO Exercises

From 1952, NATO began a series of large-scale exercises to enable the components of ACLANT to practise working together. The first such manoeuvres, Exercise *Mainbrace*, took place over ten days in September 1952 to 'test the forces of the Supreme Allied Commander-in-Chief, Atlantic, in co-operation with the forces of the Supreme Allied Commander, Europe, in defence of the northern flank of the North Atlantic Treaty Organization area.' It included 220 ships from nine NATO members and also New Zealand. The British carriers HMS *Eagle*,

BELOW A Grumman TBM-E3 Avenger AS3 of the RCN in flight during 1954. Like the RN, the RCN used these aircraft for carrier-borne ASW duties. (Library & Archives of Canada)

HMS *Illustrious* and HMS *Theseus* participated, as well as HMCS *Magnificent* and three US carriers, USS *Midway*, USS *Franklin D. Roosevelt* and USS *Wasp*. A joint statement from both SACLANT and SACEUR stated afterwards: '*Mainbrace* not only offered an outstanding opportunity for international cooperation but provided a testing ground for tactical and strategic coordination between the two NATO commands. A great number of lessons will evolve as we continue the evaluation of the exercise. These lessons will serve to better our means of cooperation.'

In September the following year, SACLANT held Exercise *Mariner*, the largest naval exercise ever held. Once again, the maritime forces of nine NATO members participated, including 300 ships and some 1,000 aircraft. On the afternoon of 23 September, the weather unexpectedly closed in on the carriers USS *Bennington*, USS *Wasp* and HMCS *Magnificent* and, shrouded in thick fog, they were unable to recover the 52 aircraft that had been launched earlier. Commodore Herbert S. Rayner, commanding the HMCS *Magnificent*, took up the story:

Without warning a blanket of fog rolled in. The aircraft were recalled at 14:40hrs but only ten managed to land. Repeated attempts were made to talk down more planes using radar and radio but the pilots could not get low enough to see the decks. We could hear the unseen approaches through the solid wall of fog. The USS *Iowa* and cruisers were ordered well astern of the carriers to eliminate the hazards of masts and high structures for the aviators… Then came a call from the US submarine, USS *Redfin* (SS 272), ten miles to the west. *Redfin* said the ceiling near her was 100ft with two miles visibility. The carriers could not reach the area by dark but the aircraft could so we decided to head for *Redfin* where the pilots could ditch in a group near the

BELOW The Avro Lancaster equipped three squadrons of the RCAF Maritime Group from the early 1950s. The final operational mission flown by an RCAF Lancaster was during the Cuban missile crisis in 1962. (Canada Department of National Defence)

LEFT The Royal Netherlands Navy Air Service MLD operated 18 Lockheed PV-2 Harpoons in the anti-submarine role during the first half of the 1950s. This Harpoon is seen at Valkenburg in 1953. (Netherlands Institute of Military History)

submarine. Just as darkness approached, there was a miracle! That is the only word for it. The fog ahead began to thin and lift a bit. We began to make out other ships. The planes were recalled and came down one by one on which ever carrier was most convenient. At 18:20hrs it was dark, and ten planes were still in the air even though their estimated fuel time had passed. But they all got down.

The size of NATO naval forces did not increase during 1953, but large-scale air-sea exercises like *Mainbrace* and *Mariner* ensured that the forces declared to SACLANT, including the air components, were sufficiently trained to be able to work together seamlessly.

BELOW Under the auspices of the Western Union (a pre-NATO alliance), 54 ex-RAF Avro Lancaster B1 and B7 aircraft were modified for the long-range maritime reconnaissance and anti-submarine roles, and supplied to the *Aéronavale* in 1951. (Jarrett)

ABOVE During the 1950s, the Royal Danish Air Force (RDAF) operated eight Consolidated PBY-5A Catalina for coastal reconnaissance around the Baltic Sea. The aircraft were also used as radio relays in support of low-level missions flown by tactical fighters. (RDAF)

Soviet Maritime Aviation in the Mid–Late 1950s

The regime change in the Soviet Union after the death of Soviet leader Josef Stalin in March 1953 was the catalyst for another change in direction for the Soviet Navy. The entry into service of the North American AJ Savage nuclear strike aircraft had made NATO aircraft carriers a serious threat to the Soviet Union, and the Soviets realized that such a threat would need to be neutralized much further out from the coast than they had previously planned. The best tools with which to perform this new task would be submarines and long-range aircraft. Admiral Kuznetsov was sacked as the head of the navy and the new approach to be taken by the Soviet Navy was spelled out by Nikita S. Khrushchev, the incoming First Secretary of the Communist Party of the Soviet Union, who announced that: 'We must concentrate on developing our defensive weapons, our means of sinking enemy ships, rather than on building up an offensive surface fleet of our own'.

LEFT The Soviet Navy air arm, the AV-MF, expanded during the late 1950s and the Tupolev Tu-16 (Badger) gave the Soviets a genuine long-range maritime strike and reconnaissance capability for the first time. The range of the Tu-16 was further increased by air-to-air refuelling, as seen here, using an unusual wingtip to wingtip technique. (NARA)

During the 1950s, naval forces were quick to appreciate the possibilities of the helicopter both for transport and ASW. The Piasecki HUP Retriever utility helicopter lands on the deck of the heavy cruiser USS *Pittsburgh* (CA-72) during a Mediterranean cruise in 1954. (US Navy)

The eventual replacement for Kuznetsov in 1956 was Admiral Sergey G. Gorshkov, under whose leadership the Soviet naval priority switched from the interdiction of the SLOC to the neutralization of US aircraft carriers. The large-scale construction of surface ships was abandoned in favour of submarine forces and long-range aircraft. The late 1950s saw the introduction of three new types of torpedo attack submarines into the Soviet Navy – the Project 627 *Kit* (Whale) (November-class) long-range nuclear-powered submarine, the Project 641 (Foxtrot-class) long-range diesel submarine and the Project 633 (Romeo-class) medium-range diesel submarines. Some Whiskey-class boats were also converted to carry guided missiles. Soviet submarine presence in the Mediterranean Sea was also bolstered by the agreement in 1958 with Albania for the establishment of a Soviet naval base at Valona. Access to the Mediterranean Sea had long been a challenge for the Soviets, as transits from the Black Sea to the eastern Mediterranean were controlled by the Montreux agreement which limited traffic through the Bosporus, and at the western end of the Mediterranean the Straits of Gibraltar were under the surveillance of the British base there. Thus, the ability to station up to 12 Whiskey-class submarines in the Adriatic Sea represented a major increase in capability, as well as a potent threat to the aircraft carriers of the USN 6th Fleet.

In parallel to submarine development, the AV-MF was modernized and upgraded. Mikoyan-Gurevich (MiG)-17 (Fresco) and MiG-19 (Farmer) fighters replaced older types for short-range fighter defence, but perhaps the most important acquisition was the Tupolev Tu-16 (Badger) long-range bomber, many of which were transferred from VVS units to the AV-MF from 1954. The range of the Tu-16 matched the Shackleton, while its performance in terms of speed and ceiling was close to that of contemporary US fighters. A Tu-16 regiment would typically consist of two squadrons of Tu-16T torpedo bombers and a squadron of Tu-16Z air-to-air refuelling (AAR) tankers. The torpedo bomber variant of the Tu-16 was short-lived since it was soon obvious that the aircraft could not get close enough to drop a torpedo against an aircraft carrier. Some aircraft were reconverted to the bombing role, while others were modified to become the Tu-16KS (*krylatyy snaryad* – winged projectile) (Badger-B) armed with the KS-1 *Kometa* (Comet) (AS-1 Kennel) guided missile. With a range of some 80km, the KS-1 gave at least some stand-off capability from the defences of a carrier group. A reconnaissance variant of the Tu-16, the Tu-16R (Badger-E), also entered service at this time. Meanwhile, the Il-18 remained in front line service and two torpedo regiments based at Dunayevka near Kaliningrad were allocated to support the Baltic Fleet.

From 1957, the AV-MF also experimented with the use of helicopters for ASW. The Kamov Ka-15 (Hen) co-axial helicopter could be flown from Kotlin-class destroyers in this role. The practice was to use three helicopters working together as a team: one was equipped with two RSL-N dipping sonars, while the second carried the SPARU-55 receiving system for the sonar and the third aircraft was armed with two PLAB-MK 50kg depth charges.

Warsaw Pact Maritime Aviation in the 1950s

In response to West Germany (Bundesrepublik Deutschland – BRD) being admitted into NATO, a collective defence treaty, the Warsaw Pact, was signed on 14 May 1955, linking the armed forces of Albania, Bulgaria, Czechoslovakia, East Germany (Deutsche Demokratische Republik – DDR), Hungary, Poland and Romania. Like their Soviet masters, the communist European countries which bordered the sea (Poland and the DDR on the Baltic, Albania on the Adriatic, and Bulgaria and Romania on the Black Sea) all had small coastal navies with little tradition of naval aviation. In the early 1950s, the 256th Maritime

ABOVE The flight deck of USS *Forrestal* (CVA 59) during shakedown operations on 12 March 1956. A North American FJ-3 Fury of VF-21 taxies towards the port bow catapult while an F2H-3 Banshee is readied on the starboard bow catapult. In the background, a second Fury has launched from a midships catapult. (US Navy)

Aviation Patrol group (*Patrula 256 Hidroaviație*) of the Romanian Navy operated some World War II-vintage floatplanes including the Arado 196 and Heinkel 114 and Bulgaria also operated a handful of similar types, but all of these aircraft were gradually phased out of service in the first few years of the decade. However, both Bulgaria and Romania formed ASW helicopter units using the Mil Mi-4MT (Hound) in 1959. In the same year the DDR formed Naval Helicopter Wing 18 (*Marinehubschraubergeschwader* – MHG 18), also with the Mi-4 at Parow, near Stralsund.

In contrast to the other Warsaw Pact navies, the Polish Navy (*Marynarka Wojenna*) had established a Naval Air Arm (*Lotnictwa Marynarki Wojennej* – LMW) in 1949. In 1951 the 33rd Naval Air Division (*Dywizja Lotnictwa Marynarka Wojenna* – DLMW) was formed comprising two regiments: the

30th Naval Aviation Regiment (*Pułk Lotnictwa Marynarki Wojenne* – PL MW), equipped with the Ilyushin Il-10 Sturmovik attack aircraft, which was based at Wrzeszcz, near Gdansk, and 34th Fighter Aviation Regiment (*Pułk Lotnictwa Myśliwskiego* – PLM), flying the Lim-2 (a licence-built version of the MiG-15) which was based at Babie Doły, near Gdynia. These units were joined by an Il-28 unit, the 15th Independent Naval Reconnaissance Squadron (*Eskadra Lotnictwa Rozpoznawczego Marynarki Wojennej* – ELR MW) which was formed at Siemirowice, to the west of Gdansk, in 1955.

US in the Mid-Late 1950s

In many ways, the commissioning of the aircraft carrier the USS *Forrestal* (CVA 59) in 1955 can be considered to be the most significant naval event of the 1950s. She was the first 'super carrier,' far larger than any previous aircraft carrier, and she set the new standard for US aircraft carriers for the next decades; she also cemented the role of the aircraft carrier as the central part of a naval strike force. With a 60,000-ton standard displacement, which was twice that of the Essex-class, the Forrestal-class ships were the first to be built specifically for jet aircraft operations and for the nuclear strike role. Four of these ships, USS *Forrestal*, USS *Saratoga* (CVA 60), USS *Ranger* (CVA 61) and USS *Independence* (CVA 62) were commissioned between 1955 and 1959. They were configured with a 10-degree offset angled flight deck and four stream catapults, and each carrier could operate up to 100 aircraft. From the mid-1950s, the USN maintained a strength of between 14 and 16 attack carriers, at least one of which was allocated to the permanently maintained Atlantic strike fleet (STRKFLTLANT).

BELOW The single-engine McDonnell F3H-2M Demon was equipped with a Hughes APG-1 radar and could be armed with four Raytheon AAM-N-6 Sparrow missiles, as well as four 20mm cannon. This example is from VF-61 aboard the USS *Saratoga* (CV 60) in 1957. (US Navy)

RIGHT Despite its resemblance to the FJ-3, the North American FJ-4B Fury was a complete redesign: it had a larger, heavier airframe with a revised fuselage and wings. Nine US Navy and three USMC attack squadrons operated FJ-4B strike fighter between 1956 and 1965. (San Diego Air & Space Museum)

With the new generation of attack carriers came a new generation of jet aircraft. In 1956 the North American FJ-4B Fury entered service. It resembled the previous variants of the Fury, but it was in fact a completely different aircraft which was larger, stronger and more capable than its predecessors. The FJ-4B was designed as a strike fighter and was capable of delivering a nuclear weapon. The same year saw the arrival of the McDonnell F3H Demon fighter, which equipped 22 squadrons, eight of which were allocated to the Atlantic Fleet. Prior to 1956, USN fighters had been armed with cannon, but the F3H-2M variant of the Demon could be armed with the Sperry AAM-N-2 Sparrow 1 radar 'beam riding' AAM. At the same time, the Philco/General Electric AAM-N-7 Sidewinder 1A infra-red homing AAM became available for the Cougar. Another arrival in 1956 was the Douglas A3D Skywarrior, a large twin-engine jet bomber which was to replace the AJ Savage in the nuclear strike role. With a 1,000-mile tactical range and the ability to carry a 12,000lb weapon load, the Skywarrior was a formidable strike platform. At the other end of the scale, the diminutive Douglas A4D Skyhawk, with a 27-ft wingspan (as compared to the 76-ft span of the Skywarrior), also joined the fleet in 1956 to fill the tactical ground-attack role, including nuclear strike. The Skyhawk was one of the most successful carrier-borne aircraft, remaining in front-line service through the next two decades. The final type to enter service in 1956 was the Douglas F4D Skyray, a delta-winged all-weather fighter. The type, which joined VC-3 in April, had set a world speed record in October 1953 and later went on to set five world time-to-altitude records. It was also the first USN aircraft capable of supersonic performance in level flight. Known colloquially as the

'Ford' because of its '4D' designation, the Skyray mounted the state-of-the-art AN/APQ-50 radar that could detect targets at ranges out to 18 miles, and could be armed with four AAM-N-7 Sidewinder AAMs. Despite its short range and unstable handling characteristics, the Skyray proved to be a very effective fighter and remained in service until 1964.

The following year marked the introduction of two day-fighter types, the Grumman F11F Tiger and the Vought F8U Crusader. Both types were armed with the Sidewinder missile as well as cannon. The Tiger was swift and manoeuvrable, but it was destined to remain in front-line service for just four years. The Tiger never fired its guns in anger, but one aircraft did manage to shoot itself down when, on 21 September 1956, Grumman test pilot Tom W. Attridge overtook the bullets that he had fired at supersonic speed and was hit by three 20mm cannon shells. The reason for the demise of the Tiger in service was that its contemporary, the Crusader, had better overall performance, particularly in speed at height and tactical radius, and it proved an altogether more versatile airframe. Despite being optimized for high-speed flight, the Crusader maintained good low speed handling characteristics thanks to the ingenious solution of a variable incidence wing: the entire leading edge of the main wing could be tilted upwards by 5° to achieve the correct angle of attack for a 130kt approach speed. The first cruise by the F8U Crusader was to the Mediterranean with VF-32 aboard Forrestal-class carrier USS *Saratoga* in 1957. With the introduction of numerous new types in the mid-1950s, carrier air groups were organized to have one day fighter squadron with Crusaders or Tigers, one all-weather fighter squadron with Demons or Skyrays and two or three attack squadrons with Skyhawks, Furys or Cougars. The larger Forrestal-class carriers also carried a heavy attack squadron flying the Skywarrior.

BELOW The final evolution of the F9F design, the Grumman F11F Tiger incorporated an area-ruled fuselage, thinner wings and an afterburning Wright J-65 engine, giving it supersonic performance. Although it was outclassed by the Vought F8U Crusader, it equipped six front-line squadrons. (US Navy)

As the Forrestal-class carriers entered service they replaced Essex-class ships, which in turn were then either refitted with angled flight decks, or re-roled to join their sister-ships for ASW (and re-designated 'CVS'). By 1958, there were 11 Essex-class ASW carriers in service with the USN. In this role they were equipped with one squadron of 20 Grumman S2F Tracker and one squadron of Sikorsky HSS-1 Seabat helicopters. The twin-engine Tracker entered service with VS-26 in 1954 and combined the role previously fulfilled by pairs of Avengers or Guardians into one airframe. Equipped with an APS-38 search radar in a retractable ventral turret and a retractable ASQ-10 MAD sensor in the tail, the Tracker carried sonobuoys in bays in the rear of the engine nacelles. It was also armed with depth bombs or torpedoes that were housed in a fuselage weapons bay. The Tracker could operate the Julie/Jezebel system of active and passive sonobuoys introduced in 1956. The Jezebel buoy was a passive system that listened for the acoustic signature of submarines, while the Julie buoy was used in conjunction with a practice depth charge (PDC), a small explosive charge dropped by the ASW aircraft. The Julie used the reflected sound from the PDC detonation for echo-ranging to locate the target precisely. The combination of both types of sonobuoy enabled a Tracker crew to locate, follow and, if necessary, attack an enemy submarine. The Seabat joined the USN inventory in 1955, and carried a dipping sonar that was used to locate submarines that could then be engaged by surface destroyers. The Tracker airframe proved to be very adaptable and two variants, the WF-2 Tracer airborne early warning (AEW) aircraft and TF-1 Trader carrier onboard delivery (COD) transport were produced. The Tracer carried an AN/APS-82 radar that incorporated a height finder and a doppler airborne moving target indicator (AMTI) which removed sea returns from the display, making it easier for the radar operator to interpret.

The mainstay of shore-based ASW operations in the USN continued to be the P2V Neptune. By the second half of the decade the P2V-7 variant was in service, in which the defensive gun armament had been removed and a fixed MAD sensor fitted in a 'sting' fairing at the tail. To improve take-off performance, a Westinghouse J34-WE-34 turbojet was mounted under each wing.

With the increased range of Soviet submarines operating from Murmansk, the narrows of the Greenland-Iceland-UK Gap (GIUK Gap) became more strategically important: submarines were forced to transit on one or other side of Iceland, which effectively formed chokepoints. USN Neptunes based at Keflavik in Iceland patrolled the seas between Greenland and the Faroe Islands, but NATO commanders also wished to operate MPA from Norwegian bases in order to hunt for submarines as

OPPOSITE The Supermarine Scimitar F1, which entered service in 1958, was the first British carrier-borne aircraft to be nuclear-armed with the Red Beard weapon. Here an aircraft from 803 NAS performs a 'bolter' after landing on but missing an arrester wire. (Jarrett)

ABOVE A Goodyear ZS2G-1 airship taking off from NAS Lakehurst, circa 1956. The US Navy continued to use airships for maritime patrol and early warning duties throughout the 1950s. (US Navy)

they rounded the North Cape. At first this was not possible because the Norwegian government had forbidden the basing of foreign aircraft on its territory; however, in 1955 permission was granted for the USN aircraft to be detached temporarily from Keflavik to fly from Norwegian bases. This arrangement was known as Operation *Neptune Journey*. In 1956, NATO ASW capabilities were further enhanced by the introduction of the Mk 44 acoustic homing torpedo. The Neptune was armed with this new weapon, which was dropped by parachute. On entering the water, the torpedo entered a search pattern and homed onto the first acoustic return that it received.

After World War II the USN had continued to use airships for ASW work and in 1955 there was still a relatively large number of the type in service. Fifteen ZSG-4 and 12 ZS2G-1 airships were based at NAS Lakehurst, New Jersey. Both types were new designs, having been introduced in 1954 and 1955 respectively. Another role fulfilled by the type was that of AEW, and 12 ZPG-2 airships were operated by Airship Early Warning Squadron 1 (ZW-1), also based at Lakehurst. The main AN/APS-20E search radar was mounted below the gondola, with the height finding radar mounted in a fairing on top of the gas envelope. In addition, there were a further five ZPG-2W early warning airships that carried a low frequency radar mast internally within the gas envelope. On 14 January 1957 a ZPG-2W commenced a ten-day patrol some 200 miles off the coast of New Jersey. The crew completed their task during a period of harsh winter conditions that had kept conventional military and civilian aircraft grounded. The following year four newly built ZPG-3W airships were delivered to ZW-1. With an overall length of 400ft – almost half the length of an Essex-class carrier – the ZPG-3W was the largest non-rigid airship ever built and incorporated a 40ft radar scanner mounted inside the gas envelope. Airships remained in service with the USN until 1962.

Conventional aircraft were also tasked with the AEW role. During the early 1950s, the Pine Tree Line, a chain of ground-based early warning radars, had been established across the 50th Parallel to detect aircraft approaching to attack the main cities of Canada and the USA from the north. The Pine Tree Line had been superseded by the middle of the decade by a chain of 90 doppler detection sites known as the Mid-Canada Line, and in 1957 the distant early warning (DEW) line was established along

Developed from the de Havilland DH110, the Sea Vixen FAW 1 was a successful all-weather fighter and the first British naval aircraft to be armed exclusively with missiles rather than guns. Four de Havilland Firestreak infra-red homing missiles could be loaded under the wings. (Jarrett)

the 69th Parallel between Alaska and Baffin Island. These ground-based chains protecting the North American continent against attacks from the north were augmented by lines of radar picket destroyers deployed some 300 miles off the eastern and western seaboards. Although the air defence of North America was the responsibility of the USAF Continental Air Defense Command (CONAD), the USN was responsible for providing early warning over the sea. As well as the AEW airships, the USN operated the Lockheed WV-121 Warning Star, a modification of the Constellation airliner that was known to crews as the 'Willy Victor', and which carried an APS-20 search radar in a ventral housing and a dorsal-mounted APS-45 height finder radar. These aircraft were used for two 'barriers' which were continuously mounted from July 1957 off the west and east coasts: the BARPAC over the Pacific and the corresponding BARLANT over the Atlantic. In the Pacific, five aircraft were continuously airborne, flying the BARPAC route between Adak Island and Midway Island. In the Atlantic, three Warning Star squadrons, VW-11, 13 and 15 flew from NAS Argentia to establish four radar orbits, spaced at 250-mile intervals, stretching between Cape Farewell, at the southern tip of Greenland, to the Azores. The year 1957 also saw the establishment of the combined USAF/RCAF North American Air Defence Command (NORAD) organization to control all air-defence activities on the North American continent. Despite NORAD being a predominantly USAF command, one USN all-weather fighter squadron, VF(AW)-3, equipped with the F4D-1 Skyray was assigned to NORAD as a shore-based asset operating from NAS North Island, San Diego, in early 1959.

One short-lived flying boat which joined the USN inventory in 1954 was the Convair P3Y Tradewind. Originally conceived as an ultra-long range MPA, it evolved into an AAR tanker which, due to its 145ft wingspan, could refuel four fighters simultaneously. Unfortunately, its Allison T40-A-10 turboprop engines proved to be very unreliable, and the 11 aircraft were taken out of service in 1958.

Britain, Canada and Europe in the Mid-Late 1950s

Like the USN, the RN modernized its aircraft carrier fleet during the mid-1950s. HMS *Eagle* was joined by her sister ship HMS *Ark Royal* (R09) in 1956; both had a similar displacement to the US Essex-class carriers. Meanwhile, the Illustrious-class ships were scrapped, with the exception of HMS *Victorious* (R38), which returned to service in 1958 after a long modernization refit that included an angled flight deck. Four Centaur-class light aircraft carriers were also commissioned between 1953 and 1959: HMS *Centaur* (R06), HMS *Albion* (R07), HMS *Bulwark* (R08) and HMS *Hermes* (R12). More capable aircraft types also began to arrive towards the end of the decade. The first swept-wing type, the Supermarine Scimitar, joined the FAA as a day fighter/strike aircraft in 1958 and the following year it was joined by the de Havilland Sea Vixen, fighter, all-weather (FAW) 1. The Scimitar, which had a nuclear strike capability carrying the British Red Beard weapon, was first operated by 803 NAS aboard HMS *Victorious*. It had a maximum speed of 640kt (M 97) at sea level and at low speed it benefitted from having blown flaps – high pressure air bled from the two Rolls Royce Avon engines was blown over the flaps, increasing their aerodynamic performance to reduce approach and landing-on speed. The Scimitar equipped four front-line squadrons, serving firstly as a strike/attack fighter and later as an AAR tanker, until 1969. Although a capable

The Fairey Gannet ASW aircraft was powered by an Armstrong Siddeley Double Mamba turboprop driving two contra-rotating propellers and carried an ASV Mk 19 radar in a retractable 'dustbin' fairing which is extended in this view. The Gannet was short-lived as an ASW platform and was replaced in role by the helicopter. (Jarrett)

RIGHT Quite possibly the ugliest aeroplane ever designed, the Short Seamew was a competitor to the Gannet. It equipped a small number of naval reserve units and was evaluated – and rejected – by the Yugoslav Air Force. (Crown Copyright)

aircraft, the single-seat Scimitar was not an easy aeroplane to fly, and over half of the FAA inventory was lost in accidents. On the other hand, the Sea Vixen was a more successful type and represented a huge leap in capability over the Sea Venom that it replaced. Not only did it have considerably better performance than its predecessor, but the GEC AI Mk18 radar mounted in the Sea Vixen could link with the Type 984 radar on the ship giving an excellent radar picture for the two-man crew to attack targets with de Havilland Firestreak infra-red homing AAM. The Sea Vixen FAW1 was first flown from HMS Ark Royal by 890 NAS and, like the Scimitar, it equipped four front-line squadrons.

The ASW role also benefitted from new aircraft with improved capabilities. Equipping 826 NAS in 1955, the Fairey Gannet AS1 shipborne ASW aircraft was first embarked on HMS *Eagle*, while in the same year the newly equipped 824 NAS embarked its Gannets on HMS *Ark Royal*. At first glance, the Gannet resembled a single-engine aeroplane, but it was in fact powered by an Armstrong Siddeley Double Mamba – two turbojets linked to a gearbox to drive two coaxial contra-rotating propellors. Each Mamba could be shut down, and the propellor feathered, to conserve fuel (and engine hours) and extend the time on patrol.

The FAA also expanded the use of helicopters in the ASW role with the Westland Whirlwind HAS7, which entered service in 1957. The Whirlwind operated in hunter/killer pairs in the same way that the Avenger had been previously deployed – one helicopter carried a dipping sonar, while the other was armed with a homing torpedo. The concept proved a success and as a result the in-service life of the Gannet was short-lived, as the Whirlwind gradually took over the ASW role from 1958.

RAF Coastal Command had returned its Neptune fleet to the US by 1957 and from then the ASW/maritime patrol role was fulfilled entirely by the Shackleton. Because of its relatively short range, the Neptune had been mainly used to patrol the North Sea areas, but the Shackleton enabled Coastal Command to patrol at a much longer range. A typical Shackleton sortie might last between 15 and 20 hours, consisting of a 1,000-mile transit to the operating area followed by three to four hours on task and a 1,000-mile return to home base. Thus, the UK-based Shackleton squadrons could reach into the North Atlantic Ocean and Norwegian Sea, while units based in Malta could cover the whole of Mediterranean Sea. The MR2 and MR3 variants of the Shackleton had been introduced, which featured an improved EMI ASV 21 airborne maritime surveillance radar mounted in a retractable 'dustbin' turret behind the bomb bay. In practice the ASV 21 could detect targets the size

BELOW The Avro Shackleton MR1 provided the RAF with a much-needed long-range MP and ASW platform. Various marks of the type would form the backbone of Coastal Command until the late 1960s. (Jarrett)

ABOVE From 1957, with the acquisition of the angled deck carrier, the RCN operated a squadron of McDonnell F2H Banshees from HMCS *Bonaventure* (CVL 22). (Library & Archives of Canada)

of a submarine snorkel mast at six or eight miles in the typical sea conditions in the Atlantic. However, later Soviet submarines were equipped with sensors that could detect ASW radar transmissions, complicating the search tactics used by MPA. Another means of detecting submerged submarines was the sonobuoy and the Shackleton was equipped with the T9003 passive buoy and the T11514 active sonar buoy. On contact with the water the sonobuoy lowered a hydrophone to a pre-determined depth to listen for acoustic returns. In the case of the passive buoy, it rotated its hydrophone slowly and could detect the signature of the Soviet Whiskey, Zulu or Foxtrot-class submarines at a range of 5,000yd. The active buoy rotated its hydrophone in 36-degree steps and emitted a 'ping' on three frequencies at each step. Any return echo enabled it to give both a range and a bearing of the contact. Once a submarine had been located the Shackleton could attack with depth bombs or the Mk 30 homing torpedo (which was similar in concept to the US-built Mk 44 torpedo). Attacks were carried out at 100ft by day and 200ft at night. The Shackleton did not carry a MAD sensor, since the airframe itself generated too much magnetic disturbance, but it was equipped with Autolycus diesel exhaust detector equipment, which 'sniffed' the air for fumes from submarine diesel engines. Unfortunately, Autolycus also detected the emissions of numerous other vessels, so its practical value was limited.

In Canada, the P2V-7 Neptune had replaced the Lancaster in RCAF Maritime Air Command on the eastern seaboard, although the Lancaster would remain in service with 407 Sqn at Comox on the west coast until 1959. The east coast Neptune squadrons were re-equipped again in 1958 with the Canadair CP-107 Argus long-range MPA, releasing the Comox Lancasters to be replaced in turn by the Neptune. The four-engined Argus was equipped with either the British ASV 21 radar or the US-built AN/APS-20 radar and a tail-mounted MAD sensor, as well as Julie/Jezebel sonobuoys, homing torpedoes and depth bombs and also an AN/ASR-3 diesel exhaust detector. Like the Shackleton in the RAF, the RCAF Argus was used for long-range patrols and the standard length of patrols by the Argus was 18hrs. Completing the upgrading of Canadian ASW capability, the RCN modernized both its aircraft carrier and its aircraft inventory by replacing the HMCS *Magnificent* with another Majestic-class carrier, the HMCS *Bonaventure* (CVL 22) in 1957. This was a more modern ship with an angled flight deck and was equipped with F2H Banshee fighters flown by VF-870 and S2F Tracker ASW aircraft flown by VS-880. The ship also carried four Sikorsky HO4S-3 (H-19) ASW helicopters equipped with dipping sonar, which were operated by HS-50.

The Royal Netherlands Navy modernized the *Karel Doorman* between 1955 and 1958 to incorporate, amongst other improvements, an angled flight deck. Her new complement of aircraft included a squadron of Hawker Sea Hawk Mk 60 fighters and a squadron of Grumman TBM-3S and TBM-3W Avenger ASW aircraft. The French Navy also carried out a refit on its carrier *Arromanches* between 1957 and 1958, introducing an

BELOW During the mid- to late 1950s, the French *Aéronavale* operated Grumman TBM Avengers in the ASW role from the carrier *Arromanches*. (US Navy)

ABOVE The Vought F4U Corsair was still in service with the *Aéronavale* and it saw combat in French colonial wars as well as during the Suez Crisis of 1956. (Bannwarth)

angled flight deck. After its update, the carrier operated mainly in the ASW role, with Bréguet Br 1050 Alizé (Tradewind) ASW aircraft flown by *Flottille* 6.F, supported by Sikorsky HSS-1 (CH-34G) Seabat helicopters. The Sud-Est Aquilon (North Wind) fighter had been introduced to *Aéronavale* in 1955, but these were not initially used for carrier operations, being flown instead as land-based fighters by *Flottille* 11.F based in Tunisia and *Flottille* 16.F based at Hyères, near Toulon. The *Aquilon* was a license-built version of the de Havilland Sea Venom and during the 1950s it was used by *Aéronavale* as a fighter bomber to support operations over North Africa.

West Germany joined NATO in 1955 and from that year it was permitted to have its own armed forces. The naval aviation arm (*Marineflieger*) was formed in 1956 and the first of its two wings, Naval Aviation Group 1 (*Marinefliegergruppe* – MFGr 1), was formed at Schleswig the following year, comprising one squadron of Sea Hawk Mk 100 jet fighters and one squadron of Gannet AS4 aircraft. MFGr 1 was based at Kiel and was responsible for the Baltic Sea area, while MFGr 2 which had formed at Nordholz, also with the Sea Hawk and Gannet, took responsibility for the North Sea area. The main role of the *Marineflieger* was to counter the activities of the Soviet Baltic Fleet, as well as the naval units of East Germany and Poland.

Meanwhile in the Mediterranean area, the Italian Air Force began to replace the Harpoon and Helldiver with the S2F Tracker from 1957. The previous year the *Aviazione Navale* had procured three Augusta-Bell AB-47 helicopters, with which 1st Helicopter Group (1° *Gruppo Elicotteri* – Gruppelicot) was formed at Catania. The group was expanded over the next few years with more AB-47s and with HSS-1 Seabat helicopters which were used for ASW.

Crises in the Middle East 1956–58

A surge of pan-Arabism in the second half of the 1950s triggered a series of crises in the Middle East which, although outside the remit of NATO, still involved the deployment of British, French and US naval forces in

BELOW Known in French service as the Aquilon (North Wind), the Sea Venom was built under license in France by SNCASE (Sud-Est) and served with the *Aéronavale* into the early 1960s. (Jarrett)

OPPOSITE TOP From 1959, the TBM Avenger was replaced in *Aéronavale* service by the Rolls Royce Dart-powered Breguet Br.1050 Alizé (Tradewind) ASW aircraft. The Alizé was equipped with a ventrally mounted retractable CSF search radar and an internal weapons bay. (Bannwarth)

OPPOSITE BOTTOM The German *Marineflieger* operated the Hawker Sea Hawk Mk 100 and Mk 101 variants. These were similar to the FGA6 variant used by the FAA but had a taller tailfin and rudder and the Mk 101 was equipped with an Ekco 38B search radar mounted in a pod beneath the starboard wing. (Jarrett)

the Mediterranean. The first such crisis occurred in November 1956 when, in response to the nationalisation of the Suez Canal by the Egyptian government, British and French forces invaded the Canal Zone. In conjunction with aircraft based in Malta and Cyprus, three British aircraft carriers, HMS *Eagle*, HMS *Albion*, HMS *Bulwark*, and two French carriers, *Arromanches* and *La Fayette*, carried out numerous airstrikes between 1 and 4 November. Their aircraft attacked airfields and other military targets in preparation for amphibious and airborne landings which took place on 5 November. HMS *Eagle* carried one squadron of Wyvern S4 (830 NAS), two squadrons of Sea Venom FAW21 (892 NAS and 893 NAS) and two squadrons of Sea Hawk FGA6 (897 NAS and 899 NAS) as well as a flight of Skyraider AEW 1 (A Flt, 849 NAS); the other two British carriers each had three squadrons embarked. The French carrier *Arromanches* had one squadron of F4U-7 Corsair (14.F) and one squadron of TBM Avenger (9.F), while *La Fayette* carried one augmented squadron of F4U-7 Corsair (15.F). During this period, US citizens were evacuated by the carrier USS *Antietam* (CVS 36), while the other 6th Fleet carriers, USS *Coral Sea* (CVA 43) and USS *Randolph* (CVA 15), monitored the situation. The landings on 5 November included an airlift by Whirlwind and Sycamore helicopters operating from HMS *Theseus* (R64) and HMS *Ocean* (R68), while the strike aircraft carried out close air support for the ground forces. Hostilities ceased the following day, after the British and French governments agreed on a withdrawal from the Canal Zone.

The following year, the 6th Fleet carried out manoeuvres in the eastern Mediterranean Sea to demonstrate US support for King Hussein of Jordan after he survived an attempted coup. The same year saw the formation of the United Arab Republic (UAR) which (temporarily) united Egypt and Syria and was loosely aligned with the USSR; then, in 1958 there was a coup d'etat in Iraq and a rebellion in Lebanon. On 14 July, the president of Lebanon requested US military support and the next day, in Operation *Blue Bat*, USMC troops landed in the country. The aircraft carriers USS *Essex*, USS *Saratoga* and USS *Wasp* had already set off from the western Mediterranean to support the landings, but they were still some distance away from Lebanon; however, USS *Essex* launched four FJ-3 Fury and seven AD Skyraiders which routed via Cyprus and, in an impressive demonstration of co-ordination, these aircraft arrived overhead just as the marines came ashore. Aircraft from USS *Essex* continued to maintain a presence overhead for the next two days. From 18 July, they were supplemented by aircraft from USS *Saratoga*.

NATO Exercises

There were numerous small-scale maritime exercises from 1955. Exercise *Fishplay*, which became an annual event, was first held from 20 May to 4 June 1955. It was designed to 'test the NATO doctrine for submarine-maritime air barrier [and]… to obtain data on the effect of air-patrol zones and submarine killer patrol zones on transiting submarines.' The exercise took place in a 200- by 400-mile exercise area northwest of Bermuda and included MPA from the US, Canada and the UK; for example, *Fishplay IV* in 1959 included five Shackletons from 203 Sqn that deployed from RAF Ballykelly to Norfolk, Virginia.

The large-scale exercise Operation *Strikeback* was held in the North Atlantic during September 1957. It involved over 140 ships and 650 aircraft. During the exercise the ASW elements of 'Blue Forces', including the hunter-killer groups led by the six ASW carriers USS *Wasp*, USS *Essex*, and USS *Tarawa* (CVS 40), also HMS *Eagle*, HMS *Ark Royal*, and HMS *Bulwark*, were tasked to prevent 'Orange Force' submarines from progressing through the GIUK Gap to threaten NATO shipping. Three carrier battle groups based on the carriers USS *Forrestal*, USS *Saratoga* and USS *Intrepid* (CVA 11) then carried out simulated strikes against 'Orange Force' positions in Norway.

In the same year, Operation *Deep Water* was held to practise operations to protect the Dardanelles from Soviet invasion. The aircraft carriers USS *Lake Champlain* (CVS 39) and USS *Franklin D. Roosevelt* (CVA 42) were involved: USMC squadrons operating from *Lake Champlain* covered landings by US marines, while Carrier Air Group 17 (CVG-17) flew sorties from USS *Franklin D. Roosevelt*.

The First Decade

At the beginning of the 1950s NATO navies had enjoyed control of the seas in the Atlantic and the Mediterranean with negligible competition from the Soviet Navy. Over the decade the USN established the role of the nuclear-capable carrier battle group as a means of projecting offensive power, and it also became an integral part of plans to reinforce the northern flank of NATO. The advent of jet aircraft and the invention of the angled flight deck during the decade significantly enhanced the operational capabilities of the aircraft carrier, and the arrival of the 'super carrier' had established the primacy of the type in naval warfare. Like their land-based counterparts, carrier-borne aircraft had seen a massive increase in performance as the decade progressed.

Initially the Soviet Navy had seen the interdiction of the North Atlantic SLOC as a priority, but reflecting the threat posed by the aircraft carrier, Soviet naval strategy changed in the late 1950s to neutralizing the carriers. As a result, by the end of the decade the Soviet Navy had grown considerably by having an increasingly large fleet of submarines as well as a large number of long-range maritime strike and patrol aircraft. The rise of the Soviet submarine force in turn had driven NATO navies and maritime air forces to develop more effective ASW capabilities. The introduction of role specific ASW aircraft and long-range MPA types, as well as advances in sonar and weapons technologies, brought major improvements to ASW tactics on both sides. By the close of the decade helicopters were also proving to be very effective in the ASW role.

The practice at working together during large-scale naval exercises had welded the individual NATO navies into a single entity and proven the tactics of both the carrier battle group and ASW operations. These were further validated during the crises in the Middle East, where aircraft flying from British and French carriers had been successful in combat operations and aircraft from US carriers had been effective in projecting US power and support into the Levant.

The busy flight deck on USS *Saratoga* (CVA 60) during the Exercise *Strikeback*, a major NATO exercise in the autumn of 1957. A Douglas A3D-2 Skywarrior of VAH-9 launches from the waist catapult, with a McDonnell F3H-2M from VF-61 being positioned on the bow catapult, while a Douglas F4D-1 Skyray of VF-101 waits its turn. (US Navy)

CHAPTER 2

CONTROL OF THE SEAS – 1960–69

'Events of October 1962 indicated, as they had all through history, that control of the sea means security. Control of the seas can mean peace. Control of the seas can mean victory. The United States must control the seas if it is to protect your security.'

President John F. Kennedy, late US Navy, 6 June 1963.

At the beginning of the 1950s NATO sea power had been wielded by a disparate group of navies operating obsolescent equipment, while the Soviet Navy had existed as a short-range coastal force. At the start of the 1960s, the situation had changed completely: a massive rearmament and re-equipment programme during the previous decade had provided the NATO navies with a large fleet of modern aircraft carriers, high performance jet aircraft and highly effective ASW aircraft. A series of large-scale exercises under the auspices of an integrated command structure had welded ACLANT into a single entity within which allied ships and aircraft operated seamlessly together. The USSR had also invested heavily in the Soviet Navy which now boasted a large fleet of modern submarines as well an extensive inventory of long-range maritime strike aircraft. While the balance of force still lay strongly in favour of NATO, Soviet naval forces constituted a significant threat in the North Atlantic, as well as the Mediterranean and Baltic Seas.

OPPOSITE Known to its pilots as the 'Scooter', the McDonnell Douglas A-4 Skyhawk was one of the most successful carrier-borne attack aircraft, with nearly 3,000 built. The type entered US Navy service in 1956 and saw extensive combat during the Vietnam War. (US Navy)

The USSR in the Early 1960s

The expansion of the Soviet submarine fleet continued during the early 1960s. A notable step was the deployment from 1961 of the Project 629 (Golf-class) diesel-electric submarine which was armed with the R-13 (SS-N-4 Sark) ballistic missile and which marked the start of the Soviet Navy taking a strategic nuclear role. However, the main focus of the Soviet Navy remained on neutralizing the NATO aircraft carrier fleet and two new classes of cruise missile-armed submarines entered service in the early 1960s to counter this threat. The Project 650 and 675 boats (Echo I and Echo II-class respectively) were nuclear powered submarines (SSN), while the Project 651 (Juliett-class) was a diesel-electric submarine. These vessels were initially armed with P-5 (SS-N-3c Shaddock) cruise missiles with nuclear warheads, but these were later replaced with the P-6 (SS-N-3a Shaddock) which was more accurate and was better suited to attacking aircraft carriers. The P-5 and P-6 missiles had a range of approximately 250 and 220 miles respectively. While this range gave protection to the launching vessel, the submarine had to be on the surface to fire both of these missiles; furthermore, in the case of the P-5, the submarine also had to remain surfaced for the time of flight of the missile in order to steer it to the target, so the submarine was still vulnerable during the attack sequence. In order to target aircraft carriers at long range 'over the horizon,' the submarine needed to have a target position given to it and the missile required mid-course guidance during its flight: these data were supplied by an MPA. From 1964 this role was fulfilled by the Tupolev Tu-95RTs (*Razvedchik-Tseleookazatel* – reconnaissance target-designator) (Bear-D) reconnaissance aircraft operated by the AV-MF. For the Northern Fleet, these huge turboprop aeroplanes were operated by the 392nd Independent Long-range Reconnaissance Regiment (*Otdelnyy Dalniy Razvedyvatelnyy Aviatsionny Polk* – ODRAP) flying from the Severomorsk-1 airfield near Murmansk. The Tu-95RTs was equipped with a suite of passive electronic support measures (ESM) sensors as well as the MTsRS-1 Uspekh-1A (Big Bulge) I/J-band search radar to find its quarry. The search radar was mounted in a large ventral radome, while a smaller chin type housed a steerable datalink antenna to enable it to communicate with Juliett and Echo II-class submarines and also their missile systems. A typical engagement profile began with the Tu-95RTs locating a suitable target using its ESM sensors and relaying the information to the attack submarine. The aircraft would then shadow the target until the submarine was approximately 150 miles from the target in position to launch. At this point the Uspekh radar picture would be

OPPOSITE A Soviet Tu-95M (Bear-A) intercepted over the Norwegian Sea some 400 miles east of Keflavik by a US Air Force F-102 on 17 March 1972. (NARA)

ABOVE A critical element of Soviet anti-carrier strategy in the early 1960s was the mission flown by the Tupolev Tu-95RTs (Bear-D) to locate targets for subsequent attack by missile-armed submarines. (US Navy)

data-linked to the submarine for missile firing, after which the Tu-95RTs would gather the missile and guide it towards the target until the terminal guidance system of the missile (usually radiation seeking) could take over.

The AV-MF also operated about 12 of the Tu-95MR (Bear-E) maritime reconnaissance variant which carried a ventrally mounted camera pack for photo reconnaissance, as well as an array of passive ELINT gathering sensors. Other variants of the Tu-95 that were operated by the VVS Long-Range Aviation (*Dal'naya Aviatsiya* – DA) also had a maritime strike role. The Tu-95K (Bear-B) could be armed with the 250-mile range Raduga Kh-20 (AS-3 Kangaroo) air-launched cruise missile. While the prime mission of this weapons system was against strategic targets, they also had a secondary role against NATO aircraft carriers. The Tu-95K was equipped with an YaD A336Z (crown drum) I-band attack radar in the nose to provide guidance to the missile. A further refinement, the Tu-95KD (D – *Dalny* – long range) variant was configured for air-to-air refuelling, giving it a much longer reach than the original version of

the aircraft; in this case a Myasishchev 3MN-2 (Bison-B) tanker aircraft would support the strike aircraft. The Tu-95KM (*Kompleks Modernizirovany* – complex upgraded) (Bear-C) variant was a further improved model of the missile launcher, incorporating passive ESM sensors to aid with target location. The maritime reconnaissance capability of the AV-MF was enhanced further from 1962 with the introduction of the Tupolev Tu-22RD (*Razvedchik Dalny* – long-range reconnaissance) (Blinder-C) which carried an array of cameras in the weapon bay.

During the early 1960s the Soviet air forces underwent a major re-organization during which some 1,500 tactical aircraft were transferred from the AV-MF to the frontal aviation (*Frontonaya Aviatsiya* – FA) of the VVS. In addition, the three AV-MF Tu-16 regiments in the Crimea were transferred to the VVS Black Sea Fleet. The AV-MF was left with about 800 aircraft which included bomber, reconnaissance and coastal ASW types. The newest of the latter was the Beriev Be-12 Chayka (Seagull) (Mail) amphibious flying boat which entered service in 1964. This turboprop powered aircraft was equipped with an APM-60Ye MAD system mounted in the tail boom and an Initsiava-2B search radar in the nose. An internal weapons bay could carry torpedoes and mines as well as sonobuoys. Two regiments of Be-12s were allocated to the Pacific Fleet, while the Northern and Black Sea Fleets had one regiment each and the Baltic Fleet was allocated a single independent anti-submarine squadron (the 49th OPRAE based in Kaliningrad). Another Beriev type, the jet-powered Be-10 (Mallow) flying boat, entered limited service in the Crimea. However, the Be-10 proved difficult to fly and was not a success.

In the meantime, the AV-MF Tu-16 regiments had been redesignated as Naval Missile Aviation Regiments (*Morskoy Raketonosnyy Aviatsionnyy Polk* – MRAP) and three regiments of the 5th Naval Missile Aviation Division (*Morskoy Raketonosnyy Aviatsionnyy Diviziya* – MRAD) were allocated to support the Northern Fleet from bases near Murmansk and Arkhangelsk. In 1961 the Tu-16K-10 (Badger-C) entered service. This variant was designed to carry the Raduga K-10S (AS-2 Kipper) anti-shipping missile, which was carried semi-recessed under the belly of the aeroplane. A distinctive flattened radome in the nose of the aeroplane mounted a YeN (Puff Ball) I-band radar which was used for target acquisition. The Il-28 remained in service, with two regiments based in the Kaliningrad SSR and Latvian SSR to support the Baltic Fleet. The inventory of the 759th OMTAP in Kaliningrad included some ten Il-28PL (*Protivolodochnyy* – anti-submarine) ASW aircraft, which were equipped with the SPARU-55 sonobuoy receiver and from 1962 armed with ASW torpedoes.

OPPOSITE The AV-MF employed the Beriev Be-12 Chayka (seagull) (Mail) amphibious flying boat for coastal ASW. The aircraft was powered by two Ivchenko AI-20D turboprops and had a range of some 2,000 miles. (NARA)

ABOVE The anti-shipping strike role was carried out in the AV-MF by the Tupolev Tu-16K-10 (Badger-C) armed with the Raduga K-10S (AS-2 Kipper) anti-shipping missile. The distinctive nose radome covers the YeN (Puff Ball) I-band radar. (NARA)

With improved air cover and possibly with submarine protection, the three Sverdlov-class cruisers that had joined the Soviet Northern Fleet in the late 1950s became a potential threat to NATO convoys in the North Atlantic. NATO intelligence considered that in time of conflict these vessels would act as commerce raiders, carrying out opportunistic attacks on NATO shipping. Despite their small number, the well-armed Sverdlov-class ships represented a significant opponent and became priority targets for NATO maritime aircraft.

US in the Early 1960s

Just as the USSR had continued its submarine building programme into the 1960s, so the USA had continued with the construction of large aircraft carriers. Three new attack carriers joined the USN in 1961: the nuclear-powered USS *Enterprise* (CVAN 65) and the first two improved Forrestal-class ships USS *Kitty Hawk* (CVA 63) and USS *Constellation* (CVA 64). Powered by eight A2W nuclear reactors, USS *Enterprise* was larger even than the Forrestal-class ships, making her the largest warship in the world when she joined the 2nd Fleet in the Atlantic Ocean. The size of the ship was reflected in her large complement of aircraft: when *Enterprise* set sail in late 1962 for a cruise of the Atlantic and Mediterranean with CVG-6 embarked, she carried one squadron each of F4H Phantoms and F8U Crusaders, three squadrons of A4D Skyhawks, and one squadron each of AD Skyraider, A3J Vigilante, WF Tracers, F8U-1P Crusader reconnaissance aircraft and Piasecki HUP Retriever helicopters, a total of over 100 aeroplanes. However, despite the commissioning of three new aircraft carriers, probably the most important development for the USN at that time was the introduction of the Lockheed UGM-27 Polaris submarine launched ballistic missile (SLBM), which took over the strategic nuclear role from naval aviation in the early 1960s.

As well as three new carriers, the year 1961 saw the introduction of two new aircraft types: the McDonnell F4H Phantom II and the North American A3J Vigilante. One of the most successful military aircraft ever built, the Phantom was designed as a carrier-borne long-range high-altitude interceptor, although it would go on to be a truly multi-role aeroplane, equally good at fulfilling the air-to-air and air-to-ground roles. With a crew of two, it was powered by two afterburning J79 turbojets and equipped with an APG-72 fire control radar in the nose. The aircraft

LEFT Derived from the short-lived North American A-5 Vigilante attack bomber, the RA-5C enjoyed a long and successful career as a carrier-borne photo-reconnaissance aircraft. This aircraft is preparing to launch from USS *Forrestal* (CVA 59) in summer 1968. (US Navy)

PREVIOUS PAGES Two McDonnell Douglas F-4B Phantoms of VF-84 photographed in 1964. The multi-role Phantom became the mainstay of the US naval fighter squadrons throughout the 1960s and 1970s. (US Navy)

was not armed with a gun; instead, the radar was used to illuminate the target for its armament of up to six Raytheon AAM-N-6 Sparrow III semi-active homing AAMs. The Phantom quickly replaced the Cougar, Demon and Skyray in service and by 1966 some 29 USN and USMC squadrons were flying the Phantom. The Vigilante was a supersonic all-weather attack aircraft, configured with an unusual 'linear bomb bay' between the jet pipes from which a B27 nuclear weapon could be ejected from the rear of the aircraft. A reconnaissance variant was also built and when the strategic nuclear role was absorbed by the Polaris submarine fleet, the strike variant Vigilantes were also converted to the reconnaissance role. In order to reduce their approach speeds for carrier operations, both the Phantom and the Vigilante benefitted from boundary layer control (BLC) – high pressure engine bleed air blown across the aerodynamic surfaces to increase their performance at low speed.

In September 1962, the USN changed its system of aircraft designations to bring them in line with the USAF (see Appendix 1). The Phantom became the F-4B and the attack and reconnaissance variants of the Vigilante became the A-5A and RA-5C respectively. With the change in designation, another type, the Grumman A2F, had become the A-6 Intruder by the time it entered service in 1963. Like the Vigilante, the Intruder was a long-range all-weather attack aircraft, but it was optimized for night/poor weather operations. The digital integrated attack navigation equipment (DIANE) gave the crew the ability to fly to and attack a target while completely 'blind,' flying solely on instruments.

RIGHT A Mk 101 Lulu nuclear depth charge mounted on an AD Skyraider. The weapon incorporated a W34 nuclear warhead with a yield of some 11 kilotons and was intended for use against Soviet ballistic missile submarines. It was used by the US, British and Netherlands maritime patrol aircraft and ASW helicopters. (US Navy)

ABOVE A Grumman A-6A Intruder of VA-42 seen aboard USS *Forrestal* (CVA 59) on 25 August 1963. Equipped with sophisticated navigation and attack sensors, the Intruder could strike its targets by day and by night, in all weather conditions. (US Navy)

The aircraft was described, as follows, in the US naval journal *Proceedings* in May 1961:

> The A2F is not what you would describe as a beautiful airplane. In fact, one person who saw it portrayed for the first time in a broadside view remarked that it looked like a tadpole. But beauty is more than skin deep. To the fleet commander, who realizes the A2F will provide him with an attack bomber that can deliver nuclear or conventional weapons with pinpoint accuracy on targets obscured completely by weather or darkness, it is a pretty beast. To the pilot who can approach a target from such a low altitude that he can avoid enemy radar detection, and who knows he can keep piloting while the second man in the cockpit manipulates the black boxes, the A2F is a beauty. To the carrier's air officer, a plane whose flight time can be reckoned in hours instead of minutes – thereby providing clear decks for the high performance 'gas hogs' who must have landing space in a hurry – the A2F is a dream.

The Phantom, Intruder and Vigilante represented a quantum leap in performance and capability over their forebears in the 1950s, and unlike those earlier short-lived types they all enjoyed long in-service lives. The Vigilante was deployed on carriers in squadrons of six aeroplanes, while an Intruder squadron typically comprised ten attack aircraft and four KA-6 AAR tankers. From 1964 early warning for the fleet was enhanced by the arrival of another aeroplane which was also to become a long-serving type, the Grumman E-2 Hawkeye. Above its fuselage the Hawkeye carried a 24-ft diameter rotodome containing the AN/APS-96 search radar, while the mission systems were integrated with the naval tactical data system (NTDS) which gave the task force commander an overall picture of the disposition of all assets under his command. Computerized systems on board the Hawkeye also assisted the three-person rear crew to interpret the tactical situation. The Hawkeye progressively replaced the E-1 Tracer on the attack carriers.

The new decade also saw new helicopter designs entering service. The Sikorsky H-3 Sea King joined the naval inventory in 1961, bringing a significant improvement in ASW capability over the SH-34 Sea Bat. In particular, both of the hunter-killer roles were incorporated into a single helicopter which could carry both a dipping sonar (a Bendix AQS-10 or -13) and a further 840lb of weapons. Unlike its predecessor, the Sea King was also fully equipped for all-weather operations. The Kaman H-2 Seasprite entered service in 1962 as a general-purpose utility helicopter, which covered many roles including search and rescue (SAR).

By the early 1960s ten Essex-class ships were operating as ASW carriers, divided equally between the Atlantic and Pacific fleets. The complement of USS *Essex* (CVS 9) in the Atlantic with CVSG-60 embarked was typical for these ships and consisted of two squadrons of S-1 Tracker ASW aircraft, one squadron each of E-1 Tracer AEW aircraft and H-3 Sea King helicopters. Three other ships of the class were re-designated as amphibious assault ships (LPH). These ships (USS *Boxer*, USS *Princeton* and USS *Valley Forge*) typically carried 30 helicopters; USS *Boxer* was allocated to the Atlantic Fleet, while the other two LPH were based in the Pacific Ocean. In 1964 there were six attack carriers and five ASW carriers allotted to the Atlantic Fleet, while the Pacific fleet had nine attack carriers and four ASW carriers.

The USN continued flying airships into the early 1960s, although a fatal accident to a ZPG-3W off the New Jersey coast in 1960 marked the beginning of a rundown of the type. The 400ft-long USS *Reliance* had crashed into the sea in July and 18 of the 22-man crew were killed. The last flight by a USN airship was in August 1962, but by then, the fixed

OPPOSITE By the early 1960s, helicopters were becoming increasingly important as ASW platforms. This piston-engined Sikorsky HSS-1 Seabat helicopter is using its dipping sonar on 15 February 1961. (US Navy)

ABOVE A Grumman E-2A Hawkeye of AEW squadron VAW-116 assigned to the USS *Coral Sea* (CVA 43) in 1967. From 1964, the type provided early warning and fighter direction for the fleet. (US Navy)

wing AEW aircraft such as the redesignated EC-121K Warning Star (formerly the WV-2) were proving far more suitable for the ever-evolving role. The Atlantic Barrier was discontinued in the summer of 1961 and replaced with a line of defence further forward, the Greenland-Iceland-United Kingdom Early Warning Barrier, abbreviated as BARFORLANT. The new barrier comprised two airborne AEW patrol stations and two surface radar pickets, with the airborne element patrolled by EC-121K flying from Keflavik.

Like the embarked aircraft types, the USN MPA fleet underwent a quantum improvement in the early 1960s. The four-engine Lockheed P-3 Orion began to replace the P-2 Neptune from early 1962. Based on the Electra airliner, the Orion was equipped with state-of-the-art electronic systems as well as a tail-mounted MAD and it could carry an extensive weapon load in its internal weapons bay. In various updated variants, the Orion would remain in service well beyond the end of the Cold War.

Britain in the Early 1960s

In 1960 the RN had five aircraft carriers in front-line service: HMS *Victorious*, HMS *Eagle*, HMS *Ark Royal*, HMS *Hermes* and HMS *Centaur*. In addition, two former carriers, HMS *Albion* and HMS *Bulwark*, had been converted to become helicopter-carrying amphibious assault ships. Equipped with Westland Whirlwind and later Wessex helicopters, the assault ships were committed to naval forces 'East of Suez' along with at least one of the aircraft carriers. Indeed, during the first part of the decade, the focus for RN carrier operations continued to be in support of national operations beyond the NATO area in the Middle and Far East.

At the start of the 1960s the Scimitar remained as the primary strike aircraft operated by the FAA, but it began to be replaced by the Blackburn Buccaneer S1 from 1962. Like contemporary US types, the Buccaneer benefitted from extensive use of BLC to enable the slow approach speeds needed for carrier operations. On the other hand, it was capable of high subsonic speeds at low level and had an impressively long range. Weapons, either conventional or nuclear, were carried in an internal bomb bay and could be aimed using the nose mounted Ferranti Blue Parrot (Airpass II) radar, which also enabled the aircraft to perform stand-off toss delivery profiles. The prime targets for the FAA Buccaneer squadrons were the Sverdlov-class cruisers of the Soviet Northern Fleet. The first unit to operate the Buccaneer was 801 NAS which embarked on HMS *Ark Royal* in February 1963 and was followed by 800 NAS (aboard HMS *Eagle*), 803 NAS and 809 NAS. The introduction of the Buccaneer released the Scimitar to be used as an AAR tanker flown by 800B Flight (known as 'The Flying Tankards'), which in turn enabled the Buccaneer, which was somewhat under-powered by the de Havilland Gyron Junior engines, to be launched with less fuel, and therefore at a lighter weight, improving its performance at launch. Once airborne, the Buccaneer could then top up its fuel load from the Scimitar.

BELOW The Grumman S-2 Tracker entered US Navy service in the late 1950s and continued to be an important ASW aircraft throughout the following decade. This is an S-2E Tracker of VS-27 with the APS-38 radome extended. (US Navy)

ABOVE A Douglas KA-3B Skywarrior AAR tanker of VAH-4 in late 1967. Like many of the type, this aircraft was later converted to a dual-use EKA-3B tanker/ electronic warfare aircraft. (NARA)

OPPOSITE The Sikorsky SH-3D Sea King began to replace the Seabat from 1961. This example is from HS-3, operating from USS *Randolph* (CVS 15). (US Navy)

The Sea Vixen was to remain as the FAA fleet air-defence fighter and its capability was expanded from 1963 with the FAW2 version, which carried extra fuel in the tail booms and was armed with the Hawker Siddeley Red Top infra-red seeking AAM. By 1960 the Fairey Gannet had been superseded in the ASW role by the Westland Whirlwind HAS7, but the Whirlwind was also progressively replaced from 1961 with the Westland Wessex HAS1. The design of the Wessex was based on the Sikorsky Sea Bat, but the Wright R-1820-84 piston engine of the American helicopter was replaced in the Wessex by a Napier Gazelle gas turbine. The new engine gave a significant increase in performance allowing the Wessex, like the USN Sea King, to carry out both hunter and killer roles in ASW operations. Two anti-submarine homing torpedoes could be carried on either side of the fuselage. The instrumentation was also improved, and an autopilot fitted, making the helicopter capable of all-weather operations. The Wessex of 815 NAS first embarked on HMS *Ark Royal* in the summer of 1961. Smaller frigate-sized ships of the RN began to receive the Westland Wasp helicopter in 1964. This machine was intended to carry out the killer role in ASW operations, operating up to ten miles away from the mother ship, which would locate the submarine.

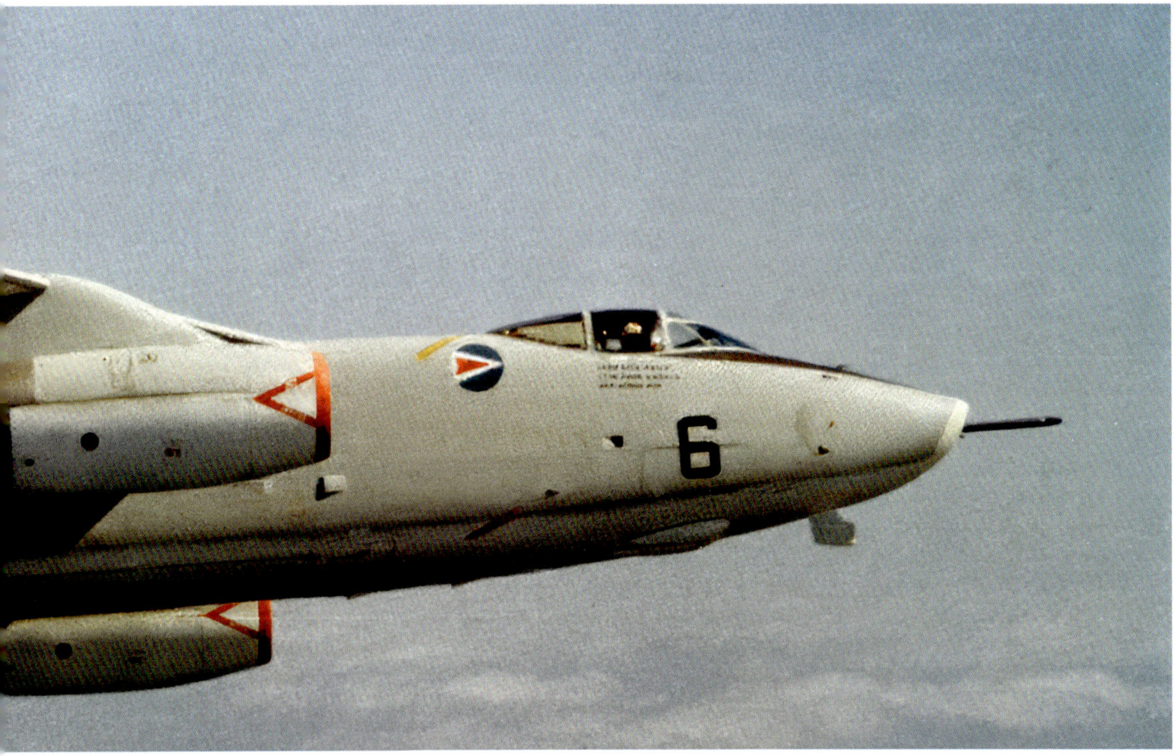
6

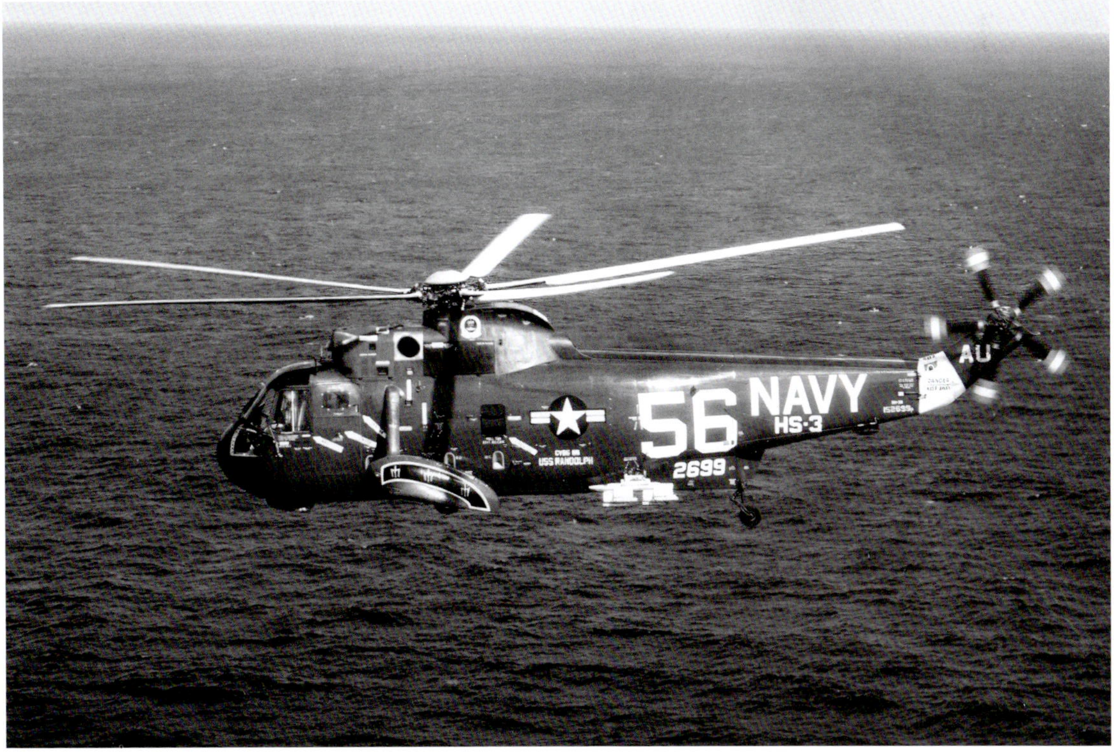
56
NAVY
HS-3
AU
2699
USS RANDOLPH

RIGHT When 800 NAS was re-formed as a Buccaneer S1-equipped unit, the type could not be catapult launched with a full weapons and fuel load. Consequently, 800B Flight was formed with four AAR-equipped Scimitars to refuel the aircraft soon after launching. The flight was known as 'The Flying Tankards'. (Pitchfork)

Loss of the ASW role did not mean the end of the line for the Fairey Gannet: indeed, the AEW3 which joined 849 NAS in 1960 ensured its longevity. The aircraft became one of the most highly utilized types in the FAA. At the heart of the aircraft was the AN/APS-20 search radar, which was mounted in a ventral radome, and which displayed its picture to the two radar observers (lookers) sitting side-by-side in a fuselage cabin aft of the wing. The Gannet AEW3 served only with 849 NAS, but aircraft of the squadron were deployed, in flights of four aeroplanes, on all five aircraft carriers.

RAF Coastal Command continued to fly the Shackleton in the maritime patrol and ASW roles. In the early 1960s there were eight Shackleton squadrons based in the UK flying the MR2 and MR3 variants, as well as a further squadron based in Malta to cover the Mediterranean Sea.

BELOW The Goodyear ZPG-3W 'Reliance' backs from its mooring prior to departing NAS Lakehurst, New Jersey. This airship was destroyed in a crash in the summer of 1960, leading to the curtailment of airship operations. (US Navy)

Canada and Europe in the Early 1960s

The Canadian armed forces underwent a major re-equipment and reorganization in the first years of the decade. In 1962 the RCAF replaced its CL-13 Sabres and CF-100 Canuks with Lockheed CF-104 Starfighters and CF-101 Voodoos respectively. The budgetary pressures from these purchases and the focus on the ASW role for the navy led to the disbandment of VF-870 in September 1962 and the withdrawal of its F2H-3 Banshee fighters. For the rest of the 1960s HMCS *Bonaventure* was equipped only with the Trackers of VS-880 and helicopters of HS 50, thus mirroring the complement of USN ASW carriers. HS 50 continued to operate the HO3S, but these were augmented from 1963 with the CHH-2 Sea King, which was identical to the USN SH-3A variant. The formation of 415 Sqn at Summerside, Prince Edward Island, brought the number of CP-107 Argus MPA squadrons to three on the east coast, while 407 Sqn at Comox on the West Coast continued to fly the Neptune.

ABOVE In the early 1960s, the Blackburn Buccaneer S1 low-level strike aircraft was painted in an 'anti-flash' white finish. This aircraft served with 801 NAS in 1963. (Pitchfork)

1960s – Flying the CS2F Tracker
Stanley Brygadyr • Royal Canadian Navy CS2F Tracker pilot

We would brief in the briefing room, get our mission, go to our aircraft, and start up. There would be normally five aircraft starting up – there's always a spare and it would be behind the fourth aircraft… Once you do your instrument checks and everyone does their run-up checks – we were flying piston-engine aircraft, these weren't jets so you have to check your magnetos and check all your temperatures and gauges – if you're ready to go, then you would launch. There were two ways you could launch fixed wing aircraft on the carrier: you can do a catapult launch, which is the preferred way, because you know you're getting airborne – when the catapult fires you, you're going airborne! The other method is what's called a 'free deck run.' Now the maximum free run on the *Bonaventure*'s deck was I think about 480ft so you had to get airborne in 480ft, but you have a head start because the carrier turns into wind and the carrier puts on speed of say 16kt or 18kt and there's a 20kt wind speed so you've already got 40kt of airspeed before you even start moving…and with full power on and 40kts starting over the deck you can get airborne in 460ft or 480ft on the carrier just by rolling down the runway. If all four are serviceable – away you go, but if anyone in the pack was unserviceable – had bad equipment it could be your backseat equipment, too – radar or some such thing – when it's your turn to go, you pull that aircraft out and the crew jumps into the spare aircraft, which is being manned by a spare pilot who wasn't going to launch – he's just starting the aircraft and doing all the checks – the crew changes aeroplanes and that spare aircraft then becomes the fourth aircraft for the launch. Then away you launch. The flights were normally four-hour duration – and then you come back and you get air traffic control – the carrier has its own air traffic control – a tower just like you have on a land base. You get put in the stack, you get a holding position and when it's time to land, you drop down into the landing pattern and it's your turn to land. It's not a very uptight situation in the daytime on a nice sunny day and calm weather, when the deck is steady – it's quite routine. On a windy day or a deck motion day when the ship is moving, it starts to get a lot trickier and at night it can be a wholly different situation. At night in itself, even on a nice day, when you're all depending on just a very few little lights to give you guidance the 'pucker factor' is pretty high. If there's a lot of deck motion it can get really hard and if it's raining and you're using wipers on your windscreen and you can't see a darned thing it can get pretty tough and pretty tense.

University of Victoria, Special Collections and University Archives, Military Oral History Collection (SC141), Stanley Brygadyr, Interview 796

A similar pattern was followed by the Netherlands Navy in that the Sea Hawks of 860 Sqn were withdrawn and the unit was disbanded when the *Karel Doornan* entered refit in 1964. By then the ASW capability of the MLD had increased considerably: Grumman S-2 Trackers had been procured from the USA and also from the RCN; these were operated onboard the carrier by 2 Sqn. Lockheed SP-2H Neptunes had also been procured for 320 Sqn based at Valkenburg, and 8 Sqn had re-equipped with the Sikorsky SH-34J Sea Bat. After its refit, the air complement of the *Karel Doornan* consisted of eight Trackers and six Sea Bats, reflecting the practice of US and Canadian ASW carriers.

The French navy retired the *Bois de Belleau* in 1960 and *La Fayette* in 1963, making space for two French-built carriers, *Clemenceau* (R 98) and *Foch* (R 99) which were commissioned in 1961 and 1963 respectively. These ships were similar in displacement to the USN Essex-class. With the new carriers came new aircraft. The Dassault Étendard IVM carrier-borne strike aircraft was introduced in 1962, serving with the front-line *Flottilles* 11.F and 17.F. The Étendard was a relatively light aeroplane, but it nevertheless combined impressive performance and easy handling with a potent weapon load. In the fleet air-defence role, *Aéronavale* chose the Vought (LTV) F-8E(FN) Crusader. This variant differed from the USN

ABOVE The Hawker Siddeley Sea Vixen FAW2 which was introduced in 1963 featured additional fuel tanks in forward extensions of the tail booms and could be armed with the Red Top air-to-air missile. These aircraft are from 899 NAS which was the last Sea Vixen squadron to disband in 1972. (Jarrett)

OPPOSITE Based on the Sikorsky S-58 design, but fitted with a Napier Gazelle gas turbine engine, the Westland Wessex took over much of the ASW role from the Gannet. Weapons were carried externally, as illustrated by this Wessex of 826 NAS. (Pitchfork)

The Fairey Gannet AEW 3 proved invaluable as an early warning aircraft. The type entered service with 849 NAS in 1960 and was to remain in front-line use until December 1978. (Cooke)

ABOVE Long-range maritime reconnaissance and ASW by the RCAF was carried out with the Canadair CP-107 Argus. Equipped with either the US-built AN/APS-20 or British-supplied ASV Mk 21 radar, the Argus was considered one of the most effective MPAs of its day. (Canada DND)

F-8E to enable it to operate from the smaller French carriers: the variable incidence leading edge was increased from 5 degrees to 7 degrees and the flaps were fully blown with BLC. In addition, the fighter was configured with the AN/APQ-104 radar to give it compatibility with the French-manufactured Matra R530 AAM with which it was to be armed. The Crusader was operated by 12.F and 14.F based, when on shore, at Lann-Bihoué in Brittany.

Lann-Bihoué was already the base for three Lockheed SP-2H Neptunes operated by 23.F, 24.F and 25.F, which had replaced the Lancaster units in the late 1950s. Two more P-2G Neptune units, 21.F and 2.F, were based at Nimes-Garons in southern France. ASW capability for the aircraft carriers continued to be provided by the Bréguet 1050 Alizé which was flown by 4.F and 9.F from Lann-Bihoué and by 6.F at Nimes-Garons. The Rolls Royce Dart-powered Alizé was equipped with a CSF DRAA-28 radar in a retractable 'dustbin' housing under the fuselage and had carried a suite of sonobuoys and depth charges.

West German and Danish air power in the Baltic approaches region (BALTAP) was co-ordinated by COMAIRBALTAP, whose command included the land-based strike aircraft in the RDAF and West German *Marineflieger*. The early 1960s saw a major re-organization of the *Marineflieger*. In 1959 MFGr 1 at Schleswig had been upgraded to full Wing strength to become Naval Air Wing 1 (*Marinefliegergeschwader* 1

– MFG 1) and in 1963 the unit was re-equipped with the Lockheed F-104G Starfighter. Initially this choice of aircraft was not a popular one, as naval pilots thought that a twin-engine type would be more appropriate for flying over the sea, but the Starfighter eventually enjoyed great loyalty from its fliers. The Starfighter variant used by the West German air arms was optimized for the low-level strike role and was the first to equipped with a Litton LN-3 inertial navigation platform. The *Marineflieger* Starfighters were armed with the Nord AS.30 air-to-surface missile (ASM) for use against Warsaw Pact surface vessels. MFG 2 was formed at Nordholz from MFGr 2 in 1960 and the unit moved to the longer runway at Eggebek at the end of 1963 in preparation for receiving the Starfighter in 1965. The Sea Hawks were withdrawn on the arrival of the Starfighter and the Gannets were gathered into MFG 3, a dedicated ASW squadron, in 1964. In the previous year the West German SAR unit had been redesignated as MFG 5, which operated a mixture of Saro Skeeter and Bristol Sycamore helicopters as well as Grumman HU-16 Albatross flying boat, Hunting Percival Pembroke and Dornier Do27 transports. MFG 5 also administered an ASW helicopter unit, 1/MFG 4, which flew the SH-34J Sea Bat.

BELOW A Sea Hawk FGA60 of the Dutch MLD squadron VSQ860 on the catapult of the *Karel Doornan* in summer 1960. The MLD Sea Hawks were withdrawn when the ship was refitted as an ASW carrier in 1964. (Netherlands Institute of Military History)

ABOVE Like a number of NATO navies, the Royal Netherlands Navy operated the Avenger in the ASW role until the beginning of the 1960s. Seen aboard the *Karel Doornan* in the summer of 1960 are Grumman TBM-3S2 and TBM-3W2 Avengers of squadron VSQ2. (Dutch MoD)

OPPOSITE From 1961, Grumman S-2A Tracker replaced the Avenger aboard the *Karel Doornan*. The aircraft were sourced from surplus US Navy and the RCN. (US Navy)

The RDAF also underwent a major re-equipment programme at the beginning of the decade, having acquired the North American F-100D Super Sabre to replace the Republic F-84G Thunderstreak in Esk 725 and Esk 727 based at Karup and Esk 730 based at Skrydstrup between 1959 and 1961. The roles allocated to the Super Sabres included tactical air support for maritime operations (TASMO) missions for which the aircraft could be armed with the AGM-12 Bullpup ASM. But despite all the modern jet inventory, maritime reconnaissance by the RDAF was still carried out by the Catalina squadron, which for the period 1961 to 1966 was renumbered as Esk 722.

In Norway, 333 Skv replaced the Catalina with the Grumman HU-16 Albatross, and a second Albatross unit, 330 Skv, was formed in 1962. Both units were based at Sola. In Norwegian service the twin-engine Albatross amphibian had an AN/APS-31A search radar mounted in a thimble-type radome on the nose and was also fitted with a MAD sensor. The type was equipped with sonobuoys, ECM and a searchlight and had a range of some 2,800 miles. However, with the increasing numbers of Soviet submarines allocated to the Northern Fleet there remained a requirement for a better NATO ASW capability in the Norwegian Sea. Exercise *Neptune Journey* continued, with USN P-2 Neptune units

operating from Norwegian airfields as forward bases for their patrols. In addition, Exercise *Cold Road* involved RAF Shackletons using Bodø and Andøya as staging posts for long-range patrols. The three Shackleton units based at Ballykelly in Northern Ireland, 204 Sqn, 240 Sqn and 269 Sqn, frequently carried out a three-day triangular patrol route with night-stops in Keflavik and one of the RNoAF bases, which enabled them to reach into the Norwegian Arctic as far as north and east as Bear Island and Spitzbergen.

ABOVE Fifteen Lockheed SP-2H Neptune aircraft were procured by the MLD in 1962, replacing the Harpoon flown by 320 Sqn at Valkenburg airbase. The Neptune served the MLD in the ASW role until the early 1980s. (Netherlands Institute of Military History)

In the late 1950s the USN had cycled detachments operating the P2V Neptune through the British naval air base at Hal Far on Malta, but it soon became clear that there was insufficient space there. Instead, a US naval airfield was established at Sigonella on Sicily. The first Neptune unit to deploy there was VP-18 in 1960 and thereafter Neptune squadrons took their turn cycling aircraft through the base on four-month detachments. Further ASW capability in the Mediterranean theatre was delivered by RAF Shackleton MR2s flown by 38 Sqn from Luqa on Malta. In addition, the ItAF continued to operate the S2F Tracker from Grottaglie and Catania, the latter also being the home of the *Aviazione Navale*. An AB-47J helicopter of the *Aviazione Navale* was first deployed aboard a frigate, the *Luigi Rizzo*, (F 596) in 1961. Based on this experience, the SH-34 Sea Bat helicopters began to be used for ASW duties aboard the helicopter cruiser *Andrea Doria* (C 553) in 1964. Unfortunately, the airbase at Fontanarossa-Catania was struck by a tornado in October 1963, completely destroying eight helicopters and seriously damaging another eight. The lost aircraft were replaced during the following year.

A Dassault Étendard IVP of 16.F landing on deck. The IVP variant of the Étendard was a photoreconnaissance fighter equipped with five OMERA cameras in the nose. Lack of more space in the nose meant that the refuelling probe was non-retractable. (Petit)

Cuban Missile Crisis October 1962

In 1960 the pro-American administration of President Fulgencio Batista of Cuba was overthrown by a communist administration headed by the revolutionary leader Fidel Castro. The following year an American attempt to overthrow Castro ended in a humiliating failure at the Bay of Pigs (during which six unmarked A4D Skyhawks had been embarked on the carrier USS *Essex* to support the landings there but were not used). This defeat had emboldened the Soviet premier, First Secretary Nikita Khrushchev, to seek an agreement with President Fidel Castro to base Soviet ballistic missiles and bomber aircraft on the island. The Soviet Operation *Anadyr* commenced in the summer of 1962, transporting 1,000-mile range R-12 (SS-4 Sandal) and 2,000-mile range R-15 (SS-5 Skean) ballistic missiles, as well as nuclear capable 2K6 *Luna* (FROG3) tactical missiles and Il-28 aircraft to the island by sea. In addition, two S-75 (SA-2 Gainful) surface-to-air missile (SAM) divisions and the 32nd Guards Fighter Aviation Regiment (*Gvardeyskiy Istrebitel'nayy Aviatsionnyy Polk* – GvIAP), equipped with the MiG-21-F13 (Fishbed), were deployed; the MiG-21s started flying from Santa Clara airfield in September 1962. As part of Operation *Anadyr*, four Foxtrot-class submarines, B-4, B-36, B-59 and B-130, from the Soviet 69th Submarine Brigade departed Severomorsk on 1 October, sailing for the Caribbean Sea. A Zulu-class boat also sailed into the Atlantic.

The island of Cuba had been under USAF surveillance since March that year, but American aircraft did not overfly the island until October. Meanwhile, US naval aircraft patrolling the sea areas around Cuba found that the Cubans were becoming increasingly aggressive and on 8 September two P-2F Neptunes operating from NAS Key West were intercepted by a MiG-17 which carried out multiple simulated gunnery passes. USN F-6A Skyray fighters were scrambled from Key West in response, but the MiG had departed by the time they arrived on scene. The US Central Intelligence Agency (CIA) reported the presence of SAM sites on the island west of Havanna on 17 September 1962. As tensions rose, F-4B Phantoms from VF-41 deployed from NAS Oceana to NAS Key West on 8 October and USAF aircraft began to reinforce the region. Then, on 14 and 15 October three flights over Cuba by Lockheed U-2F high altitude reconnaissance aircraft brought back imagery of ballistic missile launch sites near San Cristobel and an international crisis was sparked.

On 17 October, the RF-8A Crusader reconnaissance aircraft of VFP-62 (reinforced with pilots from VMCJ-2) deployed to NAS Jacksonville in preparation for Operation *Blue Moon*, a low-level photo-reconnaissance task over Cuba. Ten of these aircraft moved forward to NAS Key West two days later. Over the next days, the ASW units of the USN were deployed for operations: four Neptunes from VP-10 were sent to Lajes on 20 October; VP-7, VP-18, VP-24 and VP-45 were all detached to Guantanamo Bay, on the easternmost point of Cuba. In addition, four P-3 Orions from VP-44, which had just been declared operational with the new aeroplane, were deployed to Bermuda, while the Neptunes of VP-26 remained at NAS Key West. On 2 October, a Neptune flying from Lajes spotted the Soviet Zulu-class submarine refuelling in the mid-Atlantic. On the same day the two attack carriers of task force (TF)-135, USS *Independence* (CVA 62) with CVG-7 embarked and USS *Enterprise* with CVG-6 aboard, reported that they were in position to the northeast of Cuba and ready to strike. USS *Enterprise* had just returned from a cruise of the Mediterranean and was diverted to its new task as it returned home; her A-3 Skywarriors were flown ashore to be replaced with the A-4 Skyhawks of VMA-225, which would be better suited to the close air support of troops ashore, if that was needed. Over the next days, TF-135 sailed to take up another position, this time to the south of Cuba.

In a move that reflected the seriousness of the crisis, US forces were brought to readiness state DEFCON 3 on the evening of 22 October and the following day Operation *Blue Moon* was initiated. Three pairs of Crusaders carried out photo-reconnaissance of the island. The squadron commander Cdr Willam B. Ecker led Lt C. Bruce Wilhemy in the first pair. After completing their runs, the aircraft landed at NAS Jacksonville so that their imagery of the missile sites could be processed. Cdr Ecker then personally flew the prints directly to Washington.

A naval quarantine was established around Cuba on 24 October and a picket line was established around a 500-mile arc from the island, a distance that prevented attack by Cuba-based Il-28 bombers. The line

BELOW A Dassault Étendard IVP from 16.F is in its natural environment – at low level over the sea. (Petit)

ABOVE The Grumman HU-16 Albatross amphibian was primarily used by the rescue services of the USN, USAF and RCN. The type was used by Greece, Italy, Norway, Spain and West Germany. (US Navy)

was patrolled by both ships and aircraft. The P-5A Marlin flying boat squadrons VP-45 and VP-49 covered the north sector, while the southern part was the responsibility of the Neptunes of VP-5 from NAS Jacksonville. The ASW group led by USS *Randolph* (CVS 15) was stationed in the north and USS *Essex* was in the southeastern sector. Two days later, the standing plan for the 'Argentia Sub/Air Barrier' was actioned and a barrier line was established from Cabot Strait between Newfoundland and Nova Scotia to a point 600 miles south of Argentia. It was picketed by ten submarines patrolling southwest of the line and 17 MPAs patrolling the northeast. The Neptunes of VP-11, which had deployed to NAS Argentia at short notice that day, took responsibility for the northern portion of the patrol area and the longer-range RCAF Argus aircraft took the most southerly part. It was on that day that a Marlin flying from Bermuda reported sighting a snorkel some 420 miles north Puerto Rico; this was later confirmed to be the Foxtrot-class submarine B-130.

Daily Operation *Blue Moon* missions had continued over Cuba and on 25 October the photographs confirmed the presence of the 2K6 missiles. On the same day the Foxtrot-class submarine B-59 was sighted on the surface, by a land-based MPA, some 350 miles southwest of Bermuda. The submarine dived but was tracked for the following hours by Trackers and Sea Kings from USS *Randolph*, as well as destroyers from

ABOVE The SP-2H Neptune (here flown by VP-7) was the only variant of the aircraft to be fitted with Julie/Jezebel submarine detection gear. Auxiliary jet engines mounted in pods under the wings improved the dash speed of the aircraft. (US Navy)

BELOW The 'dustbin' housing for the ASV Mk 21 search radar is clearly visible on this Avro Shackleton MR3 of 206 Sqn. With extra fuel carried in the wingtip tanks, the aircraft had an impressive range of 3,660 miles. (Pitchfork)

the hunter-killer group, which dropped PDCs as signal to the submarine that it should surface and identify itself. Consequently, B-59 was forced to surface and was monitored as it stayed on the surface over the next 48hrs to recharge its batteries. The B-130 was seen again on the surface by Trackers from USS *Essex*, but it dived immediately and remained submerged, but tracked, until 30 October when it was forced to surface with failure of its diesel engines and batteries; it had to be towed back to the USSR. The submarine B-4 was never forced to surface, but it was tracked from 23 to 28 October as it manoeuvred to the south of the Turks and Caicos Islands. On 28 October the fourth Foxtrot-class submarine, B-36, was located by the destroyer USS *Charles P. Cecil* (DD 835) and Neptune MPAs, which subjected it to a 35-hour bombardment with PDCs, eventually forcing it to the surface. It remained on the surface for the next 36hrs before submerging again. This day marked the turning point in the crisis, for that evening Soviet First Secretary Nikita Khrushchev announced that the missiles would be returned to the USSR. On 30 October, Admiral George W. Anderson, chief of naval operations (CNO), had observed: 'the Soviets are providing excellent submarine services for exercising our ASW capability.'

ABOVE During the Cuban Missile Crisis in 1962, Operation *Blue Moon* photo-reconnaissance sorties were flown by VFP-62 equipped with the Vought RF-8A Crusader. (US Navy)

The quarantine was maintained until 20 November, with ASW patrols continuing throughout the period. A task given to the RCAF was to fly a reconnaissance patrol into the Davis Strait between Labrador and Greenland to search for any Soviet vessels that might sabotage the undersea cable link to the BMEWS station at Thule. At that time all of the Argus fleet was committed to the Cuban operation, which included a new commitment for a detachment of aircraft to operate out of NAS Brunswick, Maine to cover an additional patrol area. This left the only available aircraft, an elderly Lancaster that was still allocated to 408 Sqn, to carry out the task. Poor weather prevented flying until 4 November, on which day the aircraft flew the last operational mission by a Lancaster.

Despite the withdrawal of Soviet weapons, communist forces on Cuba maintained an aggressive stance and on 5 November two Operation *Blue Moon* Crusaders were intercepted by a pair of MiG-21s eight miles west of Santa Clara. Having seen the MiGs, the Crusaders were able to turn into them and pass the fighters head on. Then they accelerated away from the Cuban MiGs which were unable to catch them.

When the carriers USS *Wasp*, USS *Saratoga* and HMCS *Bonaventure* returned from the Mediterranean area in early November they took their places in the barrier line until the quarantine was terminated on 20 November.

Vietnam and Space

The USN picked up two major commitments during the first half of the decade which fell outside the NATO responsibilities. Between 1961 and 1962 the carriers USS *Lake Champlain,* USS *Randolph* and USS *Intrepid* were involved in the recovery of the first four Project Mercury astronauts after their capsules splashed down in the Atlantic Ocean. USS *Kearsarge* carried out this duty for the final two Mercury missions which splashed down in the Pacific Ocean in 1962 and 1963. Between them the carriers USS *Intrepid,* USS *Lake Champlain,* USS *Wasp,* as well as the amphibious assault ships USS *Guadalcanal* (LPH 7) and USS *Guam* (LPH 9), carried out the same duty for the ten Project *Gemini* missions between 1964 and 1966 and for the first three Project *Apollo* missions which splashed down in the Atlantic Ocean in 1968 and 1969.

On 2 August 1964 an attack by North Vietnamese motor torpedo boats against the US destroyer *Maddox* (DD 731) in the Gulf of Tonkin marked the beginning of nine years of direct intervention in Vietnam by the US. Initial attacks against targets in North Vietnam were carried out by aircraft operating from the carriers USS *Constellation* and USS *Ticonderoga* (CVA 14) on 5 August. Eventually 15 attack carriers as well as two ASW carriers acting in a limited attack role would participate in the Vietnam War; a further four ASW carriers supported these operations. During the nine-year conflict,

RIGHT The Douglas F-6A Skyray remained one of the principal carrier-borne fighter aircraft throughout the early 1960s, until it began to be phased out of service in 1964. (US Navy)

LEFT A pair of McDonnell F3H-2 Demon strike fighters of VF-141 in flight on 13 February 1961. Redesignated the F-3B, the type remained in front-line service until, like the F-6A Skyray, it was withdrawn in 1964. (US Navy)

ships from both the Pacific and Atlantic Fleets were seconded to Task Force 77 for combat tours. There were typically two or three attack carriers, sometimes with an ASW carrier in support, operating from the 'Yankee Station' off the coast of North Vietnam to carry out strikes over North Vietnam, while another carrier on the 'Dixie Station' would carry out 'in-country' operations over South Vietnam. Many ships completed multiple combat tours of Vietnam, including USS *Hancock* (CVA 19) which completed nine tours, the highest number by any carrier. Other ships, for example, the USS *Forrestal*, completed only one such tour. During the conflict USMC fighter and attack squadrons were also based ashore at Da Nang. In addition, USN P-2 Neptune, P-3 Orion and SP-5B Marlin MPAs were involved in Operation *Market*, flying coastal surveillance missions to prevent seaborne infiltration into South Vietnam.

BELOW During the Cuban Missile Crisis, the RCAF CP-107 Argus was employed on the longer-range patrols over the mid-Atlantic. (Canada DND)

ABOVE The Cuban Missile Crisis also saw the operational debut of the Lockheed P-3A Orion. This type was to form the backbone of the US Navy and NATO ASW forces until the end of the Cold War and beyond. (US Navy)

The USSR in the Mid–Late 1960s

On 15 November 1960, the first US nuclear-powered ballistic-missile submarine (SSBN), USS *George Washington* (SSBN-598), sailed on its debut deterrent patrol armed with 16 Lockheed UGM-27 Polaris A-1 submarine launched ballistic missiles (SLBM). By 1967 the USN had 41 Polaris submarines in service and in the same year the first of four RN Polaris A-3 boats, HMS *Resolution* (S 22), was commissioned. In seven years, the threat to the USSR posed by the NATO carrier battle group had been eclipsed by the SSBN and the Soviet Navy acted accordingly with a major change of naval strategy: from 1967 its prime focus switched to countering the SSBN, and ASW became the most important facet of its maritime policy. The Soviet approach was threefold: firstly, to balance the new threat with a counter-threat from its own SSBN force, secondly to employ hunter-killer submarines (SSN) to intercept the Polaris submarines and thirdly to use dedicated ASW surface ships and aircraft to hunt for NATO submarines.

Project 667 (Yankee-class) SSBNs armed with R-27 *Zyb* (Fang) (SS-N-6 Serb) SLBMs were deployed for the first time in 1967, giving the USSR a nuclear deterrent and counter-strike capability. Eventually some 34 of these submarines were built, the bulk of which were allocated to the Northern Fleet. A typical patrol for these vessels would last 60 days, sailing from Severomorsk, transiting through the GIUK gap to a patrol area off the east coast of the USA. They might be accompanied as far as the GIUK gap by Project 671 (Victor-class) nuclear attack submarines (SSN), acting as an escort; the Victor-class would also rendezvous with the SSBN as it approached the GIUK gap on its return to 'de-louse' it – check that it was not being followed by a NATO SSN. However, the majority of the work carried out by the Victor-class boats was to patrol the Norwegian Sea and Arctic Ocean hunting for NATO Polaris SSBNs. The proliferation of nuclear-powered submarines in the Soviet Navy from 1967 added greatly to the task of the NATO ASW forces, with submarine activity being detected in the North Atlantic, the Norwegian Sea and GIUK gap, as well as in the Philippine Sea in the Pacific theatre.

The year 1967 was a busy one for the Soviet Navy with the introduction of new submarines, ships and aircraft. This was the year that the *Moskva* ASW helicopter carrier-cruiser first joined the Black Sea Fleet. A dedicated ASW platform, *Moskva* could carry up to 14 Kamov Ka-25 (Hormone-A) helicopters. The Ka-25 was powered by

BELOW The Soviet helicopter cruiser *Moskva* (Moscow) shadowed by a Lockheed SP-2H Neptune of VP-7 during a deployment from the Black Sea into the Mediterranean Sea during 1968. None of the complement of Kamov Ka-25 (Hormone) helicopters is on deck. (US Navy)

two gas turbine engines driving coaxial contra-rotating three-bladed rotors and equipped with a dipping sonar and MAD system and could be armed with torpedoes or depth bombs. As well as being used as an active sonar, the dipping sonar on the Ka-25 could be used passively in a bistatic system using an active sonar transmitter onboard the *Moskva* as a means of locating targets accurately. A sister-ship *Leningrad* joined *Moskva* in the Black Sea Fleet two years later and both ships made regular deployments into the Mediterranean Sea.

A new aircraft type in use by the AV-MF from 1967 was the Ilyushin Il-38 (May) MPA. This development of the four-engined Il-18 (Coot) airliner was capable of eight-to-nine-hour patrols and was equipped with a Berkut STS (Wet Eye) search radar and an APM-73 MAD sensor. Two ventral weapons bays housed sonobuoys and anti-submarine weapons. The aircraft was capable of maintaining a five-hour patrol at a range of 1,000 miles from its base. The 24th Independent Long-Range Anti-Submarine Aviation Regiment (*Otdel'nyy Protivolodochnyy Aviatsionnyy Polk Dal'nego Deystviya* – OPAPD) flew the Il-38 from Severomorsk, supporting the Northern Fleet. Despite the enhanced ASW capability that these aeroplanes offered, only a small number of them (estimates vary between 30 and 60) were built.

By now the Soviet Navy had an almost global reach with its nuclear submarines, but the lack of aircraft carriers with which to extend its air-defence cover constrained it to operate mainly in the areas where land-based air cover could be provided. Fortunately for the Soviets, these areas in the Norwegian Sea and, in the eastern region, the Sea of Okhotsk

The first Soviet dedicated long-range MPA/ASW aircraft was the Ilyushin Il-38 (May), which entered AV-MF service in 1967. The chin-mounted radome housed a Berkut STS (Wet Wet) search radar. (NARA)

overlapped with the areas where Polaris submarines would have to operate to reach targets deep within the USSR. In the Baltic, there were numerous coastal airfields that were suitable for the AV-MF or the Soviet air-defence force (*Proti-Vovozdushnaya Oborona Strany* – PVO-Strany) to provide cover, so naval forces could sail relatively freely in this region. The emphasis of the Baltic Fleet was on amphibious operations against either the northern coast of the BDR to support the land campaign in Germany, or against Denmark in order to control access between the North and Baltic Seas. Further south, although the closure of the submarine base in Albania had severely limited Soviet naval activity in the Mediterranean during most of the decade, the aftermath of the 1967 Arab-Israeli conflict opened up ports in Egypt and Syria to the USSR. In the late 1960s, permanent naval facilities were established at Alexandria, Mersa Matruh and Port Said in Egypt and at Latakia in Syria to support Soviet naval operations. Airfields in Egypt were also made available for Soviet aircraft of the AV-MF such as Tu-16 and Il-38, as well as Soviet air-defence fighters. Thus, the Black Sea Fleet was less constrained by the Montreux Convention which limited access to and from its base via the Bosporus, and it could use its forward basing in the Middle East to challenge NATO in the Mediterranean Sea and in the Atlantic and Indian Oceans. A permanent Soviet naval presence, the 5th *Eskadra* (squadron) which encompassed all Soviet forces in the Mediterranean theatre, was formed in 1967. As a result, by the end of the decade there were about 50 Soviet naval vessels sailing in the Mediterranean Sea on a typical day, with air cover provided from Egyptian airbases.

ABOVE A Douglas A-4C Skyhawk is positioned on the catapult of the USS *America* (CVA 66) as Carrier Air Wing 6 conducts qualification operations, 24 April 1965. (US Navy)

Despite the range limitations of other aircraft types, VVS DA and AV-MF Tu-95s were able to venture further afield and in the late 1960s pairs of these aircraft frequently flew long-range sorties from Severomorsk, testing NATO air defences on their route. These aircraft actively monitored NATO deployments and exercises in the North Atlantic: the carrier USS *America* (CVA 66) was even shadowed by Tu-95s as she neared Gibraltar in January 1967. Meanwhile, Tu-95 regiments based in the Far East of the USSR kept watch over the USN activities in the Pacific Ocean. The Tu-16 was frequently seen over the Mediterranean and Norwegian Seas and in May 1968 a Tu-16RM (Badger-E) reconnaissance aircraft crashed into the Norwegian Sea after making a series of aggressively low passes alongside the USS *Essex*.

There was little change to the orders of battle in the limited naval air arms of the DDR, Romania and Bulgaria. In Poland a re-organization of the air force and air-defence forces in 1963 had resulted in the naval fighter regiment 34.PLM being transferred to the Polish Air Force (*Wojska Lotnicze*). However, the 7th Fighter-Attack Naval Air Regiment (*Pułk Lotnictwa Myśliwsko-Szturmowego* – 7.PLM-Sz MW), which was formed by re-numbering 30.PLM-Sz in 1967, remained under naval command, based at Siemerowice. From here it flew two variants of the MiG-17 built under licence, the Lim-5P interceptor and the Lim-6bis strike aircraft. The reconnaissance unit 15.ELR MW, which flew the Il-28R, was also retained under naval command.

NATO Maritime Aviation in the Mid-Late 1960s

In the USA, the programme of aircraft carrier construction for the USN continued into the late 1960s but at a reduced pace. Two new improved Forrestal-class carriers joined the Atlantic Fleet in the decade: USS *America* in 1965 and USS *John F. Kennedy* (CVA 67) in 1968. The policy of maintaining a force of 15 attack carriers continued, as did the policy of separating the strike and ASW roles in different ships. Having established the F-4 Phantom, A-6 Intruder, RA-5C Vigilante and A-3

BELOW A McDonnell Douglas F-4 Phantom about to land aboard the aircraft carrier USS *John F. Kennedy* (CVA 67) in December 1968 during the work-up for a Mediterranean cruise the next year. The ship had joined the fleet in September 1968. (NARA)

Sky Warrior as the pre-eminent carrier-borne combat aircraft in the early 1960s, these highly successful types remained in service well into the next decade. The other major aircraft type in the inventory was the A-4 Skyhawk, but the search for its replacement had already started in the early 1960s. The result was the Ling-Temco-Vought (LTV) A-7 Corsair II, which joined VA-147 in 1967 and saw combat in Vietnam later that same year. A subsonic design on based the F-8 Crusader, the A-7A Corsair was fitted with a more fuel-efficient Pratt & Whitney TF30 turbofan, giving it double the range and nearly twice the weapon load of the Skyhawk. Nearly 200 A-7A, 196 A-7B and 535 A-7E Corsair were ordered by the USN, but full replacement of the Skyhawk in front-line service would still take some years.

Amongst shore-based aircraft the P-3 Orion had completely replaced the P-2 Neptune in USN service by the end of the decade, by which time it equipped 26 squadrons. The P-3C variant entered service in 1969 featuring the Sperry Rand CP-901/ ASQ-114 computer that could coordinate avionics and sensor information with a multi-purpose display to enable faster, more accurate prosecution of submarine and surface contacts. It was accompanied by the introduction of the AN/SSQ-53 DIFAR (Directional Frequency Analysis and Recording) sonobuoys. This combination of better sensors and improved data processing over the previous models generated a massive increase in operational capability. AT1 Jim Cole, a former P-3C crew member, later commented that:

> Getting the [P-3C] 'Charlies' changed everything. The 'Charlie' was such a quantum leap in ASW – I don't think we'll ever see another leap like that in weapon systems again. If getting a hot contact in ASW, it was very rare for a crew of a P-2 or a P-3A/B to still have contact when going off station. The opposite was true of the P-3C; when it got a sniff with a competent crew, it hung on. With the spectrum of types I got to fly, I'd say what made the Charlie so much better than its predecessors, outside of the digital integration, was DIFAR which had so much better capability to isolate the 'fly shit from the pepper' of the underwater sound spectrum than did the older AQA-4 and AQA-5 systems.

With the exception of combat operations over Vietnam, from the perspective of US naval aviation the second half of the 1960s differed little from the earlier part of the decade. Cruises in the Pacific and Atlantic Oceans and Mediterranean Sea continued, and the carrier strike wings (CVW – the USN had redesignated carrier air groups as air wings in 1963) and ASW groups continued to exercise for their wartime roles.

Meanwhile, France, which had withdrawn from AFMED in 1959, also withdrew its forces from SACLANT command in 1963, leaving the NATO integrated command structure completely in 1966. Although these changes affected Allied Forces Central Europe (AFCENT), they made little practical difference to NATO maritime forces. The British-led AFMED in Malta was disestablished in 1967, and the removal of much of the British presence left the USN 6th Fleet as the pre-eminent NATO force in the Mediterranean region. Though the USN maintained its status quo in the North Atlantic and Mediterranean for the rest of the decade, the same could not be said for its partners and in particular the navies of Canada, Britain and the Netherlands. The Canadian Forces Maritime Command (as the former RCN was now titled after the amalgamation of the Canadian Armed Forces in 1968) ceased carrier operations in 1969 because of financial restrictions and HMCS *Bonaventure* was withdrawn from service to be scrapped. The Trackers and helicopters were transferred to shore bases.

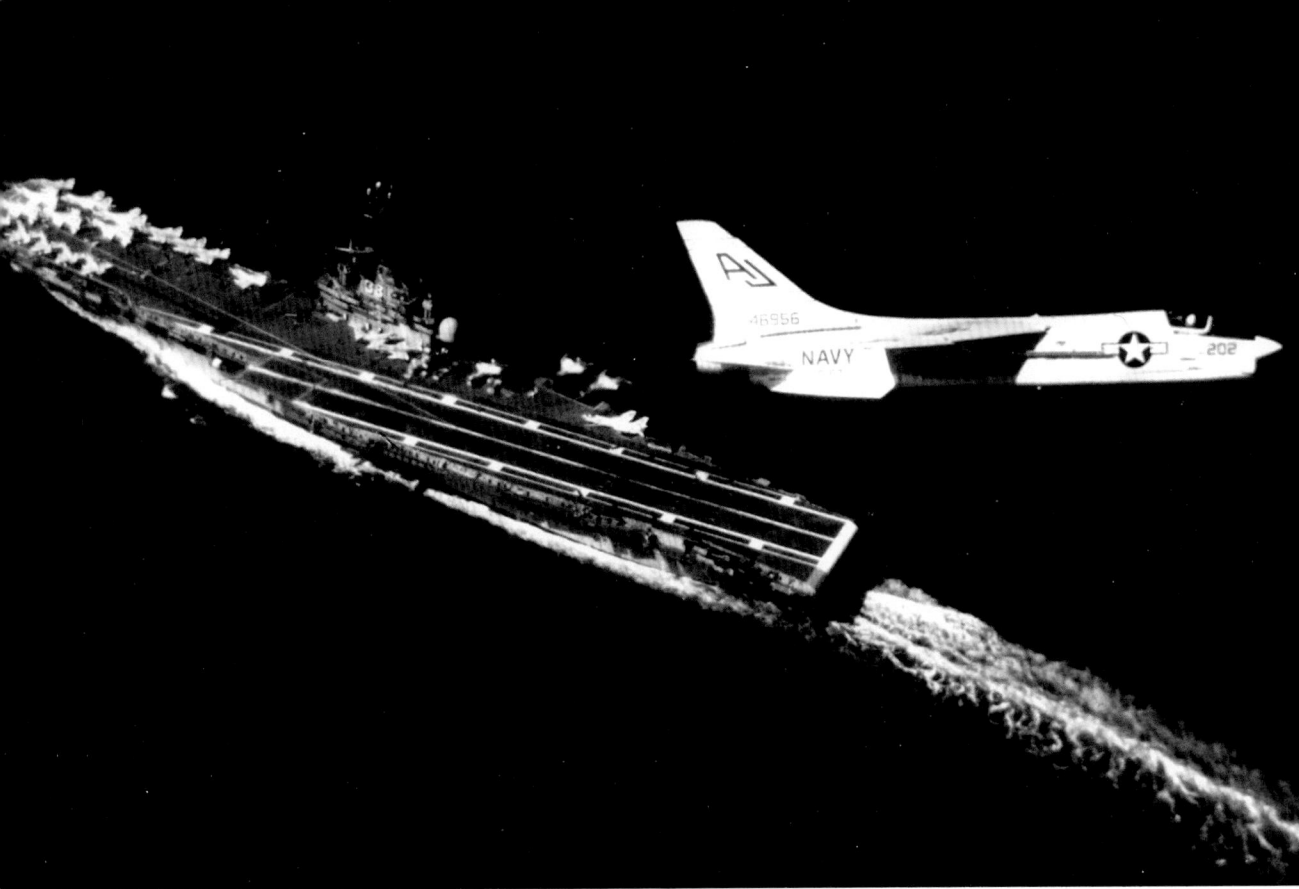

A Vought F-8C Crusader overflies the USS *Shangri-La* (CVA 38) in the Atlantic during December 1968. The ship was redesignated as an ASW carrier the following year. (US Navy)

PREVIOUS PAGES The Ling-Temco-Vought (LTV) A-7A Corsair II attack aircraft from VA-105 in flight over Cecil Field, Florida. The type entered service with the US Navy in 1967 partially replacing the A-4 Skyhawk. (US Navy)

In Britain the conflict between military ambition and economic reality reached a head in the mid-to-late 1960s firstly with the decision to withdraw from defence commitments east of Suez and secondly with the subsequent cancellation of two proposed new aircraft carriers. The older carriers HMS *Centaur* and HMS *Victorious* were withdrawn in 1965 and 1967 respectively and at the end of the decade work began to convert HMS *Hermes* as a commando carrier, leaving only two aircraft carriers, HMS *Ark Royal* and HMS *Eagle*, in service. On 14 June 1970, HMS *Ark Royal* embarked 892 NAS equipped with 12 McDonnell Douglas F-4K Phantoms (designated the Phantom FG1 in RAF service). The British variant of the Phantom, which was flown in the air-defence role by 892 NAS, differed from US Phantoms in being powered by Rolls Royce Spey turbofan engines. Other modifications including larger flaps, drooping ailerons, a slotted tailplane and an extended nosewheel leg were needed to enable the aeroplane to operate from the smaller British carrier. Only HMS *Ark Royal* was adapted for Phantom operations and the air-defence role on the other carriers continued to be fulfilled by the Sea Vixen FAW2. From 1965 the Hawker Siddeley Buccaneer S2 began to replace the Buccaneer S1 aboard the carriers in the strike role. Like the Phantom FG1, this improved version of the Buccaneer was also powered by the Spey engine, which generated 30 per cent more thrust than the Gyron Junior engine of the earlier variant. It also had much lower fuel consumption, which in turn gave the Buccaneer S2 a considerably greater range than its predecessor. Three front-line units (800 NAS, 801 NAS and 809 NAS) were equipped with the Buccaneer S2, embarking respectively on *Eagle*, *Victorious* and *Hermes*.

Part of the rationale behind cancelling the proposed aircraft carriers was that without the need for power projection beyond the NATO regions, the functions of air defence and maritime strike in the eastern Atlantic Ocean and Mediterranean Sea could be carried out by land-based RAF aircraft supported by AAR. In 1969, 43 Sqn was formed at RAF Leuchars, near St Andrews, flying the Phantom FG1 in the air-defence role and 12 Sqn was formed at RAF Honington, near Bury St Edmunds, with the Buccaneer S2 in the maritime strike role; a second RAF maritime Buccaneer squadron would be formed three years later. The RAF Buccaneers and Phantoms were tasked with TASMO missions within an area of operations stretching from the approaches to Gibraltar in the south to the furthest parts of the Norwegian Sea in the north, as well as the breadth of the Mediterranean Sea. In order to cover this vast area, forward operating bases were established at HMS Fulmar (RAF Lossiemouth) in northeast Scotland, Stornoway on the Isle of Lewis in

1960s – Learning to Fly the Buccaneer S Mk2
Mike Blissett • Royal Navy Fleet Air Arm Buccaneer Pilot

A Buccaneer at high speed and very low level is a vision of power and grace; a masterpiece of the aerodynamicist's slide rule, carved from solid blocks of duralumin by early, computer controlled milling machines. Rugged beyond the norm for aircraft of its era, I was captivated at first sight and determined to achieve RN pilot qualifications and fly one.

On 6 March 1969, with 370 hours of Jet Provost and Hunter hours in my logbook, pilot wings on my sleeve and feeling slightly nervous, I strapped myself into the Martin Baker Mk4 MSA/1 ejection seat of Buccaneer S2, XT285. My pre-start checks had been well practiced in the static simulator; I started the two Rolls Royce Spey engines. The cockpit was noisier than the Hunter, but the aircraft was smooth to steer and taxy. Acceleration on take-off provided by the 22,000lb thrust engines was far greater than anything I had previously experienced. Undercarriage raising and flaps up from 15-10-10 required swift movements and rapid cockpit checks to see that all were moving correctly within airspeed limits. Rapidly approaching 400kt climb speed I began to wonder how on earth was I going to get this monster back on the ground. All the while my staff observer provided a minimum of input in a quiet, calming manner. Very bold when you realise that there were no dual control Buccaneers ever made.

I progressed through 11hr of operational flying training (OFT) including low-level battle formation routinely flown at 50ft over the sea, strike progression, practice bombing, 2in. rocket firing, live 1,000lb bombing, air-to-air refuelling and Maddls (mirror assisted dummy deck landings). Towards the end of the course, we paid a visit to the steam catapult at RAE Bedford. This was a raised deck-like structure where you taxied up a ramp to be aligned on the gently steaming catapult track. The launch strop was placed around the catapult shuttle and fastened to the launch hooks on the underside of the fuselage. A hold back was connected at the rear and the shuttle tensioned so that the aircraft adopted a nose high launch attitude that would be optimum for flying speed at the end of the catapult stroke. Ahead of you was a very short section of runway with several sets of arrester gear and a barrier should things go badly wrong. In discussion with your observer, you check that trim settings are correct for your configuration and launch weight. With a wind-up signal and raised flag from the flight deck officer (FDO) both engines were brought to full power, thrust meter, rpms, turbine gas temperatures checked, flaps checked at 45-25-25 with blow good. A quick word from your man in the back says that he is happy and then you place the back of your right hand against the canopy to show the FDO that you are ready to launch. The FDO swiftly moves the flag to the deck level giving the executive signal to launch. A catapult launch is always hands off with your right hand locked firmly to your right thigh ready to take over at the end of the stroke. Your left hand pushing firmly against both throttles to prevent them creeping back. The kick in the back is enormous and it is impossible to breathe due to the longitudinal G force as you accelerate from zero to 155kt in 1.9sec. Suddenly, you realise that you are flying smoothly, the airstream detection device (ADD) is a nice steady note and you are climbing away cleaning up gear and flaps.

As OFT neared completion, the landing became satisfyingly routine. Great fun to run in and break at 500kt, throttles closed, airbrake out, aileron gear change at 300kt, gear going down below 225kt, flaps moving together to 45-25-25 with blow above 20 psi, gear checked with three greens ashore (four afloat with hook) and rounding finals and bringing power up to control rate of descent at 20 units of ADD indicated by the steady tone in your headset. Simultaneously you are looking to line up on the centre line with the projector sight bright white 'meatball' aligned with the green datum bars. Rate of descent is controlled with the two throttles and you land without a flare; just drive on in and as you hit the runway close the throttles and hold the nosewheel up for aerodynamic braking. Brilliant fun!

the Outer Hebrides and RAF St Mawgan in Cornwall, as well as at Gibraltar. Working in conjunction with the Handley Page Victor B(SR)2s of 543 Sqn operating in the maritime radar reconnaissance (MRR) role, the Buccaneers could carry out anti-shipping strikes while the Phantoms provided air-defence cover for the fleet. The Victor B(SR)2 which equipped 543 Sqn from 1964 was a powerful surveillance tool that was fitted with a high-definition radar and a rapid processing radar unit to process the continuous strip record of the radar pictures. A single Victor could map an area of 750,000 square miles in six hours, producing, for example, radar mosaics covering the whole of the Mediterranean Sea which would enable the position of every ship to be plotted. Five Victors could cover the whole of the North Atlantic similarly in less than seven hours.

In the Baltic approaches, the forces now available to COMAIRBALTAP included two squadrons of F-104G Starfighters flown by MFG 1 and MFG 2 and the three RDAF squadrons of F-100D Super Sabres flown by Esk 725, Esk 727 and Esk 730. In Norway the RNoAF had procured the Northrop F-5A Freedom Fighter in 1965 as well as the AGM-12 Bullpup ASM. However, of the four F-5A-equipped attack squadrons, 334 Skv at Bodø did not have a dedicated anti-shipping role at that stage. With the

A dusk launch by a McDonnell Douglas F-4K Phantom FG1 of 892 NAS. After receiving its new Phantoms, the squadron flew from USS *Saratoga* (CVA 60) in the autumn of 1969 before embarking on HMS *Ark Royal* the following year. (Cooke)

increased Soviet submarine activity in the Norwegian Sea as the decade progressed, the chronic lack of ASW aircraft in the RNoAF became an issue for NATO. A solution was found in the acquisition of five P-3B Orion MPAs by the RNoAF in 1969. These aeroplanes replaced the HU-16 Albatross in 333 Skv (for 330 Skv had already been disbanded in the previous year) and in turn the Albatrosses were sold to Greece, where they equipped 353 Naval Cooperation Squadron (*Moíra Naftikís Synergasías* – MNAS) at Elefsina airbase, near Athens.

The enhancement of maritime patrol and long-range ASW capability was also a priority for France, Germany and the Netherlands. In the early 1960s a NATO requirement for an MPA to replace the P-2 Neptune for ASW in European air arms was published. The result was the Breguet BR 1150 Atlantique, a twin turbo-prop design which was equipped with a retractable CSF radar under the forward fuselage and a MAD sensor in the tail. It could carry sonobuoys as well as anti-submarine torpedoes and depth charges. The typical patrol length for the type was 12 hours, although the aircraft was capable of 18-hour missions. The French *Aéronavale* became the largest operator of the type which replaced the Neptune in *Flottilles* 21F, 22F, 23F and 24F from 1965. In the same year the Atlantique replaced the Gannet in German service with MFG 3 at

Nordholz. For the Netherlands MLD the Atlantique was a requirement to replace the loss of ASW capability after the withdrawal of the aircraft carrier *Karel Doornan* due to costs, in 1968. In the MLD, the type was operated by 321 Sqn at Valkenburg from 1969.

Aéronavale had also procured the Sud Aviation SA 321G Super Frelon ASW helicopter for use aboard its ships. This large helicopter was powered by three Turbomeca engines and carried the usual ASW equipment of dipping sonar, search radar and anti-submarine torpedoes. In Italy the *Aviazione Navale* formed a second helicopter unit, 5º *Gruppo Elicotteri*, equipped with the Augusta-Bell AB47J to complement 1º *Gruppo Elicotteri* which now solely flew the Sikorsky SH-34.

NATO maritime patrol assets in the Mediterranean were rationalized in 1968 with the formation of the Maritime Air Mediterranean command (MARAIRMED) which gathered the SH-34 helicopters of the *Aviazione Navale*, the ItAF S-2 Trackers flying from Grottaglie and Catania, the RAF Shackletons based on Malta and the USN P-3 Orion detachments at Sigonella into a single command structure. As Commander Ralph W. Blanchard USN explained in the naval journal *Proceedings*:

> As evidence of one of the chief accomplishments of MarAirMed – the elimination of duplication – staff members point out that areas that were, at one time, patrolled by both Italian and UK aircraft, are now patrolled by one nation. For example, American aircraft, which, in the past, may have been unwittingly flying in an area just covered by a British Shackleton from Malta are now assigned areas meshed into an overall plan. The end result of this co-ordinated planning is a much larger area which can be scanned, or, on the other hand, a much more concentrated search of a given area. The information gathered may also be rapidly and uniformly distributed to the members of the Alliance.

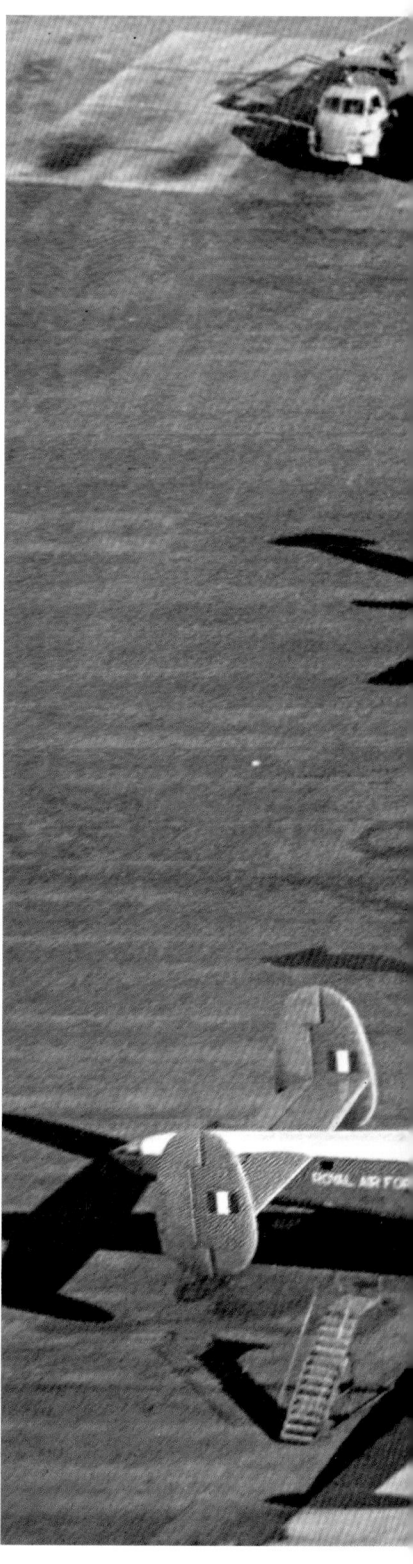

The difference in size between the Hawker Siddeley Nimrod MR1 and Avro Shackleton MR3, which it replaced from 1969, is apparent. It is also representative of the increased capabilities of the Nimrod. (Napier)

CONTROL OF THE SEAS - 1960-69

NATO Exercises

As in the previous decade, realistic 'live' exercises helped to weld the maritime forces of the various NATO members into a single cohesive force. Exercise *Dawn Breeze* VII took place off Gibraltar in late March 1962 and included the aircraft carriers HMS *Victorious* and the French *Clemenceau*, supported by Shackletons from 224 Sqn at Gibraltar and a detachment from the SP-2H Neptune squadron VP-26 based at Lann-Bihoué. As Lord Carrington, the First Lord of the Admiralty explained, during the House of Lords debate on the naval estimates:

> The task of HMS *Victorious* in the exercise was to launch a strike against an 'enemy' target – an airfield – in the face of opposition which included submarines, high-speed bombers and warships equipped with surface-to-surface missiles. Our escorts, helped by maritime patrol aircraft of Coastal Command, proved more than a match for the submarines, which were never within striking range of us. Our carrier-borne fighters were able to, and did, intercept the bombers which were sent against us at a considerable distance from the ship. And with the help of reconnaissance reports from Shackletons of Coastal Command, we were able to hit the enemy's surface force, again many miles away, with our own strike aircraft, which later on completed the carrier's mission while we were still several hundred miles from the coast. I must say that I thought this was a most impressive display, first, of the versatility and striking power of the *Victorious*; secondly, of co-operation between all three Services; and, finally, of the very difficult target which a properly escorted and supported aircraft carrier presents to an enemy equipped with even the most modern weapons.

Just three months later the carrier HMS *Centaur* participated in Exercise *Fairwind* VII in the North Sea. There was also strong involvement in this exercise from NATO MPAs flying from RAF Kinloss. RAF Shackletons from 120 Sqn, 204 Sqn and 210 Sqn were joined by Trackers from the Dutch MLD, Gannets from the German MFG 3 and Albatrosses from the RNoAF.

The annual submarine Exercise *Fishplay* continued into the 1960s and Exercise *Fishplay* VII, which was held in May 1963, included large-scale participation by MPA. The Shackletons of 203 Sqn deployed to Keflavik for the exercise, while half of 204 Sqn moved across to RAF Aldergrove, near Belfast. These arrangements made space at RAF Ballykelly for detachments of Neptunes from *Aéronavale* and from VP-24, as well as

During 1965 the Breguet Atlantique ASW replaced the Neptune in French *Aéronavale* service and also the Gannet AS4 in German *Marineflieger* service. The type was also procured by the Netherlands and Italy. (Bannworth)

four P-3A Orions from VP-8 which was normally based at NAS Patuxent River. As one resident at Ballykelly commented the P-3A aircraft 'were the centre of attraction of the remaining Shackleton crews at RAF Ballykelly, as the US crews considered them to be state of the art as far as airborne submarine hunting was concerned.'

Frequent exercises were also held in the Mediterranean region. Exercise *Deep Furrow* in 1965 was the first of an annual land-sea exercise in the eastern Mediterranean and Aegean Seas, which alternated between Greece and Turkey. US, Greek, Turkish, Italian and British forces took part, and the scenario always included a carrier battle group supporting amphibious landings. In 1965 the carrier USS *Franklin D. Roosevelt* led the group. The first of a similar exercise, *Dawn Patrol*, was held in May 1968, this time with US, Greek, Italian, French and British participation.

Learning from the benefits of the two huge maritime exercises held in the 1950s, NATO navies committed themselves to carrying out one large-scale naval exercise in the ACLANT area every four years. During the 1960s these were Exercise *Teamwork* in 1964 and Exercise *Silver Tower* in 1968. Both scenarios were based on a carrier battle group operating in the Norwegian Sea and smaller forces carrying out convoy escort duties in the Eastern Atlantic and English Channel.

One aim of Exercise *Teamwork*, which took place between 21 September and 2 October 1964, was to practise the deployment of the newly established Allied Command Europe (ACE) Mobile Force (AMF) into Norway. A carrier battle group was led by USS *Independence*, with CVW-7 embarked. *Independence* was supported by HMS *Eagle* and the ASW carrier USS *Wasp*. In addition, there was participation by MPAs from VP-21 flying from NAS Brunswick, Maine and VP-8 from NAS Patuxent River. AEW aircraft operating from Keflavik also took part, as did Convair F-102 Delta Dagger fighters of the USAF 57th Fighter Interceptor Squadron (FIS), which were also based at Keflavik. The Delta Daggers intercepted numerous Soviet Tu-95KM strike aircraft which along with Tu-16 and Myasichev 3M shadowed the NATO ships. Interceptions of Soviet aircraft were also carried out by carrier-borne Phantoms.

Exercise *Silver Tower* was held in September 1968, once again featuring a carrier battle group, this time led by HMS *Eagle*, with HMCS *Bonaventure* and USS *Wasp* providing ASW support. The carrier battle group deployed into Arctic waters and Buccaneers and Sea Vixens flying daily sorties from HMS *Eagle* provided air cover for amphibious landings on the Norwegian coast. One Buccaneer strike was against a target some 750 miles distant from the aircraft carrier. Land-based aircraft included the F-104G Starfighters of MFG 1 which had deployed to Ørland for the exercise. Meanwhile convoy operations were practised, using real merchant ships sailing from the eastern seaboard of North America into the southwest approaches of the UK and onwards into the English Channel. During this phase three Argus MPAs from 404 Sqn RCAF achieved 300 hours between them, through flying back-to-back 17-hour sorties. As with Exercise *Teamwork*, the Soviets took a great interest in the exercise, particularly in the Norwegian Sea, with numerous naval ships and submarines shadowing the NATO ships. And once again, Tu-95 and Tu-16 reconnaissance and maritime strike aircraft were also very much in evidence throughout the exercise.

The Second Decade

From the perspective of naval strategy, the 1960s was dominated by the increasing importance of the SSBN and its missile armament. By the end of the decade both sides had large numbers of missile-armed submarines in service and from a position of nuclear superiority in 1960, the USA and its NATO allies had been manoeuvred by the USSR into nuclear stalemate. With the increased submarine threat, both sides had correspondingly increased their ASW capability: in particular, longer-range, better equipped and generally more capable aircraft had been introduced during the course of the decade. The concept of the carrier battle group still dominated US Navy thinking and the USN maintained its force level of 15 attack carriers in service; nevertheless, in the ACLANT and Mediterranean regions there was a broadly even split between attack and ASW carriers. Both the Canadian and Netherlands navies had abandoned the air defence and surface attack roles from their aircraft carriers, concentrating instead on the ASW role. Although the RN saw its carrier force decline from five to two ships by the end of the decade, there was little difference to its NATO commitment, since much of the British carrier activity had concentrated on national tasking beyond the NATO area. This was also true of the French navy, with its two aircraft carriers, and although France had withdrawn from the NATO integrated military command structure, it remained a full member of the alliance.

Meanwhile, the Soviet Navy had grown in numbers both of submarines and surface ships and was beginning to venture further afield than it had done in the 1950s. Naval bases in the Middle East enabled the Soviet fleets to operate with confidence in the Mediterranean Sea as well as the Indian Ocean and the Eastern Atlantic Ocean. Soviet naval aviation was also extending its reach, having abandoned short-range tactical aircraft for long-range reconnaissance and missile-armed strike aircraft. However, the main change in Soviet naval strategy was the switch from anti-carrier operations to ASW, as evidenced by the development of SSNs and the introduction of the Il-38 MPA and the Moskva-class anti-submarine helicopter cruisers. Overall, the Soviet Navy – including the AV-MF – ended the decade in a far stronger position than it had been in at the beginning of it.

CHAPTER 3

THE FLAG OF THE SOVIET NAVY – 1970–79

'The flag of the Soviet navy now proudly flies over the oceans of the world. Sooner or later, the US will have to understand that it no longer has mastery of the seas.'
Admiral Sergei Gorshkov, Soviet Navy, 1968.

Although no-one could know it at the time, the end of 1969 marked the chronological halfway point of the Cold War. But it also marked the watershed: faced with nuclear stalemate after two decades of massive re-armament and rising political tensions, both sides realized that they would have to negotiate if they were to de-escalate the international situation. The Strategic Arms Limitation Talks (SALT), which had started in Helsinki in 1969, culminated three years later in the SALT I agreement. This limited the number of Anti-Ballistic Missile (ABM) systems that each side could deploy as well as placing a cap on the number of ballistic missiles (but not warheads) in each arsenal. Negotiations continued through the 1970s and further restrictions on numbers of delivery vehicles were agreed and introduced in SALT II at the end of the decade. Meanwhile the Mutual and Balanced Force Reduction (MBFR) talks commenced in Vienna in 1973 and in the same year, the Conference on Security and Co-operation in Europe (CSCE) opened in Geneva. The final act of the CSCE published in 1975 contained four so-called 'baskets' which covered agreements on international borders and sovereignty, economic arrangements, human rights, and the implementation process for all of these agreements including confidence building measures. Thus, where the 1960s had started with confrontation, particularly during the

OPPOSITE The last RN aircraft carrier, HMS *Ark Royal* (R09) remained in commission until 14 February 1979. During the 1970s her air wing included the McDonnell Douglas Phantom FG1 (seen here), Hawker Siddeley Buccaneer S2, Fairey Gannet AEW3 and Westland Sea King HAS1. (Cooke)

As well as missile carrying variants of the Tupolev Tu-16, the AV-MF operated the Tu-16R (Badger-E) photoreconnaissance aircraft. These aircraft frequently tracked NATO warships. (NARA)

Cuban missile crisis, the 1970s began at least with some spirit of co-existence and co-operation. Nevertheless, both sides remained deeply suspicious of each other, and they continued to improve the combat capabilities of their naval forces through both re-equipment and training.

The USSR in the Early 1970s

The Soviet Navy demonstrated its transition from a coastal force into a powerful blue water fleet in spectacular fashion, by holding a world-wide exercise between 14 April and 5 May 1970. Exercise *Okean*-70 (Ocean-70) involved manoeuvres by the Northern, Baltic, Black Sea and Pacific Fleets. Over 200 ships and submarines took part, as well as hundreds of aircraft; the Northern Fleet was represented by 60 surface ships and 40 submarines. In a remarkable display of capability, the AV-MF caried out six simultaneous globally separated simulated strikes against targets representing carrier groups. Tu-16 regiments attacked targets in the

Tupolev Tu-95 to Cuba
Sergey Lavrov • Interpreter attached to the 392nd ODRAP, AV-MF

The first time I was abroad was not on a Tu-16, but as part of the crew of the first Soviet military aircraft that landed on the American continent. In April 1970, in honour of the 100th anniversary of Lenin's birth, the *Okean*-70 exercise was conducted, during which two TU-95RTs aircraft (reconnaissance version) flew across the ocean and landed in Cuba. I was transferred from Severomorsk to Kipelovo. Since this was my first flight on these planes, then, according to flight tradition, they tried to tease in every possible way. Most of all, I remember a joke when, during a flight over neutral waters in the area of Ireland, I was tragically informed that we had been detected and in a few minutes the Lightning would fly up to us. Immediately, the warning lights and audio alarms went off, which was rather unpleasant… but for some reason I did not react in any way. Probably, I didn't 'get it'. After a few minutes, the fighters actually flew up and accompanied us for a while. The pilots were clearly visible, and they exchanged greetings and some other gestures with us. It was only after that that they explained to me that this was a common harmless escort practice.

When we landed, several jeeps with armed Cubans drove up to our plane. They started shouting at us loudly and gesticulating frantically. None of the high-ranking officials who were supposed to meet us were observed. Something was wrong… It turned out that we had landed at a military airfield, and not the international one, Jose Marti, where we were supposed to be (the difference was one degree). We quickly fixed the error…

The return flight didn't begin very smoothly either. Take-off was scheduled for 04:00hrs when the lowest daily temperature is needed to increase lift. The plane itself is heavy, plus full refuelling – 100 tons of fuel. The runway, immediately beyond which was a forest of palm trees, was already ending, and we still could not gain altitude. All the warning lights and audio alarms went off again. The pilots were extremely tense, their faces instantly covered in sweat, and it became clear that this was not a joke this time. With difficulty, the pilots still coped and in the last seconds we just cleared the palm trees. We flew back to the USSR without refuelling for 25hr. At that time, it was a record for the longest flight, which lasted so long because it was also necessary to work over the ocean. For example, we flew over the aircraft carrier *Independence*, which was 'lost' in the ocean. About two weeks later, two other crews repeated the flight. The command decided that I should fly with them again. This time they didn't make fun of me anymore because I was already a 'qualified sparrow', and everything went very smoothly. But those who saw us off from Cuba for the first time said, when we met them again, that everyone had the same reaction to our take-off: 'I feel sorry for good planes and Russians, but now they will crash into the forest …' At the end of the exercise, I was presented with a certificate on behalf of the commander of the fleet, who led the *Okean*-70 manoeuvres.

North Sea, the Sea of Japan and the North Pacific Ocean, while Tu-95 units struck targets in the North Atlantic Ocean and the Philippine Sea. These engagements were synchronized with another simulated strike by submarines and surface ships in the Mediterranean Sea. During the exercise a pair of Tu-95RTs reconnaissance aircraft flew from Severomorsk across the Atlantic Ocean to Cuba, following a flight path that took them over the Norwegian Sea and then sweeping close to Newfoundland and down to the Azores before turning for Cuba. Two more pairs of Tu-95 followed the same route over the next weeks, demonstrating the global reach of the AV-MF.

The long-range aircraft of the AV-MF underwent significant upgrades which arrived in front-line units during the early 1970s. The armament of the Tu-16 was upgraded with the Raduga Kh-26 KSR-5 (AS-6 Kingfish) anti-shipping missile. The missile, which was a smaller version of the Kh-22 (Kitchen) missile, was equipped with an active homing radar and had a range of some 350 miles; it was armed with a 1,000lb conventional high explosive warhead or a 350-kiloton nuclear warhead. After modification to carry the KSR-5, the aircraft was redesignated as the Tu-16KSR (Badger-G) and could carry two KSR-5 missiles. This modified aircraft equipped the regiments of the Baltic, Black Sea and Pacific Fleets. All three fleets continued to operate the Tu-16K-10 variant armed with the K-10S missile and this type remained the primary strike aircraft of the Northern Fleet regiments. However, some of these Tu-16K-10 airframes were also modified to carry the KSR-5 but unlike the Tu-16KSR, these aircraft retained the ability to be armed alternatively with the low altitude K-10S (Kipper) missile; they were designated the Tu-16K-10-26 variant, although they were still known to NATO as the Badger-C. The Northern and Pacific Fleets also operated the Tu-95RTs in the maritime reconnaissance role and these aircraft were supplemented with a new-build ASW variant, the Tu-142 (Bear-F). The Tu-142 featured a lengthened fuselage to accommodate the ASW equipment which included the Berkut radar and attack system (which was also mounted in the Il-38), passive ESM sensors and sonobuoys. The initial production did not incorporate MAD equipment, but this was corrected on the later Tu-142M variant, which had the MMS-106 Ladoga MAD sensor mounted at the top of the tailfin. In yet a further variant, the Tu-142MK, the Berkut system was replaced by a Korshun-K surveillance and targeting system.

With the introduction of the Project 667 (Delta-class) SSBN armed with the 4,700-mile range R-29 (SS-N-8 Sawfly) ballistic missile, the newer Soviet submarines no longer needed to sail into the Atlantic Ocean in order to reach targets in the US. They could instead remain in northern waters that were well defended by Soviet ships, aircraft and SSNs. Following on from this development, the Soviet Navy began during the 1970s to adopt a strategy of the 'bastion' in the Norwegian and Barents Seas. This concept envisioned taking control of the Norwegian Sea above the GIUK gap and denying the area to NATO aircraft carriers and submarines, perhaps even establishing their own barrier across the GIUK gap to prevent NATO navies' SSNs from entering the region of the bastion. The area was close enough to the airfields at Severomorsk for ASW and reconnaissance aircraft to patrol the area and, if necessary, for the Tu-16K-10 regiments to strike any NATO carrier group that came near. In this case it was thought that a simultaneous regimental attack by at least 20 aircraft would be needed to achieve the six to eight missile hits that were considered necessary to neutralize an aircraft carrier. Nevertheless, the older Golf- and Yankee-class submarines still needed to reach their patrol areas off the coast of North America and these submarines still had to be located and tracked by NATO naval forces throughout their cruise.

OPPOSITE TOP The Tupolev Tu-142 (Bear-F) was a bespoke long-range maritime patrol and ASW aircraft. As well as having a longer fuselage than the Tu-95 Bear variants, the Tu-142 was distinguishable by the tail mounted MAD fairing. (NARA)

OPPOSITE BOTTOM A McDonnell Douglas A-4E Skyhawk of VA-45 from USS *Intrepid* (CVA 11) escorts an AV-MF Tu-16RM (Badger-D) maritime reconnaissance aircraft, circa 1970. Equipped with the Puff Ball radar, the Tu-16RM acted in a hunter-killer team with the Tu-16K-10-26 (Badger-C) strike aircraft. (US Navy)

TOP RIGHT A pair of McDonnell Douglas F-4B Phantoms of VF-41 flying from USS *Franklin D. Roosevelt* (CVA 42) during a cruise in the Mediterranean Sea in 1973. (US Navy)

BOTTOM RIGHT An A-4D Skyhawk of VA-205 flying from USS *John F. Kennedy* (CVA 67) operating in the Atlantic, August 1971. The squadron was a reserve unit formed in 1970 to improve the combat readiness of the reserve forces. (US Navy)

Despite the emphasis on ASW, the Soviet Navy also maintained its capability to strike at NATO carrier groups. In the summer of 1971, the Northern Fleet held a large-scale anti-carrier exercise in the Norwegian Sea. A simulated carrier group passed through the GIUK gap on 25 June and over the next three days the operational area was swept by four Tu-95RTs reconnaissance aircraft, which located the group and passed on the target details. On 29 June a force of Tu-95KD from the VVS-DA carried out simulated Kh-20 attacks on the carrier group. Later on the same day, a regimental-size attack was carried out by an AV-MF Tu-16K-10 regiment followed by another attack by a VVS-DA Tu-16KSR regiment, each formation comprising some 32 aircraft. The following day, the Tu-95RTs practised providing target data for submarine launched cruise missiles.

ABOVE Flying from the carrier USS *Dwight D. Eisenhower* (CV 69) during her maiden cruise in the Mediterranean Sea in voyage 1978, this Ling-Temco-Vought (LTV) A-7E Corsair II is from VA-12. The type progressively replaced the Skyhawk through the 1970s. (NARA)

In the same year the balance of naval forces in the Baltic Sea had shifted enough to lead US National Security Advisor Henry Kissinger to comment that:

> In the Baltic it does seem clear that the Soviets have moved into a position of naval dominance. In the event of NATO-Pact hostilities, the Pact could probably gain early control of the inner Baltic although NATO has reasonable prospects of preventing egress of most of the Pact naval forces into the North Sea and beyond. However, the Pact has attained significant amphibious capability that could be used to seize the Baltic exits in conjunction with airborne forces or to conduct flanking operations to support an overland thrust across the North German Plain. Success in either of the latter two attempts would depend critically on the NATO air and ground forces that could be localized for defence.

The Baltic and Black Sea Fleets each possessed a reconnaissance regiment operating some 30 Tu-22R (Blinder-C), as well as regiments of Tu-16K-10 and Tu-16KSR strike aircraft and a further three regiments of Il-28 light bombers. These were backed up by Tu-16, Tu-95 and Tu-22 strike regiments from the VVS-DA. However, in the Mediterranean Sea the 5th *Eskadra* relied on surface ships and submarines to counter NATO carrier battle groups, rather than using the maritime aircraft like the Baltic Fleet; instead, the aircraft of the Black Sea Fleet were employed solely as reconnaissance assets.

ABOVE These two Grumman A-6E Intruders from CVW-7 embarked on USS *Dwight D. Eisenhower* (CV 69) during her maiden cruise are showing the different paint schemes in use at the time. The Intruder on the left is painted in the newer 'toned down' type. (NARA)

In the Baltic, the AV-MF was augmented by the Polish LMW, which now had an ASW capability in the four Mil Mi-4ME ASW helicopters operated by 18 Naval Rescue Squadron (*Eskadra Lotnictwa Łącznikowego MW – ELŁ MW*) based at Darlowo on the northern coast. This helicopter was equipped with search radar and MAD and could carry either the sonobuoy in the search mode or weapons in the attack mode. The unit also operated a small number of Mil Mi-2RM (Hoplite) helicopters for search and rescue duties. Meanwhile, 7.PLM-Sz MW continued to fly the Lim-6bis in the maritime strike role, and the reconnaissance unit 15.ELR MW soldiered on with Il-28R. However, increasing problems of serviceability with the elderly Il-28 led to the type being withdrawn in 1979.

US in the Early 1970s

No new aircraft carriers joined the USN fleet in the first half of the decade, for although USS *Nimitz* (CVN 68), the first of a new class of nuclear carriers, was launched in 1972 she was not commissioned until 1975. The number of attack carriers remained stable at 15, but the obsolescent Essex-class ASW carriers were withdrawn from service in the early 1970s, with the last one, USS *Intrepid*, being decommissioned in March 1974. Two Essex-class ships that had remained in the attack role, and were heavily involved in the Vietnam War, USS *Hancock* and USS *Oriskany*, remained with the Pacific Fleet until 1976. During 1970 both USS *Forrestal* and USS

Independence had deployed to the Mediterranean with eight SH-3D Sea King ASW helicopters attached to their air wings. This marked the start of combining the strike and ASW roles within a single ship and from 1971 the attack carriers were progressively modified to include the necessary equipment for the ASW role. The ships were redesignated as 'CV,' indicating their new multi-role capabilities. The first such ship was USS *Saratoga*, which was reclassified as a 'multi-purpose aircraft carrier' at the end of June 1972. In light of the new task, the composition of the carrier air wing was amended, removing 12 fighter, attack and reconnaissance aircraft to make space for S-2E Trackers and the SH-3D Sea Kings. The revised complement for a carrier air wing now included 20 F-4J Phantom fighters, 20 A-7A Corsair and nine A-6A Intruder attack aircraft, four KA-6D Intruder AAR tankers, four EA-6B Prowler EW aircraft, four E-2B Hawkeye AEW aircraft, ten S-2E Tracker ASWs and eight SH-3D Sea King helicopters, making a total of 79 aircraft.

BELOW A Vought F-8 Crusader moments before touchdown on the flight deck of USS *John F. Kennedy* (CVA 67), somewhere in the Atlantic Ocean, August 1971. The Crusader was withdrawn from service in 1976. (US Navy)

By 1970 the USN fast jet fleet had become standardized with the F-4J variant of the Phantom for air defence, the A-6E Intruder for night/all-weather strike and the A-7E Corsair for day attack missions. All of these variants of the aircraft were developments of the earlier models introducing improved avionics; in the case of the A-6E it included fitting the more powerful Allison TF-41 turbofan and the incorporation of target recognition attack multi-sensors (TRAM) and forward looking infra-red (FLIR). The F-4J update included the AN/APG-59 pulsed-doppler radar which enabled the fighter to detect low-flying targets. From 1972, some F-4J aircraft were modified to F-4N standard which incorporated a smokeless development of the J-79 engine. If the F-4 Phantom is considered the most iconic carrier-borne aircraft of the 1960s and early 1970s, then the F-14 Tomcat, its successor in the air-defence role, must surely be its counterpart in the late 1970s and the 1980s. The Grumman F-14A Tomcat was delivered to VF-1 and VF-2 on the west coast in 1973, and equipped VF-14 and VF-32 attached to the Atlantic Fleet in the following year. The twin-seat twin-engine variable geometry fighter

BELOW Handing over the baton of the fleet ASW role, a Grumman S-2G Tracker from the last Tracker unit, VS-37, breaks away from a Lockheed S-3A Viking of VS-21, the first Viking squadron, off San Diego, 28 July 1976. (US Navy)

was designed around the AN/AWG-9 radar and the Hughes AIM-54A Phoenix radar-guided AAM. With active guidance and a range of some 80 miles, the Phoenix gave the Tomcat the ability to engage targets at great distance from the carrier battle group. The F-14 could carry a war load of six Phoenix missiles, or a mix of Phoenix and AIM-9 Sidewinder AAMs. The other new type introduced to the fleet, the EA-6B Prowler, was a dedicated ECM aircraft based on the A-6 fuselage that was lengthened to accommodate the crew of four. It was built around the AN/ALQ-99 tactical jamming system and was used for electronic warfare support, which had become a vital part of strike missions.

Another important addition to the USN inventory in 1974 was the Lockheed S-3A Viking ASW aircraft. This twin-jet aeroplane had a crew of four and was equipped with the latest ASW sensors including an AN/APS-116 search radar, retractable MAD, FLIR and the AN/ALR-47 ESM system. It could carry 59 sonobuoys and had an internal weapons bay capable of accommodating four Mk 46 torpedoes or bombs, mines or depth charges. The Viking progressively replaced the Tracker in service for carrier-borne ASW.

Land-based ASW by the USN continued to be the preserve of the P-3 Orion. Detachments from the MPA squadrons cycled through Keflavik, patrolling the GIUK gap, Lajes, covering the southern sectors, and Sigonella, patrolling the Mediterranean. In all of these cases the USN aircraft co-operated closely with the MPAs of the other NATO countries. During ASW operations in the Norwegian Sea and North Atlantic when a Soviet submarine had been detected, the USN Orion squadrons would often fly six consecutive sorties in each 24-hour period, each sortie generating four hours on station overhead the submarine contact, so that 24-hour coverage was achieved and the submarine was tracked throughout its voyage.

BELOW Illustrating the inclement weather conditions that MPA crews frequently had to endure when operating from Iceland, a Lockheed P-3 Orion of VP-46 taxies along a damp flight line at Keflavik, September 1977. (NARA)

ABOVE HMS *Ark Royal* (R09) was the only RN aircraft carrier that could operate the McDonnell Douglas F-4K Phantom FG1. The British variant of the Phantom differed from the US variants in being powered by Rolls Royce Spey 201 engines. (NMNA)

In response to the concerns about Soviet dominance in the Baltic Sea, the USS *Intrepid* steamed into the Baltic in May 1971, sailing to the eastern end of the sea and to within 20 miles of Soviet coastline. This strong demonstration of political will and military capability heralded the start of regular deployments into the Baltic during the annual Exercise *Baltops* which was first held in 1972. Following its Baltic cruise in 1971, *Intrepid* joined the carrier USS *Constellation* for exercises in the Western Mediterranean Sea in June. Then, in September, *Intrepid* participated in Exercise *Royal Knight* in the Norwegian Sea, working with the attack carriers USS *Independence* and HMS *Ark Royal*. The following year, *Intrepid* sailed into the Barents Sea, again demonstrating the intention and ability of NATO aircraft carriers to contest the waters that the Soviet Navy aspired to control.

During the Arab-Israeli War of October 1973, both the USA and USSR sent warships into the Eastern Mediterranean Sea to apply political pressure on behalf of their clients. The USA reinforced Israel, while the USSR did the same for Egypt. At that time, the 6th Fleet included two carrier battle groups led by USS *Franklin D. Roosevelt* (CVA 42) and *Independence*, as well as the amphibious assault helicopter carrier USS *Guadalcanal*. Additionally, USS *John F. Kennedy* (CVA 67) and *Iwo Jima* (LPH 2), which were in the North Sea, began to sail to join them. The first task of the carrier air wings was to provide air defence cover for the Lockheed C-5 Galaxy and C-141 Starlifter transports that were carrying supplies to Israel. Meanwhile the Soviet Navy steadily increased its presence in the Mediterranean and by the end of the month there would be 96 Soviet naval units, including 23 submarines, in the theatre. The readiness state of the US Navy was raised to DEFCON 3 for two days on 26 October, which was the same day that the Soviet Navy started an anti-carrier exercise, covering all three US carriers and the two assault helicopter carriers. The confrontation ended in early November.

BELOW A Hawker Siddeley Buccaneer S2 lands on HMS *Hermes* (R12), circa 1970, the year in which the ship was decommissioned. With the demise of *Hermes* and HMS *Eagle* (R05) two years later, naval Buccaneers were passed to the RAF to form land-based anti-shipping squadrons. (Pitchfork)

1970s – First Carrier Launch in a Phantom
Chris Bolton • Royal Air Force Phantom FG1 pilot

I was scheduled for first launch in the afternoon push. One of three F4K Phantoms to carry out air intercepts and 2in. RP practice on the splash target towed 500yd astern. Taxiing out to the waist catapult, my pulse rate was probably a little elevated. The pulse rate of my observer was clearly even more so. For him, it was not just another launch, but a first launch with a rookie carrier pilot. We were expertly marshalled onto the catapult. Brakes applied. Aircraft hold back unit engaged, brakes released, nose leg extended (by 40 inches) and aircraft tensioned. The area ahead of the aircraft was no longer visible over the nose. Having clutched the stick positioning device (STP), I acknowledged correct stabilator angle as reported externally, checked internally and correct for take-off weight. Ground crew cleared away to starboard. The flight deck officer (FDO) waved his green flag over his head, and I applied maximum cold power, followed by maximum afterburner. Significant noise, vibration, and adrenalin. Heavy breathing from the rear cockpit. Wouldn't you too! All internal checks complete, I held my right hand up to the FDO. He checked for the green light from Flyco, and upon receiving it and checking all clear ahead, he lowered his green flag to the deck. This was the signal for the catapult operator to take his hands off his head and press the large circular plate in front of him, to fire the catapult. I held power at maximum top left corner lest the G retard the throttles, stick back against SPD restraint, and head firmly again the ejection seat headrest. A seemingly interminable wait as 1,120lb of superheated steam at 600°C broke the hold back unit weak link. About 60,000lbs break out force. In reality it was about 2sec. Then the very rapid acceleration to about 4G. After the 195' take off run, of about 2.5sec, airborne, and marked decrease in acceleration. Rotate from the 9 degrees to 14-degrees climb angle. Gear up, flaps up, burners out at 250kts. That was fun wasn't it! A real thrill. Only 80min to go and it would be time for my first deck landing.

Although we practised deck landings ashore using a very similar Deck Projector Landing Sight, the drama of one's first 'for real' one, was of a different order of magnitude. Conforming to our pre-briefed slot time, we recovered in echelon starboard to the ship which was already on recovery heading. This was carried out at 1,200ft and 270kt. Passing ahead of the ship each aircraft turned gently downwind at 10 second intervals. As speed reduced, gear and flaps were extended at standard speeds leaving us in full landing configuration at 150kt and 1.25nm abeam the ship. The ship looked very small. She was making forward speed to produce 30kt of wind down the angle deck. This was a combination of ship speed and natural wind. Passing abeam the landing point, I started my turn onto finals holding a constant speed of 150kt. Flying over the ship's wake, my eyes now became riveted on the sight. Real tunnel vision. Speed was critical to maintain correct angle of attack and thus correct attitude on arrival at the landing zone. There were plenty of aids to achieve this. Firstly, an ASI. Secondly there was audio angle of attack. A steady note was the optimum. High pitch tones indicated excess speed and the converse was true. Alongside the gun sight were indexers. A pointing down arrow showed excess speed and again the converse was true. A steady doughnut was optimum. As if all this was not enough, the occasionally calm voice of the observer also advised actual speed as in 'Plus Five. Minus Three' etc. Externally, there were horizontal fans of lights on the nose wheel door, enabling the LSO to observe the approach angle of attack.

Avoiding over control was important and also a little difficult with high adrenalin and a firm grip on the pole. The LSO gave advice along the lines of 'Slightly high', 'Slightly left' as appropriate. His commands were mandatory.

As previously mentioned, gear and flaps were in the full landing configuration. The hook remained retracted. This was my first time, and the plan was two rollers, then a third and final approach hook down. Three approaches was generally the limit, as concentration was stretched by then. Additionally, fuel was limited by maximum landing weight, and having sufficient to divert if necessary.

After two agricultural rollers, I was directed to 'hook down'. Crunch time, and it wasn't very pretty. I got quite low in close and caught one wire after a short taxi. The landing is always a hard arrival as no flare is made and rate of descent was about 800fpm. So, a very agricultural arrival assessed as 'Yellow' by the LSO. The 'Goofers' had not been disappointed by the new boy's performance on his first go.

Britain in the Early 1970s

The early 1970s were a time of great change for British maritime aviation. One of the most significant events was the decommissioning of HMS *Eagle* in 1972, when it proved to be too expensive to refit. The demise of the ship also marked the end of the Sea Vixen: the last Sea Vixen squadron, 899 NAS, was disbanded in January 1972. This left the RN with a single aircraft carrier, HMS *Ark Royal*, which carried a complement of just 39 aircraft comprising 12 Phantom FG1 (892 NAS), 14 Buccaneer S2 (809 NAS), four Gannet AEW3 (B Flight 849 NAS) and six Westland Sea King HAS1 (824 NAS). The latter ASW helicopter, which had entered RN service in 1970, was based on the Sikorsky AH-3 Sea King, but was powered by two Rolls-Royce Gnome engines and was fitted with British equipment, including a MEL ARI 5995 search radar, mounted in a dorsal radome, and the Plessey Type 195 dipping sonar. The fitting of the search radar enabled the British-built Sea King to operate more autonomously than its US counterpart. In addition to the above complement, HMS *Ark Royal* carried three Wessex HAS1 as 'plane guards' which provided search and rescue (SAR) cover for fixed wing operations.

The reduction in carrier-based air power was, to an extent, compensated for with the increased shore-based maritime air power in the form of the Phantom FG1 fighters of 43 Sqn RAF and Buccaneer S2 strike aircraft of 12 and, from 1974, 208 Sqns. The latter unit was formed using ex-FAA aircraft. In addition, from November 1971 early-warning radar for the UK Air Defence Region (UKADR) was enhanced by the permanent attachment of A Flight 849 NAS operating the Gannet AEW3 from Lossiemouth. Aircraft from 12 Sqn and 43 Sqn deployed to Malta for the maritime Exercise *Lime Jug* in 1970. It was during this exercise that the tactic of using the Victor B(SR)2 of 543 Sqn to locate the target and direct the Buccaneers onto it was perfected. When 543 Sqn was disbanded in 1974, the role was taken over by 27 Sqn equipped with the Avro Vulcan B2. Buccaneers and Vulcans continued to deploy to RAF Luqa, Malta in 1973, 1974 and 1975 for the annual NATO Exercise *Dawn Patrol*. The main targets for the Buccaneers were the Soviet surface action groups (SAG) and in particular those led by Sverdlov-class cruisers. The tactic was for a co-ordinated eight aircraft attack, the Alpha attack profile, during which the aircraft remained at ultra-low level to stay beneath the target radar horizon for as long as possible, before closing on the target from different directions with a mix of toss and laydown bomb deliveries.

RIGHT Exercise *Lime Jug*, which was held in Malta, November 1970, was an opportunity for the newly formed RAF Buccaneer S2 and Phantom FG1 squadrons to practise deployed operations in support of the fleet. The participating aircraft are depicted here at RAF Luqa. (Pitchfork)

There was a major enhancement of the RAF ASW capability with the introduction of the Hawker Siddeley Nimrod MR1, which began to replace the Shackleton from 1970. The Nimrod was developed from the de Havilland Comet 4 airliner and was unique in being the first jet-powered MPA to be employed in front-line service. It equipped three units, 120 Sqn, 201 Sqn and 206 Sqn, at RAF Kinloss in northern Scotland, as well as 42 Sqn at RAF St Mawgan, Cornwall and 203 Sqn at RAF Luqa, Malta. With its fast transit speed of 400kt at altitude, the Nimrod could cover a large area of sea during its patrols. It was equipped with the ASV 21 search radar, but also carried the ARAR/ARAX ESM equipment in a fairing on top of the fin, and tail-mounted MAD sensor as well as a selection of sonobuoys. State of the art data processing and a computerized tactical display ensured that despite its obsolescent search radar, the aeroplane represented a huge improvement over the Shackleton that it replaced. Like its predecessor, the Nimrod had a large ventral weapons bay that could carry a wide variety of weapons, including nuclear depth bombs. It also had underwing hardpoints for the Nord AS-12 ASM.

The Nimrod played an important part in the so-called 'Cod War' between September 1972 and October 1973, during which the Icelandic authorities attempted to enforce a unilaterally declared 50-mile exclusive economic zone around its coastal waters. RN frigates were sent to protect British trawlers from the attentions of Icelandic navy gunboats, which were attempting to cut their nets to stop them fishing in the disputed area. Continuous Nimrod patrols monitored the situation, gathering information on the relative positions of gunboats and trawlers. The task was also shared by the Bristol Britannia transports of 99 Sqn and 511 Sqn, which were called in to assist with the surveillance task in order to preserve fatigue life on the Nimrod airframes.

BELOW The first jet-powered MPA, Hawker Siddeley Nimrod MR1 acted not only as an ASW platform but also as a tactical director for the Buccaneer S2, passing updates of target positions to the strike crews. (Pitchfork)

Canada and Western Europe in the Early 1970s

Without an aircraft carrier in service, maritime aviation in the Canadian Armed Forces (CAF) was now limited to maritime patrol by the four squadrons of CP-107 Argus (404 Sqn and 405 Sqn at Greenwood, Nova Scotia, 415 Sqn at Summerside on Prince Edward Island on the east coast and 407 Sqn at Comox on the west coast) as well as the CP-121 Trackers of VS 880 which had previously flown from HMCS *Bonaventure*. While the Argus was still regarded as one of the most capable ASW aircraft in NATO service, the Tracker was handicapped by its short range now that it was shore-based. From 1974 the type was withdrawn from the ASW role and, with their ASW equipment removed, the aircraft were used instead for coastal fishery protection patrols. Reflecting the change of role to maritime reconnaissance, the unit was re-designated as MR 880. The CAF retained a more limited shipborne ASW capability through the CH-124 Sea King which was flown from Iroquois-class destroyers and Protecteur-class fleet replenishment ships. These helicopters began a modification programme, the Sea King Improvement Program (SKIP), in 1974 and over the next five years new engines, transmission and radar were fitted.

Like the CAF, the Netherlands navy no longer possessed an aircraft carrier. The Trackers of the Dutch MLD were also disposed of, leaving the two squadrons of MPA for maritime surveillance and ASW. Both were based at Valkenburg, with 320 Sqn flying the SP-2H Neptune, and 321 Sqn operating the Atlantique. Italy had also placed a late order for the aircraft and the two ItAF units, the 41st Anti-Submarine Squadron

BELOW A Canadair CP-107 Argus displaying the new logo of the unified Canadian Armed Forces. The Argus served throughout the 1970s until it was replaced by the Lockheed CP-140 Aurora. (Canada DND)

ABOVE The Breguet BR1150 Atlantique was also designated the SP-13A in the Dutch MLD which operated one squadron (VSQ321) flying the type from 1969. During the 1970s, the Atlantique was operated by the Dutch, French and German navies, as well as the Italian Air Force. (Netherlands Institute of Military History)

(41° *Stormo AntiSom*) and 30° *Stormo AntiSom* became operational respectively at Catania in 1972 and Cagliari in 1973. This meant that the Atlantique saw service in the Baltic and North Sea with the German MFG 3, the North Sea with the MLD, the Eastern Atlantic and Mediterranean with the French *Aéronavale* and the Mediterranean with the ItAF. Meanwhile, the Italian navy moved its ASW helicopter units to Sarzana-Luni, near Spezia. At the new base 1° Gruppelicot re-equipped with the Agusta ASH-3D Sea King, while 5° Gruppelicot continued to fly the AB-204AS.

Some of the surplus ex-MLD Trackers were purchased by the Turkish Naval Air Command (*Türk Deniz Hava Komutanlığı*) which established an MPA unit, 301 Squadron (*Filo*), at Bandirma, on the southern shore of the Sea of Marmara, in 1971. As well as the ex-MLD S-2A Trackers, the unit also operated S-2E Trackers bought from the USN. The fixed wing ASW fleet was complemented in early 1973 by the formation of the first Turkish ASW helicopter unit, 351 *Filo*, at Cengis Topel near Istanbul with the Agusta-Bell AB-204AS. Meanwhile on the other side of the Aegean Sea, 353 MNAS of the Hellenic Air Force continued to use the HU-15B Albatross for ASW work.

In Portugal, surplus ex-MLD P-2E Neptunes had been supplied to the FAP in the early 1960s but they were not used for in the maritime role; instead they were employed in support of colonial counter-insurgency operations in Angola, Mozambique and Guinea-Bissau. Although the 'carnation revolution' of April 1974 marked a change of government in Portugal and a rundown of military action in the colonies, the FAP Neptunes were not switched to the ASW role. Another service in receipt of surplus aircraft from another alliance member was the RNoAF, which took over 22 CF-104 Starfighters from the CAF in 1973. These aircraft were used to re-equip 334 Skv, replacing the F-5 Freedom Fighter. With the new aircraft type came a dedicated anti-shipping role. The Norwegian CF-104 could be armed with the Bullpup ASM for anti-shipping missions, but the more usual weapon load comprised four LAU-3 rocket pods carrying 2.75in. rockets, 500lb Snakeye bombs and the 20mm M61 Vulcan cannon. Tactics involved attacking as a four-ship, with each aircraft coming from a different direction. The rocket-armed aircraft would target the radar heads while the bomb-armed aircraft aimed for the hull and superstructure.

In the Mediterranean region COMARAIRMED wielded a powerful maritime surveillance and ASW force which included USN P-3 Orions operating from Sigonella, RAF Nimrods operating from Malta and periodically also from Gibraltar, Trackers flown by the ItAF and Turkish Navy, and Hellenic Air Force Hu-16 Albatrosses, as well as S-3 Vikings flown from the USN carriers of the 6th Fleet. Facing them, the submarine element of the Soviet 5th *Eskadra* in the Mediterranean had grown during the previous decade, but it was equipped with diesel-electric boats, which needed to surface to recharge their batteries. This was typically done at night, so much of the work carried out under the auspices of MARAIRMED involved night flying. Unlike the patrols in the Norwegian Sea that involved hours tracking single submarines, the ASW work in the Mediterranean was characterized by shorter contacts and much more search and reconnaissance activity.

A pair of SP-2H Neptune MPAs of squadron VSQ320 of the Dutch MLD finished in the colour scheme adopted during the 1970s. Although the type was obsolescent, the it remained in MLD service until the early 1980s. (Netherlands Institute of Military History)

> ## 1970s – The Starfighter in the Anti-Shipping Role
> Helge Andreassen • Royal Norwegian Air Force CF-104 Starfighter pilot
>
> With the arrival of the CF-104 Starfighter, 334 Sqn was designated for anti-shipping role. The CF-104 had the APG 502 radar, the Litton LN-3 inertial nav-system, a good autopilot and also the ALR-46 RWR system. The development of tactics was given to the squadron itself. Most of the training involved flights of four or six CF-104s, coordinated attack procedures and escape manoeuvres. With little or sparse target information, training often involved use of a spotter aircraft which gave the target position according to a map-grid system. The workload on the flight lead was very heavy considering he was flying a single-seat jet.
>
> Run-in to the target was via a fixed Initial Point (IP) or based on distance to the target. The four-ship would split at the IP and attack from different directions and speeds. Co-ordinated attacks were considered the most efficient and also provided a better chance of survival. The training was also practised with the RNo Navy: vessels used a towing target for us to fire on using the 20mm Vulcan cannon or 2.75in. rockets. This was practised both day and night. Night gunnery at ground ranges was normal.
>
> As for weapons, the normal load against ships was LAU-3 (19 2.75in. rockets in each pod). We did not carry and stand-off missiles. The primary targets were landing craft such as the Alligator class. Our tactics did not include attacks on ships offshore, as the order to engage an invader would not be given until after Norwegian territory/borders had been penetrated.
>
> The ALR-46 RWR gave us the opportunity to intercept Soviet naval vessels off the coast without using our own radar. We saw and heard their search radar long before they could see us on the scope. We also played with their tracking radars and knew at what altitude and distances they would break lock. In all, the ALR-46 opened a new world to us and thereby provided us with a much better understanding of the opponent's capabilities.
>
> In summary, the CF-104 provided us with a much better weapons system compared to the F-5. Even though the weapons load was not impressive, I would imagine that for the opponent, the pure fact of our existence would require some careful consideration about how to use their resources in a conflict with NATO in the north.

Hunting Submarines

The main tools used by aircraft for hunting submarines were radar and the sonobuoy, and how they were used depended on the characteristics of the quarry. It also depended on the nature of aircraft mission – in other words whether or not the aircraft needed to remain covert. ASW aircraft carried a large stock of expendable sonobuoys, of which the majority in the 1970s were passive non-directional LOFAR buoys. These could detect underwater sound and, by monitoring its frequency and applying the doppler principle, could tell whether the sound source was moving towards or away from the buoy. Intelligence sources provided a detailed frequency spectrum signature for every individual submarine, so the passive sonobuoy could also be used to identify the target. The introduction of DIFAR sonobuoys gave an additional direction-finding capability, so that the relative bearing of the contact from the buoy could also be determined. Triangulation between buoys gave the ability to locate the

ABOVE During the late 1960s and early 1970s, the RNoAF had used the Northrop F-5A equipped with the Bullpup missile in a coastal anti-shipping role. The aircraft were flown by 334 Skv which was based at Bodø. (RNoAF)

target reasonably accurately. Passive sonobuoys enabled the detection of submarines without revealing the presence of the aircraft, whereas active sonobuoys, which could determine both the bearing and the range of a target and thereby give a very accurate target position to attack, would give away the presence of an ASW aircraft.

Aircraft that were providing an anti-submarine screen for a carrier battle group, for example, were tasked to clear the way ahead and around the group. An outer screen of aircraft would drop an array of passive sonobuoys some distance away from the group to gather intelligence on any underwater activity, while an inner screen would tend to use radar and active sonar to enable them to find anything that had evaded the

RIGHT In 1973, the Northrop F-5s of 334 Skv were replaced by ex-CAF Canadair-built CF-104 Starfighters. With the aircraft cannon reinstated (it had been removed in RCAF service) the Starfighter took over the anti-shipping role. (RNoAF)

passive sensors, or to prosecute contacts that had been detected by passive means. Any submarine, whether nuclear or diesel-electric powered, would be located by active sonar, but the submarine crew would be aware of the presence of the aeroplane and could potentially manoeuvre to avoid it. In contrast to short-range ship-borne aircraft, long range MPA tended to use passive sensors in the open ocean in order to locate and follow submarines without the submarine crew knowing that they were being tracked.

Diesel-electric submarines tended to be very quiet while submerged and running on electric power, making them difficult to detect with passive sonar. However, they needed to extend their snorkel system to the surface in order to run their diesel engines periodically to recharge the batteries. At this stage they were vulnerable because the snorkel could be detected by radar and also by sonobuoy because of the noise made by the diesel engine. Thus, an MPA

BELOW The flight deck of a Lockheed P-3C Orion of VP-66, as it performs a steep left-hand turn at low level. The P-3C proved to be a highly effective ASW platform. (Stanton)

hunting a diesel-electric submarine would tend to do so from low level, dropping a barrier of sonobuoys then using its radar. However, submarines were also equipped with ESM systems to detect airborne radars, so the MPA crew could not operate their radar continuously, and instead would use it in short bursts. If a contact was found the aircraft would fly towards it and if engaging, drop a homing torpedo. It would also drop a further sonobuoy overhead the contact to mark its position, and then carry out an orbit to home in for a second torpedo attack. In theory the MAD system could also be used as a means of refining the position of the submarine as the aircraft closed on it, but in practice the MAD was not particularly reliable.

Hunting for a nuclear submarine required different tactics, since nuclear-powered submarines were able to remain submerged for the entire duration of their patrol so were invisible to radar. On the other hand, the nuclear power plant included pumps that had to run continuously and had a distinctive acoustic signature and could therefore be detected using passive sonar systems. The propeller also generated a distinctive acoustic signal. Since the submarines were also equipped with sonar equipment to listen for sounds, including aircraft noise above them, hunting for nuclear submarines was carried out from higher altitudes. The problem here was that the submarine could potentially hear the splash as a sonobuoy entered the water, so buoys had to be

One of the most impressive naval fighter aircraft of all time, the Grumman F-14A Tomcat joined the Atlantic Fleet in 1974. This aircraft from VF-14 embarked on USS *John F. Kennedy* is escorting a Tu-95RTs (Bear-D) in 1977. (NARA)

1970s – Flying the P-3C Orion from Keflavik
Don Stanton • United States Navy P-3C Pilot

After 18 intense months of flight training including six months learning to fly the P-3C, systems, and anti-submarine warfare (ASW) tactics, I checked into VP-45 as it deployed to Iceland in late 1976. We left the live oak trees and humidity of NAS Jacksonville for cold blustery Keflavik near the Arctic Circle with only 4–5 hours of light in late December.

VP-45 had 450 personnel including twelve 12-man crews and nine fairly new P-3Cs equipped with the first digital ASW based around the CP-901 computer. Our missions were to track Soviet Northern Fleet submarines transiting around the Kola Peninsula and heading either southwest through the Greenland Iceland gap for the mid-Atlantic or south through the Iceland-UK gap if they were headed into the eastern Atlantic or the Mediterranean.

After a tactics briefing and a three-hour preflight, we took off with max fuel for an 8- to 10-hour mission. When the squadron was 'FLAP-ing', round-the-clock, each crew kept flying after 12 hours' rest until the aircraft and crews wore out. We flew a two plus-hour transit north above the Arctic Circle in EMCON (Emissions Control - no radio talk) to take over hot (in contact) passive buoys from the on-station crew. We marked on the turnover sonobuoy, picked up hot buoys, and continued to track the sub by dropping buoy barriers from high altitude over the next four hours. The pilots' job was to fly a racetrack pattern at loiter speed often with #1 engine shut-down and to mark on top a buoy to maintain plot stabilization for the TACCO (Tactical Coordinator). From the beginning, it seemed to me that ASW was a combination of science and art.

Winter storms often made approaches and landings interesting. On our last deployment mission, the Skipper unexpectedly threw me in the seat for a nasty approach in driving rain. I managed to get the plane on the ground, but there was a lot of standing water on the runway with tricky crosswinds. I didn't know about hydroplaning and landed too smooth, and the plane skidded when I suddenly noticed 'magic power levers' moving as the Skipper applied asymmetric thrust to keep us centered. I was scared, but that was the day the crew accepted me because if we had diverted 700 nautical miles to Kinloss Scotland, our return to Jacksonville would have been delayed days!

The KEF routine was to fly, debrief, go to *Brass Nut* – the famous VP bar – rest, and maybe work at your ground job. We welcomed NATO crews who flew in to help prosecute Soviet subs. We interacted with RAF *Nimrod* crews from Kinloss or Dutch crews with their dark grey *Koninklijke Marine* P-3s from Valkenburg and there was a true sense of international camaraderie as we all worked together to track the Soviet missile boats during the Cold War.

dropped far enough away from the submarine to remain undetected, but close enough to ensure that the submarine sailed within acoustic range of the buoy. Initially a row of buoys would be laid across the estimated track of the submarine, which might have been generated by a previous MPA or the sound surveillance system (SOSUS) sensors on the seabed. From this first drop, a rough position and course of the submarine would be plotted. A second row of buoys would then be dropped ahead of the calculated track of the submarine and, if successfully placed, these would give a more accurate fix, enabling a more precise third row of sonobuoys to be dropped further ahead of the submarine. In this way the position of the submarine and its course could be gradually refined and continuously monitored. The US doctrine for ASW was to find, fix, track, target, engage and assess (known as F2T2EA).

A Hawker Siddeley Buccaneer S2 of 809 NAS, the last naval Buccaneer squadron, flies past HMS *Ark Royal* (R09). (Cooke)

USN P-3C Orion pilot Don Stanton recalled hunting Juliett-class submarines at night over the Mediterranean:

We flew at lower altitudes to enable use of all sensors: radar, sonar, FLIR, and our observers' eyes. Our Ops Officer worked out a set of innovative tactics for crews to hunt the Juliett on many nights. The Juliett was a big conventional diesel boat with four nuclear-capable cruise missiles with a range of 300 miles which threatened our carrier battle groups in the Med. Since they had to snorkel or surface at night to keep their batteries charged up, Dave set up a nightly plan to hunt the Juliett using over the shoulder radar and coordinating observers to scan up-moon. On an eight- or nine-hour patrol, the tactical co-ordinator (TACCO) set up a watch schedule to rotate aft observers frequently because their recognition differential (ability to alertly scan the ocean) declined rapidly after 15 or 20 min, especially in the middle of the night.

Meanwhile Soviet submarines represented a serious threat in the North Atlantic Ocean. A report to the Western European Union (WEU) in 1976 estimated that there were usually between three and five Soviet strategic submarines and between one and three Soviet cruise missile-armed attack submarines operating in the Atlantic on a typical day. ASW operations in the Norwegian Sea and North Atlantic were very much a multi-national affair and included co-ordinated missions flown by USN P-3 Orions flying from North American, Icelandic or Norwegian bases, RNoAF P-3 Orions, CAF CP-107 Argus flying from Canada or Keflavik, and RAF Nimrods based in Scotland, but frequently operating from Keflavik or Andøya.

Once a submarine contact was made by an MPA, a subsequent patrol would be tasked to take over once the first aircraft reached its endurance or had expended all of its sonobuoys. As P-3C pilot Don Stanton explained:

> Cold War sub-hunting was very complex and expensive, requiring extensive coordination between submarine, surface, and air and our Allies' ASW platforms which all contributed to round-the-clock tracking of submarines. P-3 Orions provided unique long-range and rapid reaction capabilities to support the Navy Fleet ASW and intelligence gathering. During the Cold War, the East Coast Navy deployed P-3 squadrons continuously to Keflavik, Bermuda, Lajes Azores, Rota Spain, and Sigonella Sicily. Norwegian P-3s initially tracked Russian subs as they transited around the Kola Peninsula and turned them over to the US. Our mission was to locate and/or track the subs (missile or attack) as they proceeded south to determine whether they were heading toward the G-I gap (Greenland-Iceland) which meant they were headed deep into the Atlantic or via the I-UK gap (Iceland-United Kingdom) to head down towards the eastern Atlantic or possibly by Gibraltar into the Mediterranean…
>
> At Keflavik we flew a 'high mission' and dropped sonobuoys from somewhere around 14,000ft to 16,000ft. When the sonobuoys hit the water, a string with a hydrophone deployed to pre-set depths. The buoys could be set for one-, three-, or eight-hours' life (and then sank) and our sonar operators listened and recorded potential submarine signatures passively, so the sub didn't know we were onto them. It took quite a while for the buoys to drop, and we often had problems with them freezing up on the way down, so it could be a crap shoot if they would come up and by then valuable minutes had been lost. We were constantly marking on top of a buoy to maintain plot stabilization so that we knew where the buoy pattern was in order to track a Soviet sub accurately.

P-3 squadrons were focused on tracking Russian missile boats which were a key strategic threat to the US. In 1977, the Soviets had about 33 Yankee missile boats (1,300-mile missile range) and 21 newer Delta boats (their 4,200-mile range which meant they didn't even have to go to sea to reach US targets.) The Yankees had to operate relatively close in patrol areas east of Bermuda and in the Eastern Pacific to target US cities and defence establishments with nuclear ballistic missiles. While USN submarines were the premier anti-submarine force, the P-3's job was to locate and track submarines and be ready in the event of a nuclear war, to assist in attacking Soviet 'boomers' before they launched their ICBMs or to torpedo Soviet attack boats threatening our submarines.

The Soviet Yankee-class submarines were also deployed widely in the Pacific, as Tom Spink, a P-3 navigator/ TACCO with VP-46, recalled:

Initially P-3s would transit out to the areas of the Northern Pacific, where SOSUS had detected the transit of the Yankee, and lay large patterns of 16 sonobuoys. They were called High Last Patterns because the sonobuoys were set for long life with the logic that over a long period of time the probability of the submarine coming close enough to one of the buoys for detection was great. They also were called Cadillac patterns because they cost about the same as a new Cadillac.

The USSR Pacific Fleet boats developed a predictable pattern that US forces used to our advantage. They seemed to operate within a large box 1,000 miles to the west of California. A missile boat would leave Petropavlovsk, transit across the Northern Pacific, often tracked by the SOSUS system, and enter the northern part of the box, called the Yankee East Pacific Missile Patrol Area (YEMPA). During their multiple month deployment, they would gradually move down to the southern part of the box. As their replacement would enter the northern part of the box, the on-station boat would exit the southern end and transit back to the Kamchatka Peninsula.

US VP forces did a commendable job of keeping track of these missile boats. P-3s from NAS Moffett Field and NAS Barbers Point, Hawaii, would go out on a random basis to locate Ivan. Because there isn't enough jet fuel to have a P-3 on-top the Yankee 24/7, VP forces came up with a plan. At random intervals, a squadron would be chosen for a four or five challenge event. Each event would consist of a four-hour transit, four-hour on-station period and four-hour transit home. The challenge was to go from no contact to attack criteria in as few flights as possible. In the winter, the weather added a real element

An Ilyushin Il-38 (May) flies low over the crowded deck of USS *Midway* (CV 41). Phantom, Intruder, Corsair, Hawkeye aircraft and a Sea King helicopter are all visible on the carrier. (NARA)

of discomfort. The P-3 cannot climb above the large thunderstorms that would roll across the Pacific in winter. It was a long and bumpy ride out and back in the winter. Flying at 24,000 to 30,000ft, the P-3 would have to dodge the big build-ups and thunderstorms both ways.

The Soviet anti-submarine tactics were very similar to those of the NATO forces. The Il-38 and Tu-142 used the RTS-1, RTS-2 and RTS-3 sonobuoys in similar fashion to NATO MPAs. For the Berkut-95 system used in the Tu-142, the aircraft flew between 1,500ft and 6,500ft and the system could operate in up to Sea State 4. The signals from these buoys were fed into the Berkut system which then computed the position of any submarine contact and generated an attack profile. A submarine could be engaged using the AT-1 or AT-2 anti-submarine torpedoes. However, although the Tu-142 began regular patrols of the Northern Atlantic in the late 1970s, the crews had little success in finding submarines. Apart from the difficulties in finding a submarine in a vast expanse of ocean without intelligence from SOSUS, their efforts were often disrupted by NATO MPAs. For example, in May 1979 a P-3 Orion overlayed a pattern of buoys dropped by a Tu-142 and jammed the receivers in all of the Soviet buoys; four months later an Argus employed the same tactic, thereby generating a loud whistling noise over all the sonobuoy frequencies, blotting out any submarine noises. Initially, due to

ABOVE A Lockheed P-3A Orion of VP-5 shadows the *Moskva* helicopter cruiser in the Mediterranean Sea. A Kamov Ka-25 Hormone helicopter is being readied on the deck of *Moskva*. (US Navy)

inter-service rivalry, the Soviet tactic for neutralizing the threat from SSBNs was somewhat convoluted: once a submarine was located by an MPA, its position would be transmitted to the Air Force VVS-DA headquarters. A VVS-DA bomber would then be dispatched to the location and the bomber would drop a nuclear depth bomb onto it. This unwieldy and impractical tactic was abandoned in the early 1980s.

Anti-surface Warfare

One task of maritime strike aircraft, whether carrier- or land-based, was to attack enemy surface warships, for NATO aircraft a Soviet SAG or for Soviet aircraft a carrier battle group. The general tactical principle was the same for all aircraft and was based on a multi-axis attack by a large number of aircraft to swamp the defences and ensure a hit on the target. A Soviet Tu-22K regiment would attack a surface target from high level with up to 30 aircraft, including ECM aircraft and decoys to confuse the air defences. Some 16 aircraft would then fire missiles from three different axes, launching Kh-22 missiles from 150 miles away. The Soviet Navy recognized that a carrier battle group would be a very formidable target and the doctrine was to use two regiments of ASM-armed Tu-16K Badgers, a total of 70 aircraft, against a single NATO aircraft carrier to overwhelm the fleet air defences.

In contrast to the medium-level profile adopted by the Soviets, the RAF Buccaneers planned to attack from low level, staying under the radar horizon of the target ship. The position of the target would be updated by a Victor or Vulcan maritime radar reconnaissance aircraft and passed to the Buccaneer as they approached the target area.

Buccaneer navigator Graham Pitchfork explains how such an attack would work:

ABOVE The Soviet navy received its first aircraft carrier (although it was classed as a 'through deck cruiser'), the *Kiev*, in 1976. The ship was equipped with the Yakolev Yak-38 (Forger) vertical take-off and landing fighter. (Novosti)

> At a range of 240 miles from the target the Buccaneer formation started an 'under the radar lobe' descent to sea level in order to stay outside the enemy's radar cover. By monitoring the passive radar warning receiver during the descent, the formation was able to remain outside the enemy's detection range. At 30 miles the leader 'popped up' and the navigator switched on his Blue Parrot air-to-surface radar for two or three sweeps during which time he identified and 'marked' the target before descending back to 100ft. During the attack, only the lead aircraft transmitted on radar. The navigator selected the most likely radar return as the target and the aircraft was turned to place this radar return dead ahead. To identify the target to the rest of the formation all that was needed was a pre-briefed range – normally 20 miles – and a simple codeword to tell the rest of the formation when to switch on their radars. The codeword? 'Bananas!' It was never changed, and it became the trademark attack call of the Buccaneer force. At the pre-sortie briefing one of a number of profiles, designed to provide a co-ordinated attack, was selected as the primary option depending on the defences of the planned target. We called them 'Alpha' attacks. The leader could change the option at short notice if weather or enemy ship dispositions dictated different tactics, and the new Alpha attack was broadcast with the 'Bananas' call. However, they all employed the same basic principles – suppress the enemy defences before hitting the target with the lethal weapon.

The aim of the Alpha attacks was to maintain the element of surprize by remaining outside the radar horizon of the enemy ship for as long as possible followed by a series of pre-planned splits to confuse the target defences and delay the lock-on solutions for their radar-laid anti-aircraft defences. Once we had penetrated the target ship's weapons engagement zones, we used the exceptional low-flying performance of the Buccaneer to fly at high speed and ultra-low level while sustaining high-g manoeuvres to increase the tracking problems of the enemy radars. The first attacks were delivered from a toss delivery at three miles on converging headings. Each 1,000lb bomb was fused to explode at a height of 6ft above the target, the aim being to destroy the fire-control radars and incapacitate the missile and gun crews. In the meantime, the attack force had turned starboard through 90° before rolling in to release four to six 1,000lb bombs independently from a low-level dive or laydown attack that provided the killing blow. Timing was critical if aircraft were to avoid the debris from the preceding attack. The obvious weakness of this attack was the vulnerability of the aircraft – particularly those that carried out the precision attack.

The USSR in the Mid–Late 1970s

Following on from the success of *Okean-*70 in 1970, another global maritime exercise, *Okean-*75, was held from 1 to 27 April 1975. A two-week deployment phase was followed by a five-day combat phase between 15 and 18 April, after which the deployed forces returned to their home bases. Like its predecessor, *Okean-*75 was staged on a large scale with participation by some 220 surface combat vessels from all four of the Soviet fleets. The ships included the Kara-class and Kresta II-class ASW cruisers, emphasising the importance attached by the Soviet Navy to anti-submarine operations. The scenarios faced by Soviet forces represented the Soviet view of how US/NATO maritime forces would be used in wartime: the simulated 'NATO' threats included two convoys in the North Atlantic, a carrier strike force and an ASW force in the Norwegian Sea, a SAG sailing off the West African coast, two convoys in the Pacific and an ASW task group in the Philippine Sea.

The two-week deployment phase saw Tu-95RTs detached to forward bases at Conakry, in Guinea, and at Havana, in Cuba, while Il-38 MPAs deployed to Hargeisa, in Somalia. In addition, an Antonov An-12 (Cub) surveillance aircraft was flown to Aden, in South Yemen. The first three days of the combat phase were taken up with reconnaissance, since the

LEFT The Tupolev Tu-22M2 (Backfire-B) was introduced into AV-MF service in the late 1970s. Armed with the Kh-22M (Kitchen) ASMs, the Backfire represented a major threat to NATO carrier strike groups. (NARA)

Soviet 'friendly forces' had not been told the exact location of the 'enemy forces.' This phase of exercise was a far more realistic test of maritime surveillance capability than had been seen in previous manoeuvres. Tu-95 carried out reconnaissance over the Norwegian Sea and the Pacific Ocean flying from bases in the USSR, and over the Atlantic Ocean flying from the detached bases at Havana and Conakry. Operating from the central USSR, they also transited over Iran to fly missions over the

ABOVE The main short-range ASW helicopter used by the AV-MF was the Kamov Ka-25 (Hormone-A), photographed here during the 1980s. Up to 20 of these helicopters could be carried by the Kiev-class ships. (NARA)

Until the late 1970s, photoreconnaissance for the fleet was carried out by squadrons flying the North American RA-5C Vigilante. As well as vertical, oblique and split-image cameras in the bomb-bay, a sideways looking airborne radar was mounted in a ventral fairing. (NARA)

Arabian Sea. The Il-38 May MPAs operated over the Norwegian Sea and Western Pacific from bases within the USSR and over the Indian Ocean flying from Hargeisa. With the targets now located, the simulated strike phase took place on 17 and 18 April. Missile-armed Tu-16 Badger conducted numerous simulated strikes against surface forces in the Norwegian Sea, North Atlantic, and Pacific. The new Tuplolev Tu-22M (Backfire) also took part in these missions. After the initial strikes, there was a rapid escalation of simulated hostilities, culminating in a nuclear warfare exercise in the Barents Sea on 18 April, which was observed by Admiral Gorskhov and the Defence Minister, Andrei A. Grechko. During *Okean*-75, the AV-MF had played a significant role in reconnaissance, missile strike, and ASW operations.

There was an important addition to the order of battle of the Soviet Black Sea Fleet in 1976, with the commissioning of the 'through deck cruiser' aircraft carrier *Kiev*. A sister ship *Minsk*, which was commissioned in 1982, was allocated to the Pacific Fleet. The carrier was originally intended to carry some 22 Yakovlev Yak-38 (Forger) vertical take-off and landing (VTOL) fighters, although in practice it was never seen with more than 13 aircraft on board, possibly to allow for a mixed force of fixed- and rotary-wing aircraft. In theory at least, the Yak-38 Forger gave the Soviet Navy a capability for organic air power for the first time but in reality, the aeroplane was very limited in range and performance, proved to be extremely difficult to fly and was very unreliable. Of six Forgers carried on *Kiev* during a Mediterranean cruise in 1976 only

three were serviceable at the start of the voyage and only one was still serviceable by the end of it. The aircraft was powered by an afterburning Turmansky R27V-300 vectored-thrust engine and two Kolesov RD36-35FV lift jets. It had under-wing four hardpoints for weapons, but only two were used, it had no on-board radar, and it had a radius of action of only 60 miles. Thus, despite being a step forward in bringing carrier aviation to the Soviet Navy, the Kiev-class ships brought little change in operational capability in terms of naval aviation. They did, however, carry a potent battery of P-500 *Bazalt* (Basalt) (SS-N-12 – Sandbox) cruise missiles, which received targeting data and mid-course guidance from the Ka-25Ts (Hormone-B)helicopters carried on board. These aircraft were equipped with the same Big Bulge radar that was fitted in the Tu-95RTs.

The Kiev-class carriers also carried up to 20 Ka-25 Hormone-A helicopters for ASW work. A larger ASW helicopter, the Mil Mi-14PL (Haze), entered service in 1975 but was too large for the Kiev-class ships and as a result was mainly shore-based. Based on the Mi-8 (Hip) the Haze was optimized for the ASW role and was equipped with an Oka-2 dipping sonar, some 36 sonobuoys, a towed APM-20 Orsha MAD sensor (mounted in a torpedo-shaped casing which was stowed externally at the rear of the fuselage) and an Initziativa-2M surface search radar in a radome under the nose. A mine-clearance variant, the Mi-14BT (Haze-B) which featured a towed mine countermeasures sled, was also employed by the DDR and Bulgarian navies.

The Bear-D and Bear-F variants of the Tu-95/142 and the Il-38 May continued to be used by the AV-MF for long-range reconnaissance and ASW. Supporting the Northern Fleet were one regiment each of Tu-142 and Il-38 based at Fedotovo, near Vologda (some 700 miles south of Murmansk), one regiment each of Tu-95RTs, Tu-16R reconnaissance variant and Be-12 at Severomorsk, and two further regiments of Tu-16KSR at Lakhta, near Arkhangelsk and Olenya, near Murmansk. In all, some 280 Tu-16 continued in service in the maritime strike role, of which approximately 100 were allocated to the Pacific Fleet, with the remainder serving with the Northern, Baltic and Black Sea Fleets. These aircraft were armed with the KSR-5 missiles. A Tu-16 regiment would typically comprise two squadrons of 12 Tu-16K-10 or Tu-16KSR strike aircraft, with a third squadron operating a mixture of Tu-16N tankers and Tu-16P ECM support aircraft. A partial replacement for the Badger entered AV-MF service in the mid-1970s in the shape of the Tupolev Tu-22M2 (Backfire-B), some 40 of which were allocated to the Northern and Baltic Fleets. The variable-geometry Backfire could carry up to three 300-mile range Kh-22M ASMs and with a supersonic performance, it represented a quantum leap in capability over the Tu-16. The Il-38 and Be-12 MPAs were also allocated to all four Soviet Navy fleets, for the maritime surveillance and ASW roles, and air support for the Baltic Fleet was

A pair of Ling Temco Vought A-7E Corsairs from VA-66 embarked on USS *Dwight D. Eisenhower* (CVN 69) during 1978. (NARA)

enhanced with the addition of Sukhoi Su-17M2 (Fitter-D) strike aircraft. These were operated by the 846th Independent Guards Maritime Assault Aviation Regiment (*Otdel'nyy Gvardeyskiy Morskoy Shturmovoy Aviatsionnyy Polk* – OGvMShAP) which was based at Chkalovsk, Kaliningrad from 1975. The single-seat variable geometry Su-17M2 could be used to support naval infantry during amphibious operations or to attack NATO surface vessels in the Baltic Sea. A regiment of Su-17s was also allotted to the Pacific Fleet.

US Maritime Aviation in the Mid–Late 1970s

Two new aircraft carriers joined the USN in the second half of the 1970s: USS *Nimitz* (CVN 68), the first of a new class of nuclear-powered aircraft carriers, was commissioned in 1975 and was followed two years later by a sister ship, USS *Dwight D. Eisenhower* (CVN 69). With a fully laden displacement of 91,400 tons, the Nimitz-class ships were even larger than USS *Enterprise*. The arrival of these two powerful carriers enabled the release of the two remaining Essex-class ships, USS *Hancock* and USS *Oriskany*, from service. The complement of USS *Nimitz* was 85 aircraft and in 1977 it included two squadrons of F-14A Tomcat fighters and two A-7E Corsair II attack aircraft, and one squadron each of A-6E/ KA-6B Intruders, RA-5C Vigilantes, EA-6B Prowler EW support aircraft, S-3A Viking, E-2B Hawkeye AEW aircraft and SH-3D Sea King ASW helicopters. Most of the Forrestal-class ships still carried the F-4 Phantom for air defence. The remaining F-4J variants were upgraded from 1977 to F-4S standard which incorporated the smokeless engines already fitted to the F-4N and introduced leading edge slats to improve manoeuvrability and low-speed handling. In the late 1980s the RA-5C Vigilante ended its service, the last aircraft being withdrawn in 1979.

The cruise made by CVW-3 while embarked on USS *Saratoga* in 1976 is typical of the experiences of USN carrier and aircraft crews. The air wing embarked on 6 January 1976 and sailed for the Mediterranean, where it took over from USS *John F. Kennedy* in the Eastern Mediterranean on 16 January. Over the next two months, nine- or ten-day operational periods in the Western and Eastern Mediterranean and in the Ionian Sea alternated with port calls, lasting between four and ten days, at Malaga, Palma di Mallorca, Taranto and Brindisi. In mid-March USS *Saratoga* exercised with USS *Independence* in the Tyrrhenian Sea, after which operational periods once again alternated with port calls at Naples, Split, Cannes, Palma, Genoa, Monaco and Barcelona. On 7 May USS *America*

ABOVE The relative sizes of two Douglas Aircraft Company products, the EA-3B Skywarrior and the Douglas TA-4J Skyhawk, can be compared as the former acts as an air-to-air refuelling tanker. Both designs originated in the 1950s and remained in service through to the end of the Cold War. (NARA)

arrived to join USS *Saratoga* in the Eastern Mediterranean, and the opportunity was taken for a simulated strike against the new carrier as she sailed to join up. During the exercise the S-3 Vikings from USS *Saratoga* were used as a decoy force, which successfully drew off the F-14 Tomcats from USS *America*, enabling the strike force from USS *Saratoga* to carry out an undetected approach and mount a simulated attack on USS *America*. Between 3 and 12 May, both carriers took part in Exercise *Dawn Patrol*, which also included the French carrier *Clemenceau*. During this exercise, enemy forces were simulated by USAFE F-4E Phantoms and F-111s. On 18 July, after a port call at Rota, Spain, USS *Saratoga* was relieved by USS *Nimitz* and returned to Norfolk on 26 July.

There was drama on 14 September 1976 during the NATO maritime Exercise *Teamwork 76*, when a F-14A Tomcat was lost overboard from USS *John F. Kennedy* some 75 miles northwest of the Orkney Islands. The aircraft was taxiing towards the catapult when one engine suffered an uncommanded run up to full power and the pilot could not prevent the aircraft from skidding over the side of the deck. The crew, Lt John L. Kosich, and Lt L. E. Seymour, ejected safely, but the aircraft, which was armed with a Phoenix AAM, sank to a depth of 1,800ft in international waters. Naturally the Soviets were keen to salvage the wreck, in order to gain intelligence about the new aircraft and also the new missile; the USN were equally determined to prevent this happening. Seaward, a deep-sea salvage company based in Falls Church, Virginia, was contracted to recover the Tomcat, but before they could begin the salvage, firstly the ships needed to sail to the area and secondly the aircraft wreck had to be located. All of this took nearly two weeks and when the aircraft was eventually found, it transpired that the Soviets had already located the wreck and had attempted to tow it away using trawler nets. Luckily for the US salvagers, the towing cables were not strong enough and failed, freeing the aircraft from the nets and causing the Soviets lose their prize. Having found the Tomcat, the salvage team towed it to shallower water and were then able to raise it on 11 October. The Phoenix missile had also been found and was recovered in a separate operation.

Almost exactly six months later, a second Tomcat crashed into the North Atlantic off the Virginia Capes after a ramp strike while attempting to land on USS *America*, which was sailing approximately 50 miles northeast of Norfolk, Virginia. Lt G. A. Quist and Lt J. G. Stevens of VF-143 ejected safely, but their aircraft sank in some 8,000ft of water – too deep for a recovery attempt.

British Maritime Aviation in the Mid–Late 1970s

Another 'Cod War' took place between November 1975 and June 1976 when Iceland unilaterally declared a 200-mile exclusive economic zone around its coast, thereby pushing British trawlers even further away from the rich coastal fishing grounds. Once again Nimrod-equipped squadrons were called in to monitor the activities of trawlers and Icelandic gunboats. By this time the Britannia had been retired from RAF service, so the four ageing Handley Page Hastings T5 radar training aircraft of 230 Operational Conversion Unit (OCU) were utilized to relieve the Nimrod task.

NEXT PAGES The view from a Grumman A-6A Intruder during recovery to the carrier USS *Franklin D. Roosevelt* (CVA 42) in the Caribbean Sea, after simulated Alpha strike package at the Atlantic Fleet weapons range in Puerto Rico. The Intruder is from VA-176 and the Phantoms from VF-84. (US Navy)

OPPOSITE As electronic warfare evolved during the Cold War, there was a growing need for specialist aircraft. The Grumman EA-6B Prowler, equipped with the AN/ALQ-99 tactical jamming system, was introduced into service in 1971. (NARA)

Equipped with the H2S Mk 9 radar, the Hastings was probably better equipped for the task than the Britannia had been. Nevertheless, the 'Cod War' caused friction between NATO allies as well as distracting the Nimrod force from its prime submarine hunting role. From 1977 the Nimrod aircraft were progressively modified to the MR2 standard with significantly upgraded avionics. A new FM1600D computer was fitted which gave increased data processing and was compatible with the improved GEC AQS-901 acoustic processor (and therefore able to use more modern sonobuoys) and the Loral EW-1017 Yellow Gate ESM system, which enabled it to locate and track surface emitters (including submarine antennas), was fitted in wingtip pods. Most importantly, perhaps, the Nimrod MR2 was equipped with the EMI Searchwater radar which was the most capable maritime search radar of its day. As well as the usual spectrum of torpedoes and depth bombs, the Nimrod could be armed with the Hawker Siddeley-Matra Martel ASM.

From 1975, the RAF Buccaneer force was also armed with the Martel ASM, which gave it some stand-off capability against enemy ships. A typical weapon load on the four under-wing pylons of a Buccaneer would comprise one AS 37 anti-radiation missile (ARM) and two optically-guided (TV) AJ 168 missiles, with the digital link pod for controlling the TV-guided missiles loaded onto the fourth pylon. Martel was a distinct improvement over the US-built Bullpup, as it was controlled by the navigator in the Buccaneer so that the pilot could manoeuvre during the attack, whereas the Bullpup had been controlled by the pilot who had to continue to fly towards the target while controlling both aircraft and missile. The Alpha attack profile was amended to include an all-missile attack and in the Alpha Six attack profile, the Buccaneers fired a salvo of Martel ARM at a range of ten miles from the target and then followed with the TV-guided missiles.

The FAA continued to operate the Buccaneer and Phantom from HMS *Ark Royal* until the ship was withdrawn from service in November 1978. With the demise of the ship, the FAA fixed-wing squadrons were disbanded, and their aircraft were then distributed amongst RAF squadrons. However, HMS *Hermes* had emerged from another refit in late 1973 reconfigured once more, this time as an ASW carrier. Initially she carried Sea King HAS1 ASW helicopters, but these were replaced from 1977 with the upgraded Sea King HAS2, which featured improved engines, sensors and weapons systems. The Westland Lynx HAS2 entered service in the second half of the decade and began to replace the Wasp flown from RN frigates and destroyers. The Lynx was a very effective ASW and anti-shipping helicopter, being equipped with the Ferranti Sea

ABOVE Another aspect of electronic warfare was the use of anti-radiation missiles to suppress enemy air defences. This Grumman A-6E Intruder of VA-85 is armed with a General Dynamics AGM-78 Standard ARM. (NARA)

Spray radar and armed, when required, with anti-submarine torpedoes or the BAC Sea Skua semi-active ASM.

For all the improvements in FAA and RAF ASW capability, the British interests in the Mediterranean region suffered a blow in 1979 with the forced closure of RAF Luqa on Malta. The resident Nimrod unit, 203 Sqn, had already been disbanded at the end of 1977 in anticipation of the closure, but the abandonment of Malta left British forces without a permanent base in the central Mediterranean. Instead, the airbases at Gibraltar at the Atlantic end of the sea and RAF Akrotiri, Cyprus at the eastern end continued to be used as forward operating bases for maritime aircraft on temporary detachment.

Canada and Western Europe in the Mid–Late 1970s

The equipment and capabilities of the CAF maritime air component was little changed during the late 1970s. The CP-107 Argus continued as the prime ASW aircraft, augmented by CH-124 Sea King helicopters operating from ships. Similarly, the RNoAF P-3 Orions continued their work over the Norwegian Sea, with the CF-104 Starfighter providing an anti-shipping strike capability. The RDAF also continued to employ the F-100D Super Sabre in the anti-shipping role in the Baltic, armed with the Bullpup missile. However, the German *Marineflieger* had replaced the Bullpup on the F-104G Starfighter with the EADS AS.34 *Kormoran* (Cormorant) in 1976. The new missile had a range of some 20 miles, which enabled the launch aircraft to stand off from the anti-aircraft defences of the target vessel, which typically reached out to 14 or 15 miles. The *Kormoran* used inertial guidance, with active radar homing in the terminal phase. To launch the missile, a Starfighter pilot would locate the target on radar and use a radar fix to update the target co-ordinates in the missile inertial navigation system then, when within range, fire the missile. The pilot would then break away and avoid the target defences.

The Netherlands MLD formed the maritime patrol (MARPAT) group in 1977 as an overarching command for the two MPA squadrons (320 Sqn and 321 Sqn) and the MPA conversion unit (VSQ2), which continued to operate both the Neptune and the Atlantique in the maritime patrol/ASW role. Like the RN, the MLD procured the Westland Lynx, designated the SH-14C in MLD service, in 1977 for ASW and ASuW missions from its frigates. The Lynx Mk2(FN) was also purchased by the French *Aéronavale* in 1979.

Although they were not integrated into the NATO command structure, French forces played a full part in NATO exercises. The carrier *Clemenceau* participated in the Exercise *Dawn Patrol* in the Mediterranean in 1976 and 1979 (with out of area deployments to Djibouti and the Gulf of Aden in between). At this time, the complement of *Clemenceau* comprised ten F-8E(FN) Crusaders for air defence, 16 Étendard IVM strike aircraft, four Étendard IVP reconnaissance aircraft, eight Alizé ASW aircraft, two Super Frelon ASW helicopters and two Alouette light helicopters. The Dassault Super Étendard began to replace the Étendard IVM on board from 1978. This new variant of the Étendard had a more powerful version of the SNECMA Atar engine, a revised wing and an improved avionics suite that included a Thomson-CSF Agave radar. With this radar, the aircraft could be armed with the AM-39 Exocet ASM,

OPPOSITE A foretaste of things to come: a McDonnell Douglas F-4N Phantom from VF-51 intercepts a Libyan Air Force Tupolev Tu-22 (Blinder) in 1977. Four years later US Navy aircraft would be in combat with Libyan aircraft. (NARA)

RIGHT An unlikely candidate as an MPA, the Handley Page Hastings T5 of 230 Operational Conversion Unit (OCU) was pressed into service during the 'Cod War' of 1975-76 to conserve hours on the Nimrods. (Pitchfork)

LEFT The RDAF used the North American F-100D Super Sabre for tactical air support for maritime operations (TASMO) in the Baltic Sea. The type could be armed with the AGM-12 Bullpup missile for such missions. (RDAF)

which entered service in 1979. The Super Frelon helicopter was also modified to carry the Exocet.

The Portuguese *Escuadra* 61 disbanded in 1977 and its Neptunes were withdrawn, so they were never in fact used in the MPA role. Instead, during the late 1970s, limited coastal patrols and SAR flights were carried out by transport aircraft such as the C-130 and CASA 212 Aviocar. In Greece, the Hellenic Air Force continued to operate HU-16B Albatross for maritime duties.

Both Italy and Turkey continued to operate the S-2 Tracker in the ASW role, as well as expanding their helicopter operations in the second half of the decade. In Italy 5° Gruppelicot re-equipped with the twin-engine Agusta-Bell AB-212ASW for operations from frigates, from 1976. The helicopter represented a major increase in capability over the AB-204, and was equipped with radar, FLIR, MAD and an AN/AQS-18 dipping sonar. The Turkish Marine Naval Air Base Command (*Deniz Hava Üs Komutanlığı*), which was formed in 1976, also procured AB-212ASW helicopters to equip 351 *Filo*.

OPPOSITE HMS *Ark Royal* (R09), the last conventional aircraft carrier operated by the RN, was paid off in 1979. (Pitchfork)

An *Aéronavale* Crusader F-8E(FN) being prepared for a mission at Saint Dizier in eastern France. The type entered French service in 1964 and remained with front-line units until after the Cold War had ended. (Bannwarth)

NATO Exercises

Throughout the decade, NATO continued to hold regular large-scale exercises so that naval and air forces could practise and perfect their ability to reinforce and resupply the European theatre, including amphibious landings. Crucially, these events were an opportunity to validate the concept of the carrier battle group and to demonstrate the importance of air power on maritime and coastal operations. Carrier aircraft established air defence over the fleet and provided anti-submarine protection, while strike aircraft carried out simulated attacks on coastal installations as well as surface ships. Exercise *Northern Wedding* was held in the Atlantic and Norwegian Sea every four years from 1970, while Exercise *Ocean Safari* was another exercise in the Atlantic that was held bi-annually on odd-numbered years from 1973. HMS *Ark Royal* took part in Exercise *Northern Wedding* in 1970, and again in 1978 when she and USS *Forrestal* headed two separate task groups to support amphibious landings in the Shetland islands and on Jutland. USS *Independence* took part in *Ocean Safari* 75, while HMS *Ark Royal* participated two years later.

In September 1972 Exercise *Strong Express*, held in the Norwegian Sea, was the largest sea, air and land exercise organized by NATO up until then. It involved amphibious landings in Norway and included three carrier battle groups led by USS *John F. Kennedy*, USS *Independence*, and HMS *Ark Royal*. Helicopters from HMS *Albion* were also used to deploy some troops into the landing areas. Meanwhile, MPA aircraft continued to search for and track Soviet (and NATO) submarines and Victors of 543 Sqn carried out radar reconnaissance sorties to track the Soviet vessels that were monitoring the exercise.

Continuing from the exercise series initiated in the 1960s, Exercise *Teamwork* 76, which was held in September 1976, had an even greater participation than Exercise *Strong Express* had enjoyed four years earlier, making it the largest ever NATO exercise. Some 200 ships, 30 submarines and 900 aircraft took part in this NATO demonstration of its determination and capability to maintain control of the SLOC as well as its ability to reinforce its vulnerable northern flank. It was during this exercise that the new F-14A Tomcat was lost overboard from USS *John F. Kennedy*. Naturally MPA played an important role in neutralizing

A Dassault Étendard IVM carrier-borne strike fighter of 11.F. A lightweight and manoeuvrable aircraft, the Étendard was popular with its pilots. (JJ Petit)

the submarine threat to the SLOC and nine P-3Cs from VP-49 flew intensively out of Keflavik during the 11 days of the exercise, flying a total of 43 missions. At the same time other NATO MPA assets carried out ASW exercises in the western approaches to Gibraltar.

Another carry-in from the 1960s was Exercise *Dawn Patrol*, which was an annual exercise in the Mediterranean. These exercises usually included the resident US aircraft carriers from the 6th Fleet and in the late 1970s also included French aircraft carriers. The aircraft of COMARAIRMED played a full part in the proceedings, augmented by RAF Buccaneers operating from Malta and later Cyprus or Gibraltar. Exercise *Display Determination*, which also took place over the Mediterranean in the autumn of 1978, was the last NATO exercise in which HMS *Ark Royal* and her air wing participated.

The Third Decade

The 1970s marked a significant shift in the balance of forces at sea: the Soviet Navy had demonstrated in the *Okean* exercises that it was a truly global blue water force and that it posed a real threat to NATO. Any improvements in the Soviet submarine force were mirrored in the AV-MF. The decade saw regular long-range deployments of Tu-95 variants, including the Tu-142 version which was specifically designed for maritime warfare. The Il-38 MPA was also deployed over Middle Eastern waters. In theory, at least, the addition of the through deck cruiser *Kiev* to the Black Sea Fleet enhanced the air-defence capability of the fleet, although in

While the Kiev-class/Yak-38 Forger combination was not tactically very effective, it did mark the entry of the Soviet Navy into the world of carrier-borne aviation and realised the ambitions of Admiral Gorshkov. (Novosti)

practice the Yak-38 did not prove to be particularly effective. In the Norwegian Sea, and to an extent in the Sea of Okhotsk, the adoption of the 'bastion' strategy challenged NATO countermeasures against the threat by Soviet SSBN. It was also a direct challenge to the NATO strategy of using carrier battle groups to facilitate the reinforcement of the northern flank in Norway. The Soviet Baltic Fleet included a disproportionately large AV-MF element that could potentially support amphibious operations on the coasts of northern Germany and Denmark. However, further south NATO naval air forces undoubtedly still held the upper hand over the Mediterranean.

While its allies scrapped their aircraft carriers, the USN continued to build on and improve its own carrier fleet. The arrival of the first Nimitz-class carriers in the 1970s marked a step up in fighting capability. So, too, did the introduction of aircraft types like the F-14A Tomcat and the S-3A Viking. The Tomcat in particular, armed with the Phoenix AAM and long-range radar system, gave the carrier battle group greater freedom of action within a secure air-defence environment. The shift among the British air arms from carrier-borne to land-based maritime strike aircraft undoubtedly reduced the flexibility of the RN, but the long range of the Buccaneer meant that by deploying to forward airstrips, for example in Norway or Gibraltar, it could still reach nearly all the areas where it would have been flown from a carrier. However, the argument for land-based naval air defence is less compelling.

The great strength of NATO maritime air forces was the ability of MPA to detect and shadow Soviet submarines. In the P-3C Orion, Nimrod and Argus NATO operated extremely effective long-range aircraft; these were complemented by the shorter range Atlantique in German, Dutch, French and Italian service. Consequently, despite the boast by Admiral Gorshkov that, 'the flag of the Soviet Navy now proudly flies over the oceans of the world', US and NATO naval forces and those of its allies still remained the dominant power at sea.

CHAPTER 4

A COMMON GOAL – 1980–89

'Americans and Europeans share a common goal – to build an enduring peace based on freedom.'

Senator John McCain, late US Navy, 2007.

The progress towards more peaceful relations between the two sides of the Cold War made during the 1970s was tempered by the Soviet invasion of Afghanistan in late 1979 and the Soviet deployment of nuclear-armed Soviet RSD-10 *Pioner* (Pioneer) (SS-20 Saber) intermediate range ballistic missiles (IRBM) in eastern Europe. The NATO response was the 'Dual Track' approach in which it threatened to deploy both Pershing II IRBM and ground launched cruise missiles (GLCM) into western Europe unless the SS-20 IRBMs were withdrawn. Since no such withdrawal was forthcoming, the deployment of the American weapons went ahead, which increased tension with the USSR and also caused considerable popular criticism in Europe. At a time when Europe was undergoing an economic recession, political in-fighting across the NATO membership threatened the unity of the alliance in the early 1980s; however, despite the many political differences amongst its members, NATO pulled together during the decade under strong US leadership. Indeed, the whole progress towards rapprochement between the two sides of the Cold War was influenced by changes of leadership in both the US and USSR during the 1980s.

The Soviet First Secretary Leonid Brezhnev died in 1982 and was replaced in quick succession by Yuri Andropov (1982–84), Konstantin Chernenko (1984–85) and finally Mikhail Gorbachev in 1985. Although he had successfully driven the USSR to military parity with

OPPOSITE
Two Grumman F-14A Tomcats from VF-143 fly past the aircraft carrier USS *Dwight D. Eisenhower* (CVN 69), July 1988. (NARA)

ABOVE The second Soviet carrier *Minsk* under way in 1984. Some of her complement of Yakovlev Yak-38 (Forger) can be seen on deck. Both *Minsk* and her sister ship *Novorossiysk* were allocated to the Pacific Fleet. (NARA)

the USA during his nearly 20-year tenure, Brezhnev had done so at the expense of the Soviet economy, which had stagnated in the late 1970s. By the time that Gorbachev took the reins there was an urgent need of economic and political reform in the USSR, which his twin policies of openness (*glasnost*) and restructuring (*perestroika*) were intended to achieve. At the same time the rise of the trade union Solidarity (*Solidarność*) in the Gdansk shipyard had triggered martial law in Poland in 1981, and the first cracks within the Warsaw Pact began to widen. Meanwhile, in the USA Ronald Reagan, who became president in 1981, took a more confrontational approach to the USSR than his predecessor had done. Nevertheless, he also forged a personal relationship with his Soviet opposite number and the Reykjavik Summit between them in 1986 proved to be a starting point for better relations between the two sides.

During the 1980s, the USSR sought to consolidate its newly gained position as a global maritime power, while at the same time the US attempted to maintain its strategic advantage at sea. Steady advances in naval technology, particularly in submarines and missile systems, meant that maritime aviation had to adapt accordingly to counter new threats. For both countries and their allies, the decade brought military challenges outside the Cold War arena: the USSR faced a ten-year guerrilla war in Afghanistan, while the USA faced down continuous low-level aggression by Libya between 1981 and 1989. In addition, the British fought a successful long-range amphibious war in the South Atlantic to regain the Falkland Islands in 1982.

The USSR in the Early 1980s

A third Kiev-class carrier, the *Novorossiysk*, joined its sister ship *Minsk* in the Soviet Navy Pacific Fleet in 1982. The ships continued to operate the Yak-38, although its short range, small payload and lack of radar meant that the type had only very limited use: indeed, a short trial with four Forgers in Afghanistan served only to emphasize their tactical impracticality. A more successful type was the Kamov Ka-27PL (Helix) ASW helicopter which began to replace the older Ka-25 in AV-MF service in 1981. Like the Ka-25, the Ka-27 had co-axial rotors, which negated the need for a tail rotor. The helicopter operated in hunter-killer pairs, with the 'hunter' equipped with either a dipping sonar or a MAD system, or a load of 36 expendable sonobuoys, while the 'killer' carried either torpedoes or depth charges.

Another addition to the Soviet Navy surface fleet was the *Sovremennyy*, the first of a class of anti-shipping destroyers, which was commissioned in 1980. Six more of these ships were commissioned over the next five years. The anti-shipping capability of these vessels made them prime targets for maritime strike aircraft. So, too, were the nuclear-powered missile cruisers *Kirov* and *Frunze*, which entered service in 1980 and 1984 respectively. With a displacement of 28,000 tons, these ships were approximately the same size that HMS *Victorious* had been in the 1960s.

BELOW Deck crew working on a Yakovlev Yak-38M (Forger-B) on a Kiev-class carrier. Amongst the improvements incorporated into the Yak-38M were a more powerful engine and a steerable nosewheel. (NARA)

However, the most important step forward for the USSR was in submarine design, as evidenced by the deployment of the nuclear-powered Victor III-class attack submarines and Project 949 *Granit* (Granite) (Oscar I) cruise missile submarine in the early 1980s. These boats had benefitted from the revelations by the Walker spy ring in the US which sold naval secrets, including submarine technology, to the USSR during the 1970s. A later design, the Project 941 Akula (Shark)-class (Typhoon-class) submarines, which became operational in the mid-1980s, were further improved due to the illegal sale of Norwegian-manufactured Kongsberg computer-controlled machine tools to the USSR by the Japanese electronics company Toshiba. Having acquired this specialized equipment, the Soviet shipyards were able to machine much more intricate – and importantly much quieter – propellers for the latest submarines that dramatically reduced the acoustic signature, and therefore their detectability. Hunting these submarines represented a massive challenge for NATO ASW forces and sonobuoy technology, causing tactics to be improved in order to counter these quieter vessels. The 5,200-mile range of the R-39 *Rif* (Reef) (SS-N-20 Sturgeon) ballistic missiles carried in these submarines meant that they could remain in a remote and well-defended 'bastion' area in the Barents Sea, or the Sea of Okhotsk, further complicating the task of NATO ASW forces.

BELOW Introduced in 1982, the Kamov Ka-27PL (Helix-A) was the successor to the Ka-25 (Hormone) ASW helicopter. Retaining the contra-rotating main blades and obviating the need for a tail rotor kept the design compact. (NARA)

ABOVE A Grumman F-14A of VF-142 aboard the USS *Dwight D. Eisenhower* (CVN 69) and flown by Lt Cdr Greg Quist and Lt Randy Dewar escorts a Soviet Tupolev Tu-95RTs (Bear-D) during Exercise *Readex* 83-1 near Puerto Rico. (NARA)

The composition of the AV-MF changed little during the early 1980s: four fleet air forces controlled the aviation divisions within their fleet regions. Maritime patrol, locating and tracking NATO surface vessels, was carried out by some 50 Tu-95RTs and 100 Tu-16 long-range reconnaissance aircraft, supported by 50 Il-38 MPA, 45 Tu-142 and 90 Be-12 in the ASW role, as well as Tu-16N AAR tankers. Strike operations would be carried out by the 100 Tu-22M2 and 220 Tu-16K-10/KSR in the inventory. All of these aircraft could be armed with ASMs such as the Raduga KSR-5 which had a 400-mile range and the option of a conventional or nuclear warhead. The AV-MF element of the Northern Fleet comprised the 5th MRAD with three regiments of Tu-16K based across the Murmansk and Arkhangelsk regions, and the 35th Long-Range Anti-Submarine Aviation Division (*Protivolodochnaya Aviatsionnaya Diviziya Dal'nego Deystviya* – PLAD DD) which comprised two regiments of Tu-142 operating from Fedotovo near Vologda. The Tu-16K-10 of the 5th MMAD were replaced by Tu-22M2 in the late 1980s. In addition, several units existed outside the divisional structure, reporting directly to the fleet headquarters: the 24th Independent Long-Range Anti-Submarine Aviation Regiment (*Otdel'naya Protivolodochnaya Aviatsionnaya Polk Dal'nego Deystviya* – OPLAP DD) which flew the Il-38 May from Severomorsk-1 near Murmansk, but also frequently deployed aircraft to Syria for patrols over the Mediterranean Sea, and the 392nd Independent Long-Range Reconnaissance Aviation Regiment (*Otdel'nyy Dal'niy Razvedyvatel'nyy Aviatsionnyy Polk* – ODRAP) operating the Tu-95RTs from Fedotovo.

The bulk of Tu-22M2 aircraft were allocated to the Pacific Fleet with the regiments of the 143rd MRAD based at the Alekseyevka airbase at Mongokhto, on the coast of eastern Russia some 570 miles north of Vladivostok. Alekseyevka was also the base for the 310th OPLAP, which

A Tu-16RM-2 (Badger-F) ELINT and reconnaissance aircraft flies past the destroyer USS *Hewitt* (DD-966) in the South China Sea during a cruise by the USS *Midway* (CV 41) battlegroup in summer 1983. (NARA)

RIGHT During the 1980s, the AV-MF operated some 50 Ilyushin Il-38 (May) MPA in the ASW role, sometimes deploying them as far south as Asmara, Ethiopia (now Eritrea). (NARA)

BELOW A Beriev Be-12 (Mail) amphibian flying boat continued in use by the AV-MF for coastal ASW and maritime patrol duties beyond the end of the Cold War. (NARA)

flew the Tu-142M. During the 1980s the 310th OPLAP began to fly beyond the confines of the Sea of Okhotsk and the Sea of Japan. Flying through the Korean Strait, or routing to the east of Japan, they typically completed a nine-hour sortie before landing at Cam Ranh in Vietnam.

From 1980, an additional anti-ship striking capability was also provided by the Soviet Air Force Long Range Aviation, the VVS DA, which began to upgrade its Bear-B/Cs to the Tu-95K22 (Bear-G) standard. This variant could be armed with the AS-4 ASM. The first AV-MF Tu-22M3 (Backfire-C) regiments were formed at Kulbakino airbase near Mikolayev in Ukrainian SSR during 1984. This variant, which offered further improvements over the Backfire-B, featured re-designed

intakes for its more powerful engines, a revised nose and improved avionics, including a Leninets PNA-D attack radar and satellite datalink to receive targeting information. The deployment of these aircraft in the Black Sea Fleet, augmenting the 943rd MRAP which had flown the Tu-22M2 since the mid-1970s, posed a significant threat to NATO surface warships in the Mediterranean Sea.

In the Baltic Fleet, the AV-MF wielded a significant force of Tu-16K-10/KSR strike regiments with which to attack NATO surface vessels; another independent Il-38 May unit, the 145th Independent Long-Range Anti-Submarine Aviation Squadron (*Otdel'naya Protivolodochnaya Aviatsionnaya Eskadril'ya Dal'nego Deystviya* – OPLAE DD) flying from Riga, provided an ASW capability. In addition, the 49th Independent Anti-Submarine Squadron (*Otdel'naya Protivolodochnaya Aviatsionnaya Eskadril'ya* – OPLAE) operated Be-12 ASW amphibians from Khabrovo in the Kaliningrad SSR. A priority of the Baltic Fleet was the control of the Denmark Straits, for which it was equipped with landing craft and some 10,000 naval troops for amphibious landings, which would be supported by the Su-17M fighter-bombers of the 846th Independent Guards Maritime Assault Aviation Regiment (*Otdel'nyy Gvardeyskiy Morskoy Shturmovoy Aviatsionnyy Polk* – OGvMShAP). The Baltic Fleet was a central part of the large-scale Warsaw Pact Exercise *Zapad*-81, which, amongst other objectives, was intended to send a powerful message to Poland to put its house in order. The exercise included a huge amphibious landing exercise near Gdansk, which was supported by the carrier *Kiev* and its Yak-38 fighters.

The US in the Early 1980s

Like the Soviet Navy, the equipment and order of battle of the USN changed little in the 1980s. Whereas most aircraft types from the 1950s had enjoyed a relatively short in-service life as they were made obsolete by rapidly advancing technology, the emphasis now was on modernization programmes to the robust and well-designed aircraft types that had been established in the 1960s and 1970s. The in-service life of aircraft was now measured in decades rather than years. The third Nimitz-class aircraft carrier USS *Carl Vinson* (CVN 70) joined the US Navy in 1982. At this point the USN order of battle included 13 aircraft carriers: two Midway-class, three Forrestal-class, USS *Enterprise*, four Kitty Hawk-class and the three Nimitz-class, with another two Nimitz-class under construction and nearing completion.

NEXT PAGES Crewmen prepare a McDonnell Douglas F/A-18A Hornet for launch from the USS *Constellation* (CV 64) during the first sea deployment of the Hornet in the spring of 1985. The Hornet would eventually replace the F4N/S and the A-7E. (NARA)

ABOVE A McDonnell Douglas F-4J Phantom of VF-102 in 1980, shortly before the squadron re-equipped with the Grumman F-14A Tomcat. By the end of the decade the Phantom had been replaced in front-line naval service by the F-14 Tomcat and F/A-18 Hornet. (NARA)

OPPOSITE An LTV A-7E Corsair II of VA-72 launches from the waist catapult of USS *America* (CV 66), circa 1982. By the mid-1980s, the Corsair equipped 22 front-line US Navy squadrons, but by the end of the decade the type was being progressively replaced by the F/A-18 Hornet. (US Navy)

The first McDonnell Douglas F/A-18A Hornets were delivered to the USMC in 1980 and two squadrons, VFMA-314 and -323, joined USS *Coral Sea* for her Mediterranean cruise in 1983. As indicated by its 'F/A' designation, the Hornet was equally capable of air-defence and ground-attack missions. The first USN units to receive the type were VFA-25 and -113 which converted from the A-7E Corsair in 1983. Their first deployment was with USS *Constellation* sailing to the West Pacific in 1985. Although the F/A-18 was the only new aircraft type to join the USN inventory during the 1980s, the decade saw other types either being replaced or upgraded. The A-7E Corsair II, which at the height of its service in the mid-1980s equipped 22 front-line squadrons, would eventually be superseded by the Hornet at the end of the decade. The F-4 Phantom was progressively replaced in the air-defence role by the F-14 Tomcat, which eventually equipped 28 front-line squadrons. The last F-4J was withdrawn in 1982 and F-4N was finally withdrawn from service in 1984, but the F-4S variant continued to be operational until 1986, when it was retired from the front line, marking the end of 27 years of operational naval service by the Phantom.

Meanwhile, some aircraft types received significant upgrades. The target recognition-attack multi-sensor (TRAM) system for the A-6E Intruder had been first introduced in 1979, and modification was incorporated into 228 Intruders during the early part of the 1980s. The AN/AAS-33 TRAM turret mounted beneath the nose of the aircraft housed a FLIR sensor, and a laser designator and rangefinder, which combined with the new AN/APQ-156 radar into an integrated targeting system. A terrain-following function improved the ability of the Intruder to attack targets in any weather conditions. From 1984 the EA-6B Prowler went through a second stage of capability improvement, known as ICAP II. This introduced the AN/ALQ-99D tactical jamming system and compatibility with the AGM-88 high-speed anti-radiation missile (HARM). The reconnaissance role which had been carried out by the

RA-5C Vigilante in the previous two decades was taken over by the Tomcat by means of the tactical airborne reconnaissance pod system (TARPS), an externally carried reconnaissance pod containing optical and infra-red cameras, which could be loaded onto the aircraft according to mission requirements.

Under the Update II programme which started in 1979, the P-3C Orion fleet was modified to receive the AGM-84 Harpoon anti-ship missile. With a range in excess of 60 miles, the Harpoon gave the Orion enough stand-off distance to make it a substantial threat to Soviet surface warships during the next decade. Update II also included enhancements to the P-3C suite of sensors. USN destroyers and frigates began to receive the SH-60B Seahawk helicopter as a replacement for the Kaman SH-2 Seasprite from 1983. The Seahawk was equipped with a towed MAD, sonobuoys, FLIR sensor and an APS-124 search radar, and could employ both torpedoes and ASMs against both submarines and surface vessels.

In August 1981, the carriers USS *Forrestal* and *Nimitz*, deployed with the 6th Fleet to the Gulf of Sidra, commenced a live firing exercise in the Gulf of Sirte, off the Libyan coast. Libya had claimed sovereignty over the Gulf in 1973 and what Libyan president Muammar Gaddafi described as the 'Line of Death' was established along the line of the 32° 30' North Parallel which defined the limit of the Libyan claim. However, this unilateral declaration was never recognized by the USA and their ships and aircraft frequently exercised a freedom of navigation within the Gulf of Sidra. On the first day of the exercise on 18 August, the exercise was periodically interrupted by more than 60 Libyan aircraft which flew into the live firing area during the course of the day. These aircraft were intercepted and escorted from the area by F-4J Phantoms from USS

BELOW NATO Exercise *Ocean Safari* 85 was held in the Atlantic Ocean and Norwegian Sea in late summer 1985. A Grumman F-14A Tomcat of VF-33 is launched from USS *America* (CV 66) for an exercise sortie. (NARA)

ABOVE A Grumman A-6E Intruder of VA-34 about to land on the aircraft carrier USS *America* (CV 66) during a 1983 cruise of the Mediterranean Sea and Indian Ocean. (NARA)

Forrestal and F-14 Tomcats from *Nimitz*. Early on the second day of the exercise it seemed that the pattern would be repeated when two F-14 Tomcats from VF-41 aboard the *Nimitz* manoeuvred to intercept two Libyan Su-22 (Fitter-F) fighter-bombers. However, this time as the Tomcats closed on the Libyan aircraft, the lead Su-22 launched a Vympel K-13 (AA-2 Atoll) AAM at the lead Tomcat, which was flown by Cdr Henry 'Hank' Kleemann and Lt David 'DJ' Venlet. The Atoll missed its target and the Number 2 Tomcat flown by Lt Lawrence 'Music' Muczynski and Lt JG James 'Luca' Anderson subsequently shot down the lead Su-22 with an AIM-9L Sidewinder AAM while Cdr Kleeman accounted for the Libyan wingman with another Sidewinder. These were the first air-to-air kills by the Tomcat.

A crisis erupted in Lebanon after the Israeli army invaded the country in the summer of 1982. A US-led multi-national force (MNF) deployed in August 1982 to keep the warring factions apart, but on 23 October 1983 the US Marines barracks in Beirut was bombed, triggering a deepening of the crisis. TARPS-equipped F-14 Tomcats from USS *John F. Kennedy* and USS *Dwight D. Eisenhower* (which was later replaced by USS *Independence*) flew reconnaissance missions over Lebanon in support of the MNF, and on 3 December 1983 a Tomcat was fired on by a Syrian SAM system. A reprisal raid was planned the next day against Syrian anti-aircraft sites near the village of Hammana, some 16 miles to the east of Beirut. Unfortunately, the airstrike was not well planned and during the mission two aircraft were shot down by Soviet-supplied 9K32 Strela-2 (SA-7 Grail) missiles. An A-6E Intruder from VA-85, flying from USS *John F. Kennedy*, was hit over Beirut and although both crewmembers were seen to eject, the pilot Lt Mark A. Lange was killed, and the bombardier Lt Robert O. Goodman was captured by Syrians. An A-7E Corsair was also hit, but the pilot Cdr Edward T. Andrews ejected safely and was rescued. A-6 Intruders and A-7E Corsairs from USS *Independence* had also been in action in the Caribbean Sea supporting the US landings in Grenada in October 1983.

Britain in the Early 1980s

Having lost its last aircraft carrier in 1978, the RN regained some of its former capability in July 1980 with the commissioning of HMS *Invincible* (R05), a 'through deck cruiser' design which was classed as an 'ASW carrier'. The ship was the first of a of three-ship class, and carried an air wing equipped with British Aerospace (BAe) Sea Harrier FRS1 VTOL fighters and Sea King ASW helicopters. The ships were also sometimes classed as 'STOVL carriers' indicating that the Harriers would carry out

The RN returned to aircraft carrier operations in the 1980s with the British Aerospace Sea Harrier FRS1 flying initially from HMS *Hermes* (R12) and then from Invincible-class through deck cruisers. This aircraft is from 800 NAS. (Cooke)

a short take off and vertical landing. Unlike the similarly configured Yak-38 Forger, the Sea Harrier was a very effective weapons system and the Ferranti Blue Fox radar and AIM-9L Sidewinder AAM combination made it a potent interceptor. The prime task of the Sea Harrier was air defence of the fleet, but its pilots also practised the surface attack and reconnaissance roles, too. The concept of operating Harriers from aircraft carriers was not new, having been proved with the experimental Hawker Siddeley Kestrel VTOL aircraft operating from HMS *Ark Royal* during trials in 1963 and again from HMS *Bulwark* in 1966. The difference with the new carrier was the concept of a short take-off and vertical landing (STOVL), for which the take-off performance was enhanced by a seven-degree 'ski-jump' ramp at the bow of the ship. The ramp imparted an upward vector to the aircraft, launching it at lower speed into a parabolic trajectory which enabled it to accelerate quickly to flying speed. The Invincible-class ships could also be used by RAF Harrier GR3 ground-attack aircraft.

A second ASW carrier, HMS *Illustrious* (R06) joined the fleet in 1982, but in the meantime the commando/ASW carrier HMS *Hermes* had been refitted with a 12-degree 'ski-jump' and began to carry Sea Harriers from 1981. It was not long before the carrier/Sea Harrier combination was put to the test operationally: in early 1982 Argentina invaded the Falkland Islands in the South Atlantic Ocean and a task force which included the two carriers HMS *Invincible* and HMS *Hermes* was dispatched to retake the islands. In addition to its complement of Sea Harriers, HMS *Hermes* also carried the Harrier GR3s of 1 Sqn RAF. In the first days of the conflict, RN helicopters from the destroyer HMS *Antrim*, the frigates HMS *Brilliant* and HMS *Plymouth*, and the ice patrol vessel HMS *Endurance* (A171) were involved in the retaking of South Georgia. During this operation the Argentinian submarine *Santa Fe* was neutralized near Grytviken on 25 April by the Wessex HAS3 from HMS *Antrim* dropping depth charges, followed up by Wasps from HMS *Plymouth* and HMS *Endurance* firing the Nord AS.12 ASM. The main task force and its aircraft carriers arrived off the Falkland Islands on 1 May and the Sea Harriers were in action almost daily from then until the Argentine forces surrendered on 14 June. During those six weeks, Sea Harriers carried out air-to-air combat, during which they were credited with 16 confirmed kills, as well as airstrikes against Argentine ground forces and military installations. The Harrier GR3s were also employed in the ground-attack role. Two Sea Harriers and two Harrier GR3s were shot down by ground defences during air-to-ground missions and another five carrier-borne aircraft were lost to accidents during operations.

ABOVE From the late 1980s the Hawker Siddeley Nimrod was upgraded to MR2 standard, which included the installation of the EMI Searchwater radar. These aircraft are performing a flypast at RAF Kinloss after the Falklands campaign. (Crown Copyright/MoD)

RN Sea Kings provided ASW cover for the task force during operations in the South Atlantic, but the air defence of the task force ships was hampered by a lack of an AEW platform. As a result of this shortcoming, two Sea King HAS2 were hastily modified to carry a palletized Searchwater radar, under Project LAST (low-altitude surveillance task). The radar scanner was mounted on a hydraulically powered swivel bracket on the starboard side of the helicopter where it was protected by an inflatable radome. The aircraft, which were flown by D Flight 824 NAS, were dispatched to the Falklands after the conflict in mid-1982 with HMS *Illustrious*. Later, ten Sea King HAS2 were modified to become AEW2 helicopters with the addition of the Searchwater radar mounting and from 1985 they were operated by 849 NAS. The Sea King HAS5 improved ASW variant was introduced from 1981, featuring updated avionics and the provision for sonobuoys.

1980s – Flying the Nimrod
Norton Hatfield • Royal Air Force Nimrod Pilot

On a typical 'MedEx' going from Gibraltar to Cyprus we would take off from Gibraltar, climb to 1,000ft circuit height and then descend to our normal, much lower, 'on task' operating height. Typically, at this point we would throttle back one of the outboard engines and leave it to cool down for a few minutes before shutting it down to save fuel. The aircraft would climb happily on two engines at max take-off weight once we were safely airborne. In daytime we could go down to 200ft for photography and visual inspection, or 300ft at night. Generally, on a surface surveillance exercise we would stay below cloud and vary the height to optimise radar; in a busy area such as the Mediterranean there generally wasn't much point in going above 1,000ft.

At some stage the flight engineer would work out if it was worth shutting down the other outboard engine. There was a calculation which came out with the minimum drag speed, a minimum height and a maximum weight: above that weight the aircraft wouldn't climb on one engine (if an engine failed while using just two engines), but there was sufficient time available to get one of the shutdown engines back up and running should one of the live engines fail above the calculated height. Below the calculated weight the aircraft would climb on one engine provided that the aircraft remained above the minimum drag speed. The engines produced a large increase in thrust at power settings over about half a per cent at 86%, so we would often fly the Nimrod with the middle two engines thrusting, one outer engine at idle and the other outer engine shutdown. The reason we shut down the outbound engines, besides for ease of asymmetric handling, was that the middle two engines each had two hydraulic pumps, whereas the outboards only had one.

When manoeuvring the rule of thumb for max angle of bank was 'ten degrees AOB more than the height in feet,' ie 30 degrees at 200ft, 40 degrees at 300ft, 50 degrees at 400ft and 60 degrees at 500ft (which was in practical terms the maximum bank for turning as 2.0g was the normal g limit). When trying to catch a submarine using the magnetic anomaly detector (MAD) (the long sticky out bit at the back) the navigation computer would command the flight director to fly a perfect circle, the diameter of which equated to a 30-degree banked turn in still air. We would fly this at 300ft day or night, and the effect of wind made this an interesting exercise! We also tried to minimise power changes, as the MAD would even detect the power changes due to the slight variation in the output of the electrical generators.

During the conflict the Nimrod MR2 fleet was also involved in long-range patrols to monitor Argentine naval forces. Back at home, against the background of quieter Soviet submarines, the RAF Nimrod fleet was equipped with Australian 'Barra' sonobuoys from 1980. These passive Sonobuoys comprised two sections: a surface float containing a transmitter, and a canister suspended below it which deployed a horizontal hydrophone array. The array could give accurate directional information and two such buoys could be used to track the movement of multiple submarine contacts. Amongst the 'spin offs' from the South Atlantic War was the provision of an AAR capability to the Nimrod fleet, which, in turn, extended the operational range of the aircraft well north into the Barents Sea. In addition, the Nimrods were modified to carry both the Harpoon ASM and the BAe Sting Ray light weight acoustic homing torpedo.

OPPOSITE The British Westland-built variant of the Sea King, the Sea King HAS2 differed from the US Sikorsky Sea King in its Rolls Royce Gnome engines and its avionics, including the dorsally mounted EKCO AW391 search radar. (NARA)

The RAF moved the Buccaneers of 12 Sqn and 208 Sqn to Lossiemouth in northern Scotland in 1980, putting them nearer to their most likely operational area. The Martel ASM continued in use through the early 1980s, but it was replaced by the BAe Sea Eagle anti-shipping missile in 1985. The new missile had a longer range than its predecessor and had an active seeker head so it could be launched 'over the horizon' without the launch aircraft having to penetrate the target defences. If necessary, mid-course guidance could be provided by a Nimrod.

Canada and West Europe in the Early 1980s

The CAF began to replace its aging CP-107 Argus with the Lockheed CP-140 Aurora in 1980. The Aurora was a P-3 Orion airframe, but it was equipped with the same avionics suite as installed in the more modern S-3 Viking. This included a Wescam MX-20 electro-optical/Infrared (EO/IR) system, MAD antenna, airborne imaging radar systems (AIRS), an ESM system and sonobuoys. The aircraft had an endurance of 17 hours, but the typical mission length was eight to ten hours. Originally 24 Auroras were ordered but six of them were subsequently cancelled because of budget cuts; the remaining 18 aircraft were allocated to 405 Sqn and 415 Sqn at Greenwood, Nova Scotia on the east coast and 407 Sqn at Comox on the west coast. The last Argus was withdrawn in July 1981. The CAF airborne ASW forces also included the CH-124 Sea King, now enhanced through the SKIP, which continued to operate from Iroquois-class destroyers and Protecteur-class fleet replenishment ships.

BELOW With the demise of the Fairey Gannet AEW3 and the consequent gap in long range early warning radar cover, 12 Shackletons were fitted with the AN/APS-20 search radar taken from the Gannets, to become Shackleton AEW2. (NARA)

ABOVE During the mid-1980s the Lockheed F-104 Starfighter was replaced in Norwegian and Danish service by the General Dynamics F-16A. Those in RNoAF service would eventually be armed with the Kongsberg Penguin anti-ship missile. (RNoAF)

In Norway the RNoAF received its first F-16s to replace the F-5 and F-104 in 1980. The second F-16 unit to become operational was 334 Skv at Bodø and it retained its anti-shipping strike role with the new aircraft. However, the Bullpup missile was not used on the F-16, being replaced instead by the Kongsberg Penguin ASM which entered service in 1987. Originally intended for use by fast patrol boats, the Penguin ASM incorporated an inertial platform and passive infra-red sensor to home in on its target and had a range of some 30 miles. Maritime patrols and ASW work by the RNoAF continued to be carried out by the P-3B Orions of 333 Skv, flying from Andøya. During the 1980s, the squadron carried out daily surveillance missions along the coast of the Kola peninsula as far as 40 degrees East. Like the RNoAF, the RDAF also started its conversion to the F-16 in 1980, replacing both the F-104G Starfighter and the F-100D Super Sabre with the new type. In 1982 it also acquired three Gulfstream III-SMA3 for maritime patrol duties. These aircraft, flown by Esk 721, were fitted with an APS-127 search radar produced by Texas Instruments, and were used predominantly in the Baltic Sea, but they also patrolled as far away as the Faroe Islands.

While the Netherlands, Belgium, Norway and Denmark had chosen to replace the F-104 with the F-16, West Germany selected the Panavia Tornado for both the *Marineflieger* and the air force (Luftwaffe). The two-seat Tornado heralded a massive increase in capability over the Starfighter, including all-weather operations, and could carry two *Kormoran* missiles on its under-fuselage pylons. MFG 1 received its Tornados in 1982, but MFG 2 continued to operate the F-104G Starfighter through the first half of the decade. The ASW role continued to be discharged by those Atlantique of MFG 3 based at Nordholz. Some of these aircraft had been modified for the SIGINT role and they were

ABOVE By 1984, the Lockheed P-3S Orion had replaced both the Lockheed SP-2H Neptune and Breguet Atlantique in Dutch service. As part of the MARPAT group the MLD frequently operated the Orion from Iceland. (Netherlands Institute of Military History)

active in the Baltic Sea gathering intelligence data during flights along the coasts of Warsaw Pact countries. MFG 3 also formed a third squadron equipped with the Westland Lynx Mk 88 for both ASW and ASuW operations from small warships.

Between 1982 and 1984, the MARPAT group of the Netherlands MLD acquired 13 P-3C Update II.5 Orions (a modification state which incorporated all of the improvements in Update II and some of those in Update III). The first unit to re-equip with the aircraft was 320 Sqn (now titled VSQ320) since the SP-2H Neptune was already obsolete. In VSQ321, the Atlantique was phased out in favour of the P-3C during 1984, making Valkenburg an all-Orion base from that year. Once it was fully combat ready with the new aircraft, MARPAT established a permanent detachment at Keflavik in 1985 to participate in the joint NATO ASW operations from Iceland.

The two French aircraft carriers *Foch* and *Clemenceau* continued to operate the Super Étendard, Étendard IVP, F-8 Crusader and Alizé during the 1980s, as well as Super Frelon helicopters. The Alizé was modernized early in the decade with a Thomson-CSF *Iguane* radar and updated avionics, enabling it to remain an effective ASW platform through the decade. Like the US carriers of the 6th Fleet, both French carriers took turns to support peace-keeping forces during the Lebanese civil war and Super Étendards from *Foch* bombed Syrian artillery positions in September 1983 after the Syrians fired on French forces. In 1984 Foch carried out exercises of the Libyan coast in the Gulf of Sidra. Throughout the decade, *Aéronavale* continued to use the Atlantique as its prime land based MPA.

There was little change in the composition of NATO naval aviation in the Mediterranean Sea during the 1980s. ItAF maritime patrol and ASW work was carried out by the Atlantique in 88° *Gruppo* at Sigonella and 86° *Gruppo* at Cagliari Elmas. The Italian Navy also continued with the ASH-3D Sea King and both the Italian and Turkish navies operated the AB-212ASW helicopters. The S-2 Trackers of the Turkish Air Force continued to carry out ASW duties in the Black Sea and the Eastern Mediterranean from Topel on the far north-eastern arm of the Sea of Marmara. The Hellenic Navy established a Naval Helicopter Command (*Dioíkisi Elikoptéron Naftikoú* – DEN) at the Amfiali helicopter station, Athens, in 1980. The unit was equipped with the AB-212ASW and was complemented in this role by the HU-16B Albatross of the Hellenic Air Force.

NATO Maritime Tactics in the 1980s

In NATO, the concepts of strategic ASW and forward operations reached maturity in the 1980s. The strategic approach involved all aspects of ASW working together within a unified command structure and was an excellent demonstration of co-operation across allies and across fighting services. All US ASW forces (and therefore in practice all NATO forces) in the North Atlantic Ocean came under the command of Commander, Submarine Forces, US Atlantic Fleet (COMSUBLANT) and the tactical control of the Commander Task Force (CTF) 84 based at Keflavik. The forces allocated to CTF-84 included surface warships, attack submarines (SSN) and MPA, as well as undersea surveillance systems including the SOSUS network. The MPA bases included Keflavik, Lajes and Rota (Spain). There was a similar arrangement in the Mediterranean region under CTF-67. CTF-84 kept a close watch on the Soviet submarine

bases in the Kola peninsula. Every Soviet SSBN was shadowed by a NATO SSN throughout its cruise from the moment that it left port. It was also tracked by NATO MPAs which kept a virtually constant presence overhead. Initial tracking would probably be by RNoAF Orions from Andøya, which would hand over the RAF Nimrods from Kinloss and then as it passed through the GIUK gap to USN or MLD Orions, or CAF Auroras, operating from Keflavik. Once they entered their patrol boxes in the western Atlantic, the submarines would be constantly tracked by NATO aircraft flying from Bermuda, Lajes or other bases around the Atlantic coasts. During these tracking operations of Soviet SSBNs, the aircraft would use covert passive sensors so that they remained undetected by their target. On the other hand, if the Soviet submarine was an attack submarine, MPA crews would aim to achieve attack parameters as quickly as possible and carry out a simulated attack. The strategy was to be in a position to neutralize Soviet SSBNs either by MPA or SSN as soon as hostilities started.

In the late 1970s much thought was given as to how to counter the threat to carrier battle groups posed by the Tu-22M2/ Kh-22 weapons system. The speed of the Tu-22M2 and range of the Kh-22 made it essential to neutralize the threat as far away as possible from the carrier group. One part of the solution was to deploy specialist anti-aircraft ships ahead of the carrier, while the other part was to push fighter aircraft as far out from the carrier group as possible. The question was how best to achieve this most efficiently. The first concept was known as *Vector Logic*, in which the F-14 Tomcats were sent to distant CAPs and were then

OPPOSITE The French aircraft carrier *Foch* (R99) under way during NATO Exercise *Distant Drum* in the Mediterranean Sea during summer 1983. The complement of Dassault Super Étendard multi-role fighters can be seen near the bows. (NARA)

BELOW Equipped with the Thomson-CSF Agave radar, the Super Étendard could be armed with the Aérospatiale AM 39 Exocet anti-ship missile. This Exocet-armed aircraft is launching from *Foch* (R99) off the Lebanese coast in early 1986. (NARA)

ABOVE A Vought F-8E(FN) Crusader of 12.F. During the late 1980s the *Aéronavale* aircraft underwent a modernization and refurbishment programme to extend their operational life until the Dassault Rafaele entered service. (Petit)

maintained on station for as long as possible by AAR tankers. However, this technique placed a heavy burden on the tanker aircraft and also precluded them from supporting the strike aircraft. An alternative solution, which found favour between 1984 and 1987 was known as Operation *Chainsaw*, in which the Tomcats were cycled out from the carrier along the most likely attack tracks out to their maximum range, before returning to land on the carrier. As one fighter began its return leg, the next one launched from the carrier to patrol along the same track. The fighter tactics were also integrated into the E-2C Hawkeye mission profiles to give the fighters early warning and tactical direction. The problem with *Chainsaw* was that it increased the number of launch and landing cycles for each fighter, which took its toll in fatigue life and thus reduced their combat effectiveness. The final tactical iteration, Operation *Tank Saw*, in the late 1980s was a hybrid of the two previous profiles in which fighters were 'pulsed' out along the expected attack tracks but also had AAR support, so that rather than landing on the carrier, they refuelled and set out once more along their designated track. This system enabled multiple pulses by each aircraft and reduced the number of launch and landing cycles.

Another passive measure to protect the carriers from the air threat was that of Forward Operations, which involved pushing carrier battle groups through the GIUK gap and then dispersing them amongst the Norwegian fjords. Here they would be difficult for the Soviets to locate or attack but they would still be able to launch their aircraft close enough to fly well into the Soviet 'bastion' areas in the Barents Sea. The concept was tested during the NATO Exercise *Ocean Safari* in 1985. The main problem here was that the air-defence zone around the NATO strike fleet might extend out to some 300 miles from the carrier, so when the battle group sailed into the Norwegian Sea, its air-defence zone (ADZ) began to overlap the Norwegian ADZ. This greatly complicated airspace management, particularly as the USN insisted on maintaining separate, but co-ordinated arrangements, rather than integrating the carrier battle group into the existing air-defence management system in the Defence Command North Norway. This state of affairs had already been the case during operations in the GIUK gap where the strike fleet air-defence zones overlapped with the UKADR. The solution was the Coordinated Air Defense in Mutual Support (CADIMS) concept which formalized procedures to deconflict friendly aircraft within the overlapping areas. A similar arrangement was therefore agreed in the late 1980s with the Commander North Norway (COMNON), in which the airspace was divided along a line parallel to the Norwegian coastline, with the strike fleet taking responsibility for air defence on the seaward side and COMNON taking responsibility for the landward side. Another teething problem which was encountered during Exercise *Ocean Safari* was the need to establish forward supplies of fuel and weapons to be used by the naval aircraft.

BELOW A Grumman F-14A Tomcat of VF-102 embarked on USS *America* (CV 66) during 1982. As well as their traditional fighter role, the squadron was the first to use the tactical airborne reconnaissance pod system (TARPS) pod in the reconnaissance role. (NARA)

Warsaw Pact in the 1980s

Warsaw Pact amphibious forces in the Baltic region were given a substantial boost to their air support with the formation in the DDR of Naval Flight Wing 28 (*Marinefliegergeschwader* – MFG-28) at Laage near Rostock. It was formed in great secrecy in 1985 and its existence was not admitted until 1987. MFG-28 operated 24 Su-22M4 (Fitter-K) ground-attack aircraft in two squadrons. It was tasked with offensive support for the 'united Baltic Sea Fleets.' One reason for the formation of MFG-28 was the doubt over the reliability of Polish forces given the unrest in the country. The two squadrons of the Polish 7th Naval Fighter Bomber Regiment (*Pułk Lotnictwa Myśliwsko-Bombowego Marynarki Wojennej* – 7.PM-B MW), which was based at Siemirowice, were due to replace their Lim-6bis with Su-22M4R in 1984. However, the re-equipment did not take place for budgetary reasons and instead the regiment soldiered on with its obsolete Frescos until it was disbanded in 1988. Another less ambitious plan to equip a single naval squadron with the Su-22M4 by reforming the 15th Independent Reconnaissance Aviation Squadron (*Samodzielnej Eskadry Lotnictwa Rozpoznawczego MW* – SELP MW) also came to nothing.

The Polish navy continued to use the Mi-14PL helicopters for ASW work, flown by 16 Special Naval Aviation Regiment (*Pułk Lotnictwa Specjalnego MW* – PLS-MW) at Darłowo. The Mi-14PL was also used by the East German Naval Helicopter Wing18 (*Marinehubschraubergeschwader* – MHG 18) at Parow near Stralsund in the ASW role from 1980. The unit also flew the Mi-14BT (*Buksirovschich Tralov* – mine countermeasures sled tow) (Haze-B) mine clearance variant of the helicopter. The Mi-14PL were also flown by the Bulgarian navy in the Black Sea from 1980. Romanian naval aviation during the early 1980s comprised just a handful of obsolescent Mi-4 helicopters with a limited ASW capability.

BELOW The 'eyes of the fleet' providing early warning radar cover and fighter direction, a Grumman E-2C Hawkeye prepares to launch from the aircraft carrier USS *America* (CV 66) during air operations off the coast of Libya in 1986. (NARA)

LEFT The carrier onboard delivery (COD) was a vital if unglamorous part of carrier operations, transporting personnel, equipment and supplies between ship and shore. Here a Grumman C-2A Greyhound aircraft lands on USS *Forrestal* (CV 59) during NATO Exercise *Ocean Safari* in the Andfjorden, Norway, autumn 1987. (NARA)

The USSR in the Mid–Late 1980s

The fourth Kiev-class carrier *Baku* was commissioned in 1987 and was allocated to the Northern Fleet. Like her sister ships, *Baku* carried the Yak-38 fighter and Ka-27 helicopter. The ships now operated an improved variant of the Yak-38, the Yak-38M, which was introduced from 1985. It was fitted with the Tumanskiy R-28-300 vectored-thrust main engine which was some 10 per cent more powerful than the R27V-300 that had powered the previous variant. The two separate lift engines were also upgraded, giving a similar increase in thrust. Nevertheless, the type still

BELOW A Mil Mi-14PS (Haze-C) search and rescue helicopter of the Polish navy. The Polish navy regiment 16. PLS-MW also operated the Mil Mi-14PL (Haze-A) ASW variant. (NARA)

Monitoring NATO Exercise *Northern Wedding* 86, Tupolev Tu-16RM (Badger-E) reconnaissance aircraft overflies participating warships in the Norwegian Sea. The Soviet navy took great interest in the progress of the exercise. (NARA)

had little practical operational value. A more conventional aircraft carrier, launched in 1985 as *Brezhnev*, but renamed *Tblisi* in 1987, carried out sea trials in the late 1980s with Sukhoi Su-27K (*Korabyelny* – shipborne) (Flanker-D). The ship featured a 'ski jump' ramp at the bow which enabled aircraft to take off from the vessel without the use of a catapult; the aircraft would land using the conventional wire arrestor system. However, neither carrier nor its aircraft were destined to see service during the Cold War, for she was not commissioned until 1990, after assuming her third identity as *Admiral Kuznetsov*.

The AV-MF Tu-16 regiments in the Northern Fleet began to replace their elderly aircraft with the Tupolev Tu-22M3 (Backfire-C) in 1985. In the Tu-22M3, the Tupolev design bureau had re-designed much of the aircraft, including fitting it with more powerful Kuznetsov NK-25 engines and re-profiling the engine intake ramps; the nose was also lengthened to incorporate an AAR capability, the wing sweep schedule was revised, and the avionics suite was updated and improved. This included equipping the aircraft with the Leninets PNA-D attack radar which used doppler beam sharpening and the SMKRITs satellite targeting datalink receiver. The new type equipped two former Tu-16 regiments, the 574th MRAP and 924th GvMRAP in Arkhangelsk and Murmansk respectively, as well as re-equipping the 5th GvMRAP in the Crimea. The mid-1980s also saw the introduction of a new nuclear air-launched missile, the Kh-15 (AS-16 Kickback). Tu-22M3 could carry six of these missiles on a rotary launcher carried in the internal bomb bay, but the prime weapon for anti-shipping missions remained the Kh-22 which was carried semi-recessed under the fuselage. The Tu-95RTs could provide mid-course guidance for both of these missile types. Another variant of the Tu-95/142, the Tu-142MR (Bear-J) was a specialized relay platform for communication with Soviet strategic submarines while they were submerged, including sending them the authorisation codes to launch ballistic missiles. The *Oryol* (Eagle) mission equipment included a 9,000m VLF radio antenna cable which was extended in flight and towed behind the aircraft. During the 1980s AV-MF Tu-95RTs aircraft made increasing numbers of flights from their bases northern Russia across the North Atlantic to land in Cuba. These surveillance sorties were used to monitor and gather intelligence on US and NATO forces, and included entering the air defence identification zone (ADIZ) off the eastern seaboard of the USA to gauge the response. Bear-F aircraft also began regular flights to San Antonio de los Banos, Cuba from 1983. In addition, there was a permanent detachment of pairs of Tu-95RTs and Tu-142 at Camh Ran Bay, Vietnam, with each aircraft remaining there for 60-day periods. During this time, they would venture into the Pacific and the Sea of Japan. Tu-95RTs aircraft were frequently deployed to Angola and Il-38 MPAs were deployed in pairs both to Syria and Libya as well as to Asmara in Ethiopia. Soviet tactics for attacking NATO carrier battle groups with aircraft were further developed during the 1980s. Instead of regimental attacks, each carrier group would be attacked by an entire AV-MF division, a total of around 100 Tu-22M and Tu-16K. Of these aircraft, some 70-80 would be armed with Kh-22 ASMs. Since the NATO Exercises *Northern Wedding* and *Team Sprit* regularly involved three carrier groups and the AV-MF fielded only two divisions each in the Northern and Pacific Fleets, extra aircraft would need to be provided, if necessary, by the VVS DA. The attack formation would also be supported by a regiment of Su-15TM (Flagon-F) long-range interceptors who would act both as a decoy element and a fighter escort, as well as targeting the E-2 AEW aircraft when they reached the target area. Target updates for the strike element would be transmitted by Tu-95RTs during the ingress to the target. The strike formations would split into two or more elements to confuse the defences, using chaff and ECM to confuse and distract the defenders still further. The doctrine was for all aircraft to fire the missiles in a salvo, within a minute-long time window, in order to saturate the defences with an almost simultaneous arrival of the missiles, some of which might also carry nuclear warheads. The Soviets estimated that their attrition rate for such missions would be 50 per cent.

For all the ingenuity in its design, the development of the remarkable – and unique – Alekseev Project 903 *Lun* (Duck) ekranoplan was abandoned by the Soviet navy in the late 1980s. (Napier)

The Soviet Navy held its largest ever maritime exercise in the summer of 1985. Codenamed '*Summerex*' by NATO, it took place in July and August and was even bigger in scale than *Okean* 75 had been ten years previously. *Summerex* was a major sea control exercise in which the Northern Fleet was augmented by elements from the Baltic and Black Sea Fleets to establish control over the Norwegian Sea and thereby prevent NATO from reinforcing its northern flank. Five separate submarine barriers were established in the North Sea, the Eastern Atlantic Ocean, the GIUK gap and two across lines in the Norwegian Sea. Apart from attempting to deny the Norwegian Sea to NATO carrier battle groups, the barriers were also intended to protect and defend Soviet SSBN in the 'bastion' area of the Norwegian and Barents Sea. The carrier *Kiev* participated in the exercise, sailing from Murmansk on 18 July to be in position off the west coast of Norway by 21 July. On 20 July, a Yak-38 from *Kiev* ditched in the Norwegian Sea some 80 miles to the southwest of the Lofton Islands and its pilot was rescued by the RN Type 42 destroyer HMS *Newcastle* (D 87).

Two clandestine operations were carried out by Soviet submarines in order to test the US and NATO anti-submarine defences during the 1980s. In both Operation *Aport,* in the summer of 1985, and Operation *Atrina* in the spring of 1987, a group of five Project 671RTM *Shchuka* (Pike) (Victor-III) submarines from the 33rd Submarine Division (*Diviziya Podvodnykh Lodok*) left their base at Zapadnaya Litsa, near

Murmansk, together and sailed for the Sargasso Sea. In both cases NATO ASW forces, which expected Soviet submarines to sortie singly, were overwhelmed and the Victor-III boats were able to slip through the NATO defences. The Soviet Navy believed that the submarines remained undetected throughout their voyages, but US and NATO sources dispute this. In Operation *Aport* the submarines used the temperature variations in the Gulf stream to disguise their presence, and in Operation *Atrina* the submarines routed under the Polar ice cap and down the western coast of Greenland to avoid the SOSUS detectors in the GIUK gap. The submarines also used sonar countermeasure devices and noise simulators during their cruise to throw NATO ASW forces off their track. While P-3C Orions from Lajes and Brunswick, and CP-140 Auroras from Greenwood, searched for the submarines, four Tu-142M from the 35th Long-Range Anti-Submarine Aviation Division (*Protivolodochnaya Aviatsionnaya Diviziya Dal'nego Deystviya*) operating from San Antonio de los Banos, Cuba, monitored the actions of the NATO MPAs to assess their tactics.

During the 1970s, the Soviet Navy had commissioned a number of experimental 'wing in ground effect' vehicles, known as ekranoplans. These hybrid machines resembled flying boats, but were much bigger and heavier, taking advantage of the cushioning of 'ground effect' when a wing passes over the surface at a height of only a few feet. The trials culminated in Project 904, the Alekseev A-90 *Orlyonok* (Eaglet) ekranoplan which was a transport vehicle capable of carrying 250 troops or two BTR-60 armoured personnel carriers. The nose section was hinged to allow access to the payload bay. The Orlyonok class were powered by two NK-8-4K jet engines in the nose and a tail mounted NK-12MK turboprop, giving a cruise speed of 220mph at a height of 15 ft. It could operate in a sea state of up to 6ft waves. Three production models of the Orlyonok class were built between 1977 and 1983 and allocated to the Black Sea Fleet where they were operated by crews who had experience from flying the Be-12 amphibian. However, rather than being employed over the Black Sea, they were instead based at Kaspiysk in the Dagestan SSR and mainly operated in the Caspian Sea. An original order for 24 of these machines was later cancelled and the funding transferred to the SSBN programme. The Alekseev bureau also produced a much larger ekranoplan, the Project 903 *Lun* fast attack missile carrier. Powered by six NK-87 jet engines, it was armed with six 3M-80 *Moskit* (Mosquito) (SS-N-22 Sunburn) anti-shipping missiles, in other words two more launchers than were carried on the Sovremennyy-class destroyers. Travelling at much higher speeds than a ship and at much lower altitude than aircraft,

Two Grumman F-14A Tomcat aircraft are serviced aboard the aircraft carrier USS *America* (CV 66) during Exercise *Ocean Venture* 84 in the Gulf of Mexico. (NARA)

the Lun class would evade enemy defences (including mines and barriers which it would overfly) to reach its missile launch point undetected. Only one Lun-class ekranoplan was built, being delivered to the Black Sea Fleet in March 1987, but like the Orlyonok class its service was limited to trials in the Caspian Sea.

US in the Mid–Late 1980s

The US carrier building programme continued through the late 1980s with the commissioning of USS *Theodore Roosevelt* (CVN 71) in 1986. The next ship in the class, USS *Abraham Lincoln* (CVN 72), was launched in 1988 and commissioned in the last days of the Cold War in 1989. With these ships in the fleet, and excluding the ships undergoing refit, the USN now had 14 aircraft carriers in its current order of battle. When she deployed for her first cruise to the Caribbean Sea and thence to the North Atlantic Ocean, USS *Theodore Roosevelt* carried some 90 aircraft from CVW-8, comprising two fighter squadrons of F-14A Tomcats, two fighter/strike squadrons of F/A-18A Hornets, two all-weather strike squadrons of A-6E Intruder, an early warning squadron of E-2C Hawkeye, a squadron of S-3A Viking, an electronic warfare squadron of EA-6B Prowler and an ASW helicopter squadron of SH-3H Sea King.

BELOW A Lockheed P-3C Orion aircraft from VP-49 passes Mount Etna as it returns to its deployment base at Sigonella, Sicily, after a submarine hunting mission. Many US-based Orion squadrons rotated through Sigonella for temporary detachments. (NARA)

ABOVE A Lockheed S-3A Viking is launched from the flight deck of the USS *Forrestal* (CV 59) during NATO Exercise *West Wind* 88, in the North Atlantic. (NARA)

During the early 1980s Libya had sponsored a number of terrorist attacks against US civilians and servicemen. In October 1985 the cruise ship *Achille Lauro* was hijacked by Palestinian terrorists in the Mediterranean and an American passenger was murdered. The terrorists left the ship in Egypt and were put on a flight to Tunisia, but their Boeing 737 was intercepted by F-14A Tomcats from VF-74 under direction of an E-2C Hawkeye from VAW-125, all operating from USS *Saratoga*. The Boeing 737 was escorted to Sigonella in Sicily, where the terrorists were captured. As a result of this incident the USA initiated Operation *Attain Document*, which was intended to increase pressure on Libya by operating carrier battle groups, which formed Task Force 60 (TF60), in the Gulf of Sirte. Phase One of the operation took place between 26 and 30 January 1986, when USS *Saratoga* and USS *Coral Sea* sailed into international waters in the Gulf of Sirte. The battle groups were protected by 24-hour combat air patrols (CAPs) by their Tomcats. The Libyan response was minimal, although on the first day some Libyan aircraft approached the CAPs, possibly intending to drag the US fighters into the missile engagement zone (MEZ) of their S-200 (SA-5 Gammon) SAM battery. Phase Two, between 12 and 15 February, repeated the exercise, but this time there were 150 sorties by Libyan aircraft towards the CAPs, although there were no air-to-air engagements. For the final phase three of *Attain Document*, USS *Saratoga* and USS *Coral Sea* were joined by USS *America*. On 24 March a SAG consisting of the missile cruiser USS *Ticonderoga* (CG 47) and two destroyers crossed the 'Line of Death' in the Gulf of Sirte, under air cover provided by the three aircraft carriers. This time the Libyans

A Sikorsky SH-3H Sea King ASW helicopter of HS-15 hovers over the flight deck of the USS *Forrestal* (CV 59) which was leading one of the two battle groups participating in the NATO Exercise *Team Work* 88 in the Norwegian Sea. (NARA)

responded by firing two S-200 SAMs at Tomcats from VF-102 from *America*, which were on the southernmost CAP. The American fighters evaded the missiles by descending to low level, with the support of EA-6B Prowlers which also provided electronic countermeasures.

This hostile act triggered Operation *Prairie Fire*, a US contingency plan which enabled TF60 to take offensive action against Libya. A Libyan La Combattante-class fast attack boat which headed towards the SAG was engaged by two A-6E Intruders from VA-34 aboard USS *America*, which sank the Libyan boat with two AGM-84 Harpoon missiles. This was the first use of the Harpoon in combat. Meanwhile, A-7E Corsairs from VA-81 and VA-83 had launched from USS *Saratoga* and when they were locked up by the S-200 site they fired AGM-88 HARM at the target acquisition radar, disabling it. That evening a Libyan Nanuchka-class missile corvette was bombed by A-6E Intruders from VA-34 and VA-85 (from *Saratoga*) using Rockeye cluster munitions which heavily damaged the Libyan ship. Another Nanuchka-class corvette was engaged by Intruders in the early hours of the next

morning: aircraft from VA-55 flying from USS *Coral Sea* disabled the ship with Rockeye missiles, after which Intruders from VA-85 sank it with Harpoon. After two more days which were uneventful, the SAG withdrew from the Gulf of Sirte on 27 March.

However, this military action failed to stop Libyan-sponsored terrorist atrocities: on 2 April a bomb exploded on board a TWA flight to Athens, killing four US citizens, and three days later a bomb blast at the La Belle discotheque in Berlin killed another 70 including off-duty US servicemen. The USA then responded in the early hours of 15 April by launching Operation *El Dorado Canyon*, which involved simultaneous co-ordinated airstrikes against the military infrastructure in Libya. USAF F-111 strike aircraft attacked targets near Tripoli, while the USN 6th Fleet provided aircraft from USS *America* and USS *Coral Sea* to hit targets near Benghazi. Six Intruders from VA-34, supported by HARM and Shrike ARM-loaded Corsairs, attacked the terrorist training facility in the Jamahiriya barracks with 1,000lb Mk 82 bombs and although they missed most of the complex, they destroyed four MiGs which were being stored nearby. At the same

RIGHT A Boeing-Vertol UH-46D Sea Knight utility helicopter of HC-6 carrying out vertical replenishment operations between the carriers USS *Forrestal* (CV 59) and the USS *Theodore Roosevelt* (CVN-71) during the NATO Exercise *Team Work* 88. (NARA)

time eight Intruders from VA-55, with F/A-18 Hornets providing the ARM support, struck the airfield at Benina, on the eastern outskirts of Benghazi, destroying several aircraft there.

After taking part in *El Dorado Canyon*, USS *America* remained in the Mediterranean Sea until the end of August 1986 when she was relieved by USS *John F. Kennedy*. As an illustration of a typical cruise profile, the carrier arrived in Benidorm for a port visit, followed by four days at sea before another port call at Toulon. After five days in Toulon, the ship took part in the three-day Exercise *Display Determination* with the USS *Forrestal* and the French carrier *Foch*. At the end of the exercise on 13 October, USS *John F. Kennedy* sailed to Haifa for another port call.

During the previous decades, the USN fleet air reconnaissance squadrons had carried out electronic signals intelligence (SIGINT) missions around the globe. By the 1980s the two active squadrons, VQ-1 and VQ-2, operated the EP-3E airborne reconnaissance integrated electronic system (ARIES), which was a modified Orion airframe, from shore bases, and the EA-3B Skywarrior both from the shore and from aircraft carriers. During the 1980s VQ-2 was based at Rota, Spain, with six EP-3E and six EA-3B and covered the Mediterranean as well as the Atlantic and Indian Oceans. The EA-3Bs were operated singly from the on-duty aircraft carriers that were cruising in those waters. An unfortunate accident occurred on board USS *Nimitz* on 5 January 1987, when an EA-3B Skywarrior from VQ-2 crashed while attempting a night landing. All seven crew members were killed. The incident served to underline the risks of both carrier operations and of the intelligence-gathering role of the fleet air reconnaissance squadrons.

Modification programmes were initiated in 1987 for both the S-3A Viking and the F-14A Tomcat. The Vikings were progressively modified to S-3B standard by the fitting of the AN/APR-137 radar, improved avionics and ESM suites, and compatibility with the Harpoon ASM. The main part of the Tomcat upgrade was the replacement of the troublesome and surge-prone Pratt and Whitney TF30 engine with the improved General Electric F110-GE-400 engine. The re-engined Tomcat was initially designated the F-14A Plus, which later became the F-14B.

There was a final combat in the Mediterranean with Libyan forces in early 1989, when once again the 6th Fleet carrier battle group had been tasked to exercise freedom of navigation near the Libyan coast. On 4 January two Libyan MiG-23 (Flogger) fighters headed towards a pair of F-14A Tomcats from VF-32, which were flying a CAP about 40 miles north of Tobruk to protect the USS *John F. Kennedy* carrier group. The Tomcats manoeuvred away from the MiG-23s several times in an attempt to avoid direct confrontation, but at every change of direction, the MiG-23s turned towards them and continued to close on the US aircraft. When an engagement became inevitable and the Libyan aircraft were declared hostile, the lead Tomcat, flown by Cdr Joseph B. Connelly with Cdr Leo F. Enwright, shot down one MiG-23 with an AIM-7 Sparrow AAM, and the number two Tomcat, crewed by Lt Herman C. Cook with Lt Cdr Steven P. Collins, accounted for the second MiG-23 with an AIM-9 Sidewinder.

BELOW A typical flight deck scene aboard the USS *America* (CV 66) circa 1986. In the background, behind the Grumman A-6E Intruder and Grumman F-14A Tomcat, is a Douglas EA-3B Skywarrior ELINT aircraft of VQ-2. (NARA)

A pair of British Aerospace Sea Harrier FRS1s of 800 NAS embarked on HMS *Illustrious* (R06) approaching the deck of the USS *Dwight D. Eisenhower* (CVN 69) in the autumn of 1984. The aircraft are painted in the low-visibility finish adopted during the Falklands campaign. (NARA)

Update III to the P-3C Orion was introduced in the mid-1980s. Amongst the enhancements, an IBM Proteus acoustic processing system and a single advanced signal processor (SASP) brought a more robust and capable means of linking to sonobuoys and of interpreting their acoustic signals. With Update III, the Orion was far better equipped to find, track and if necessary, neutralize the more modern quiet Soviet submarines.

NATO in the Mid–Late 1980s

The third Invincible-class ASW carrier, HMS *Ark Royal* (R 07), was commissioned in 1985, replacing the elderly HMS *Hermes* which had been decommissioned the previous year. With one ship undergoing refit at any time, this enabled the RN to retain a front-line strength of two carriers, each with its own squadrons of Sea Harriers and Sea Kings. Both the HAS5 and AEW2 variants of the Sea King were operated from the carriers. There was a major enhancement to the striking power of the Fleet Air Arm with the integration of the Sea Eagle ASM into the Sea Harrier fleet in 1987. With both RAF Buccaneers and RN Sea Harriers armed with Sea Eagle, and Nimrods carrying the Harpoon, the British maritime forces had an impressive anti-shipping capability in the second half of the decade.

In the late 1980s there was no change to the way in which the ASW role was performed by Britain, Canada and the Netherlands: the Nimrod MR2, CP-140 Aurora and P-3C Orion continued working very much hand-in-glove with the Norwegian and USN P-3 Orion force over the Norwegian and Barents Seas and the North Atlantic Ocean. The efforts of NATO MPAs were complemented by shipborne ASW helicopters, primarily variants of the Sea King.

In Norway the Penguin ASM was integrated onto the F-16 in 1987 and two years later the RNoAF acquired an additional four P-3C Upgrade III Orion to join those P-3B Orion already in service with 333 Skv. The newer aircraft were needed to counter the more modern and quieter classes of Soviet submarines that were now sailing into the Norwegian Sea. Meanwhile on 13 September 1987 a Sukhoi Su-27 (Flanker) from the Soviet 941st IAP attempted a close pass on a RNoAF P-3B Orion, which was monitoring Soviet warships in the Barents Sea. The Soviet pilot Senior Lt Vasiliy Tsymbal misjudged the closure and his port tailfin hit the starboard outer propeller of the Orion. Debris from the propeller badly damaged the airframe and the engine had to be shut down, but the Orion pilot 1st Lt Jan Salvesen was able to divert safely to Banak airfield in northern Norway.

A Panavia Tornado IDS of the West German *Marineflieger* MFG1 armed with the Messerschmitt-Bölkow-Blohm (MBB) AS.34 *Kormoran* (Cormorant) 2 anti-shipping missile. (USAF)

The West German *Marineflieger* completed its conversion from the F-104G Starfighter to the Tornado in 1986, when MFG2 re-equipped with Tornado. It now fielded two groups of *Kormoran*-equipped Tornados for anti-shipping tasks, a group of Atlantique aircraft for ASW and a squadron of Lynx for both the ASW and anti-shipping roles. The Netherlands also operated the Lynx Mk27, known in MLD service as the UH-14A, in the ASW role, while the long-rage ASW role in the MARPAT was fulfilled exclusively in the late 1980s by the P-3C Orion.

The French Navy continued to operate its two conventional aircraft carriers *Foch* and *Clemenceau*, but its F-8E(FN) Crusaders were reaching the end of their useful lives. Rather than purchasing new aircraft which might jeopardize the eventual procurement of the Dassault *Rafale*, which was due to replace the Crusader in the late 1990s, a modification and refurbishment programme was designed to keep the Crusader in service until the *Rafale* could replace it. Seventeen airframes entered the programme in the late 1980s to become F-8P (*Prolongé* – extended). The *Aéronavale* fleet of Atlantique aircraft had been enlarged by the acquisition of the surplus Dutch aircraft when the MLD retired the type in 1984. In 1989 the Atlantique 2 joined the *Aéronavale* MPA force. Amongst the improvements in this new variant of were new engines, updated avionics and the ability to carry the AM-39 Exocet ASM.

The Portuguese FAP, which had carried out only limited coastal patrols during the late 1970s and early 1980s using transport aircraft, purchased six ex-RAAF P-3B Orions in 1986. Over the next two years, these aircraft were modified to become P-3P Orions, bringing them to a similar standard to the P-3C Update II.5. They were operated by *Esquadra* 601 from Montijo airbase near Lisbon and gave the FAP, for the first time, a credible ASW capability.

A Spanish navy Hawker Siddeley AV-8S Matador aircraft in flight over the aircraft carrier *Dédalo*, circa 1988. (NARA)

Spain had joined the NATO alliance, but not its integrated military structure, in 1982, and its navy, the *Armada*, had operated the aircraft carrier *Dédalo* since 1967. From the *Dédalo*, which had previously sailed as the USS *Cabot* (CVL 28), the *Armada* operated the McDonnell Douglas AV-8S Matador, a variant of the AV-8A Harrier VTOL attack aircraft. The aviation complement on *Dédalo* comprised eight Matador strike aircraft of the 8th *Escuadrilla* and four SH-3D Sea Kings of the 5th *Escuadrilla* which fulfilled the ASW role. Unlike the RN carriers, the Spanish ship did not incorporate a 'ski jump' so the take-off weight of the Matador was somewhat limited in comparison the Sea Harrier. The air force (*Ejercito del Aire* - EdA) carried out the MPA/ASW role, for which 221 Squadron (*Escuadron*) of the 22nd Patrol Wing (*Ala de Patrulla 22*) based at Jerez de la Frontera operated six P-3A Orions which were leased from the USN. Another five P-3B Orions were sold to the EdA by the RNoAF when the latter acquired its P-3C Orions in 1989. In the same year, four of the original EdA P-3As were returned to the US at the end of their lease.

The other European nation to possess an aircraft carrier was Italy, which commissioned the STOVL carrier *Giuseppe Garibaldi* (C 551) in 1985. Unfortunately, an Italian law dating from 1937 forbade the navy from operating fixed wing aircraft, which were deemed to be the preserve of the air force; even so, the ship was constructed with a four-degree 'ski jump' in the expectation that the law would be changed. The ship was used initially as a helicopter carrier for ASH-3D Sea Kings and AB-212ASW helicopters until a change in the law in early 1989 resulted in the order for 16 AV-8B Plus Harriers. These aircraft were delivered in 1991. During the late 1980s, the ItAF continued to use the Atlantique MPAs in the ASW role.

Meanwhile, the Hellenic Air Force continued to use the obsolete HU-15 Albatross of 353 MNAS for maritime surveillance and ASW work. The AB-212ASW helicopters of the DEN moved to Kotroni naval base at Marathon in 1986. In Turkey, the maritime task was similarly split between the S-2E Tracker MPAs of the Air Force and the AB-212ASW helicopters of the Turkish Navy.

NATO Exercises in the 1980s

The pattern of NATO exercises that had been established in the 1960s and 1970s continued through the 1980s. Exercise *Northern Wedding* took place every four years, while *Teamwork* and *Ocean Safari* were biennial on even and odd years respectively. All of these exercises included the reinforcement of the northern flank in Norway and typically they involved some 150 ships and about 250 aircraft. They were invariably monitored closely by the Soviet Navy.

The exercises always included the NATO STRIKFORLANT with at least one carrier battle group. Exercise *Teamwork* 1980 involved the USS *Nimitz*, while USS *Forrestal* took part in Exercise *Ocean Safari* 81. The first Exercise *Northern Wedding* of the decade took place in September 1982 with participation by USS *America* with CVW-1 embarked and *Independence* with CVW-6. During this exercise, the amphibious landings were made in Jutland. Unfortunately, there were two fatal flying accidents in the course of the exercise: the crash of a CH-46 Sea Knight from the amphibious assault ship USS *Guadalcanal* resulted in eight deaths and the pilot of an AV-8B Harrier from the amphibious assault ship USS *Nassau* (LHA 4) was killed when his aircraft crashed after take-off in poor weather. *Ocean Safari* 83 was the last exercise undertaken by HMS *Hermes* before she was decommissioned. During the exercise her complement consisted of 12 Sea Harriers, ten Harrier GR3s and ten Sea Kings. Exercise *Ocean Safari* 83 also saw the operational debut of the Dutch MLD P-3 Orions which operated from Lajes. Until 1984, the A-6 Intruder was not allowed to use Norwegian airfields during NATO exercises because of the nuclear role of the aircraft. The Norwegian government considered that operations by such aircraft would be an unnecessary provocation to the USSR. However, the ban was rescinded by the Norwegians in 1984 and the USMC A-6 Intruders were able to operate from Bodø during Exercise *Teamwork* 84. The carrier USS *Independence* led the strike fleet during this exercise.

A EA-3B Skywarrior of VQ-2 lands aboard the aircraft carrier USS *Coral Sea* (CV 43) during flight operations off the coast of Libya. VQ-2 operated both the EA-3B and the Lockheed EP-3E Aries electronic reconnaissance aircraft.(NARA)

Night Sortie in a Sea Harrier
Tim Eastaugh • Royal Navy Fleet Air Arm Sea Harrier Pilot

'Launch the Alert 5 SHAR'. I hear it, but the plane captain has already given me the 5-finger salute and the yellow coat has rotated his wand. Slide the canopy closed, confirm the seat is live and start the donkey. The NAVHARS is already aligned, so it's just a normal rapid start, and I'm ready to go in 3 minutes. The head-up display (HUD) horizon levels up, FLYCO gives an amber deck, and the chain lashings are removed. Maintainers hoist them and the Sidewinder noddy caps triumphantly for my inspection.

Eyes now on the yellow coats, as they taxy me forward to the calculated launch bracket. With every roll, I speed up or slow down as the jet moves across the deck. With the hard right command on the wand, I finish up on the centreline. Toe brake on. With a flourish, two wands twitch then point at the FDO. The boardman arrives with an updated heading scribbled on his board, and I carefully overtype the ship's heading into the NAVHARS.

All eyes turn to FLYCO. Engine up to 55 per cent. Power set. FLYCO goes green. FDO green wand. I decide to slam as the ship is halfway down her nod. Keep toe brakes ON, skid, skid, release. Accelerate! A catapult launch it is not, but I will still hit 85kt in 3sec to 4sec as the jet exits the ramp. Keep her straight, confirm full power, move hand to the nozzle lever, guard the stick. A thump in the gut as the jet goes up the slope. Ramp exit! Pull the nozzle lever back 35 degrees to the STO stop, and wait… the jet's ballistic at first, but with a trajectory of 12-degrees up, I should accelerate to flying speed before I level off. 80ft above the sea, in the black hole scanning the red symbols of truth in the HUD. Fight the somatogravic illusion; just leave the stick alone! The alpha builds towards 12 units but stabilizes. I slowly nozzle out, clean up and climb on my opening vector.

As often happens, the 'hack the Shadower' – intercept is a Bear-D – is a futile exercise… all I do is swan around, seemingly getting close… but it's just 'No Joy' again. The Blue Fox is a highly capable pulse radar, so I'm confident that if there was anything out there, I would have found it. The fun (was it, really?) is over, and I'm given instructions to recover. The only diversion, Keflavik, disappeared along with my fuel some while ago.

Approaching the top of drop, decelerate using 20 degrees then 40 degrees of nozzle. A third of a mile before the drop, select 60-degrees nozzle, apply power to stay level. *'Start your descent now'*. The CCA controller speaks. Reduce the power, lower the attitude and keep 8 units alpha Speed is 130kt–140kt now and I am almost completely thrust-borne. At this speed the jet is skittish.

I level off at 200ft with a bunch of power and look for the meatball. *'Half a mile'*. The last and vital call from the controller. It's the cue to select hover stop, power up and check that, yes, I do have hover performance. I bring the nozzle lever back to the hover stop, keep the attitude and wings level *'On the Roger'*, the LSO pipes up from FLYCO. What can I see? There must be a ship there because I can see the ball, some centre-line lights and a tiny reverse L shaped pattern from the FDO as he indicates landing spot with the wands.

Up to now, it's been relatively comfortable, but as I approach the hover alongside, it's becoming fraught. Hellishly busy at 80ft above the invisible sea. The descent is good thankfully, and I only need a tiny bit of air brake stop to establish in a hover alongside. Must be a big wind over deck, because I need to pop the lever a degree or two forward of the stop to maintain a good hover attitude.

Stabilize, wait for the deck to steady up. I've got to get on with it; after all I'm burning fuel at 300lb a minute and there's not much left. Look ahead, 90 degrees right, ahead, 90 degrees right. Smidge of right stick to transition across. Keep it on the centre line. Keep it level. And down. Half an inch of power off and I meet the deck with a thump and bounce.

Exercise *Ocean Safari* 85 was remarkable in being the first opportunity to prove the concept of forward operations. The exercise saw USS *America* sailing into Vestfjorden, between Bodø and the Lofoten Islands, from where she successfully launched her aircraft while remaining hidden from Soviet reconnaissance aircraft and protected from submarine or missile attack. The French carrier *Foch* also took part in the exercise. The Vestfjorden was used again the following year by *Nimitz* during Exercise *Northern Wedding* 86, which also saw participation by HMS *Ark Royal* and the amphibious assault ships *Saipan* and *Inchon*. The exercise was closely monitored by Soviet *Krivak*-class frigates and auxiliary general intelligence (AGI) trawlers, as well as Tu-95 and Tu-16 aircraft. A variation of the forward operations was trialled by USS *Forrestal*, which operated within the Andfjorden immediately to the north of the Lofoten Islands during *Ocean Safari* 87, and during the largest NATO maritime exercise to date, Exercise *Teamwork* 88, the three carriers USS *Theodore Roosevelt*, USS *Forrestal* and HMS *Illustrious* all operated within Norwegian fjords.

All of the major maritime exercises involved full participation by land-based aircraft as well as those from aircraft carriers. The full inventory of NATO MPAs, Nimrods, Orions and Auroras all took part as did shore-based strike aircraft such as the RAF Buccaneers, RNoAF F-16s and *Marineflieger* Tornados.

The Final Decade

Just like the previous two decades of the Cold War, the fourth decade was dominated at sea by the balances of power on the one hand between the Soviet submarine and NATO ASW forces and on the other between the US aircraft carrier and Soviet naval air forces. The emergence of ever more capable and acoustically efficient submarines in the Soviet Navy during the 1980s presented an enormous challenge to NATO ASW forces. The also claimed to have gained the upper hand through Operation *Aport* and Operation *Atrina*, although NATO sources dispute the Soviet claim that the submarines evaded detection. Certainly, the rapid advances in acoustic sensor technology and computer processing that were introduced across the NATO MPA fleet during the decade offset much of the advantage gained by the newer generations of Soviet submarines, but in the 1980s the contest between the submarine and the aeroplane was more evenly balanced than it had previously been.

The security of the NATO northern flank had always depended heavily on the ability of the NATO STRIKFORLANT to keep the SLOCs open and to land reinforcements in Norway. Battlegroups based on the aircraft carriers of the USN had always been powerful forces and the Nimitz-class ships of the 1980s, with their advanced

Two Grumman A-6E Intruder aircraft of VA-35 embarked on USS *Nimitz* (CVN 68), November 1986. Upgrades including incorporation of the target recognition attack multi-sensor (TRAM) system ensured that the type remained fully modernized. (NARA)

and capable aircraft, perhaps represented the pinnacle of naval striking power. Such forces represented a serious challenge for the AV-MF which was charged with neutralizing the threat. The sheer power of the US aircraft carriers meant that whole air divisions of AV-MF strike aircraft would have to be deployed against them to swamp the defences, and that such attacks would draw a very high rate of attrition. However, the introduction of the Tu-22M3 and of long-range ASMs in the second half of the decade gave the AV-MF a much better chance of success and NATO had to concede that it would be unwise to operate its carriers for extended periods in the Norwegian and Barents Seas.

Both the Soviet and NATO navies were forced to find ways to protect their assets from attack and to practise their new strategies. For the Soviets, the answer lay in the 'bastion' strategy, placing the Soviet SSBNs in a defended area at the extremes of reach of NATO forces. This was practised during 'Summerex 85'. For NATO, the protection of the aircraft carriers

A fine illustration of the concept of 'forward operations': the USS *America* (CV 66) under way during NATO Exercise *Ocean Safari* 85 in the 155-km long *Vestfjorden* (Western Fjord), Nordland, Norway where the ship was well concealed by the surrounding mountains. (NARA)

was achieved through 'forward operations', concealing the ships in Norwegian fjords where they were difficult to detect and were virtually immune to submarine and missile attack. This was practised during all of the major maritime exercises in the second half of the 1980s.

The fourth decade of the Cold War was to prove to be its final decade. Events at sea during the 1980s were framed against the backdrop of political difficulties in the USSR and popular resentment against the communist regimes in eastern Europe. A landslide victory by the *Solidarność* in free elections in Poland during 1989 destroyed the credibility of the communist government and within a year the communist regimes in Poland, East Germany, Czechoslovakia, Hungary and Romania had all collapsed. The symbolic end to the Cold War came on 9 November 1989 when thousands of East Berliners spontaneously flooded across the Berlin Wall and into West Berlin. The Cold War had ended abruptly. Germany was reunified in 1990 and the Warsaw Pact was formally dissolved in Prague on 1 July 1991; by the end of that year the USSR had also ceased to exist.

CHAPTER 5

THE NEUTRALITY OF A PORT – 1949–89

'Never break the neutrality of a port or place, but never consider as neutral any place from whence an attack is allowed to be made.'

Lord Nelson, Royal Navy, 1804

In the immediate aftermath of World War II when Europe found itself divided between the western and eastern blocs, there were seven countries which were not, for various reasons, aligned to either side. Austria, Eire, Finland, Spain, Sweden, Switzerland and Yugoslavia all fell outside the east-west split and remained neutral. Of these, Austria and Switzerland were landlocked, but the other five countries each had coastlines to defend, and coastal waters to keep under surveillance. Just as the reasons for and circumstances around their neutrality varied, so the maritime threats and the responses to those threats varied greatly. In the Baltic Sea there was mutual suspicion between the Warsaw Pact countries on the one hand and Sweden and Finland on the other. Similarly, in the Adriatic Sea, Albania and Yugoslavia were seen as potentially hostile by NATO and, although unaligned, Spain allowed the US to base aircraft within its borders.

Sweden

Sweden had adopted a policy of neutrality in the mid-19th century and, thanks in large part to its well-equipped armed forces, it had successfully remained neutral during World War II. In the post-war years, Sweden

OPPOSITE A SAAB 37 Viggen low over the surface of Lake Vattern. The AJ 37 Viggen took over the maritime strike role from the SAAB A 32A Lansen (Lance) in the early 1970s. (FlygHistoria)

continued to update and upgrade its armed forces in order to defend its neutrality by having forces strong enough to inflict serious damage to any potential aggressor. By the early 1950s the Swedish Air Force (*Flygvapnet*) was thought to be the fourth or fifth largest air force in the world, with a strength of some 800 combat aircraft. A doctrine of 'peripheral defence' required air and naval forces to be able to meet any attacker with massive force before they reached the borders of Sweden. Although strictly neutral and with no official links to NATO, unofficial bilateral ties did exist with both Norway and Denmark. Swedish defence planners perceived two possible threats from the USSR: firstly, an amphibious invasion of southern Sweden in order to reach the Kattegat and Skagerrak between Sweden and Denmark and thereby control access to the Baltic Sea, and secondly a land invasion of Finnish and Swedish Lapland to use it as a route to cross into Norway.

Within the *Flygvapnet* order of battle, the 1st Air Group (*Första Flygeskadern* – E1) contained four surface-attack air wings (*Flygflottilje*) based in the south of Sweden, whose primary role was to defend the country against the possibility of amphibious attack by Soviet and Warsaw Pact forces. At the start of the Cold War, the *Flygflottilje* of E1 were equipped with a mixture of SAAB A21 attack aircraft and SAAB B18 medium bombers, but most of these were replaced in the early 1950s by jet aircraft. *Flygflottilj* F14 based at Halmstadt re-equipped with the de Havilland Vampire FB50 (designated A28B) while F6 at Karlsborg and F7 at Såtenäs both received the SAAB A29B (known as Tunnen – Barrel). However, these early jet types were intended as temporary solutions, awaiting the arrival of the SAAB A32A Lansen (Lance). F17 at Ronnerby, which had continued to fly the SAAB T-18B, was the first unit to receive the two-seat Lansen in 1956, followed by the remaining three *Flygflottilje* over the next four years. Specifically designed for the maritime strike role, the aircraft was equipped with an Ericsson PS-431/A radar which was

BELOW In Swedish *Flygvapnet* service, the Consolidated PBY-5A Catalina was designated the Tp47. Three of the flying boats were operated by the *Flygvapnet* for maritime reconnaissance in the late 1940s and early 1950s but one was shot down by Soviet fighters in 1952. (FlygHistoria)

The SAAB A32 Lansen

Alf Ingesson Thoor • Swedish Air Force Lansen Pilot

The cockpit was covered by a teardrop canopy with the radar operator's seat slightly lowered than the pilot. Pilot and radar driver sat on SAAB-designed ejection seats equipped with stabilizing fins on the sides of the headrests; these were made of transparent plastic so as not to block the rear view.

Flight behaviour was excellent, stable and docile up to Mach 0.9 with fast pitch or roll response, but when that speed limit was exceeded, the aircraft became difficult to steer as the hydraulic systems that moved flaps and ailerons became less efficient and had a slower response; under these conditions the G limit dropped to just three. The rate of turn was excellent for those times: at 6,000ft and 250kt the Lansen turned pulling 6G without losing speed but the A32 needed to select the afterburner to perform the manoeuvre. To increase the range, an auxiliary tank in the shape of a half egg was soon designed and was positioned under the fuselage giving a funny and very characteristic appearance to the Lansen. This tank was not detachable in flight and could contain 600 litres of fuel. The airframe was incredibly robust as it could handle 12 positive and up to eight negative G, much more than pilots could handle.

Starting in 1959, the attack Lansen were integrated with the Robot 04 missile, the first launch-and-forget device in the world, capable of flying for 15 to 31km depending on drop altitude to the target, thanks to a solid-propelled rocket. The missile could have been programmed to hit a single unit or a fleet; in the latter case it would have armed itself only if it had identified at least 10 ships in close proximity. However, it was a very large weapon, it weighed 600kg (half of which consisted of explosives that could have split a medium-sized ship in two) and had a wingspan of 2m and was 4.45m long. Only two missiles could fit under the wings, attached to special pylons equipped with side struts. The introduction of RB-04 greatly increased the credibility of the Swedish defences by integrating with a dense network of coastal defences consisting of bunkers and artillery at the entrance to the country's main fjords.

LEFT Originally designed as a reconnaissance bomber, the SAAB B-18 evolved into an anti-shipping aircraft. The type carried a crew of three and remained in service until 1959. (FlygHistoria)

ABOVE Armed with the SAAB Rb04 anti-shipping missile, the SAAB A 32A Lansen equipped four air wings whose role was to defend against Soviet amphibious forces in the Baltic Sea. (FlygHistoria)

optimized for use with the SAAB Rb04 anti-shipping missile. The Rb04, which had a range of some 15km, was a 'fire and forget' weapon with its own internal radar system for active guidance. In 1961, F14 was replaced in E1 by F15, another Lansen unit, which was based further north than the other *Flygflottilje*, at Söderhamn on the coast of the Gulf of Bothnia.

The 4th Air Group (*Fjärde Flygeskadern* – E4) was responsible for three reconnaissance *Flygflottilje*. Sweden, just like the members of the NATO alliance, relied on reconnaissance and ELINT to ascertain the intentions of the USSR and Warsaw Pact countries in the region, and two Douglas DC-3 Dakotas (designated Tp79 in Swedish service) were used by the National Defence Radio Establishment (*Försvarets radioanstalt* – FRA) for this purpose. A major diplomatic incident involving these aircraft, known in Sweden as the 'Catalina Affair' (*Catalinaaffären*), occurred on 13 June 1952, when an FRA Tp79 failed to return from an intelligence-gathering sortie over the eastern Baltic. It soon transpired that the aircraft had been shot down by a Soviet MiG-15 fighter, but the wreckage could not be located and *Flygvapnet* aircraft continued to search for possible survivors for the next three days. On the third day, a Consolidated PBY-5A Catalina (designated Tp47 in Swedish service) was also intercepted and shot down by Soviet fighters near the Bogsskär lighthouse, some 80 miles east of Stockholm. The crew was rescued by a passing German vessel, the MV *Munsterland*. Apart from the diplomatic ructions that ensued, the affair emphasized the weakness of the Swedish air defences and their lack of an integrated early warning system. As a result, an air-defence quick reaction alert (QRA – *Incidentberedskapen*) was established and the battle management and early warning service (*Stridsledning och Luftbevakning* – STRIL) systems were developed. In the meantime, another aircraft, a Vickers Varsity (designated Tp82) was procured by the FRA to replace the lost Tp79 Dakota. The Tp82 would remain in service until 1973, while the two remaining Tp47s were retired from search and rescue duties in 1966.

ABOVE When the SAAB AJ 37 Viggen replaced the Lansen in service, it was also adapted for the SAAB Rb04 anti-shipping missile as shown here or the Maverick or RBS-15 ASMs. A maritime reconnaissance variant, the SH 37 was optimized for maritime surveillance. (FlygHistoria)

The Swedish Navy (*Marinen*) had surrendered its air arm to the air force in 1926, but in the early Cold War years, the naval staff had seen the potential of the helicopter for ASW work, SAR and for transport to and from ships. However, at that stage the *Flygvapnet* had no interest in helicopters, so the *Marinen* procured nine Vertol 44A helicopters (designated the Hkp1 in Swedish service) for the ASW role in 1958. These aircraft, which were equipped with dipping sonar, were allocated to the Naval 1st Helicopter Squadron (1.*Helikopterdivisionen*) at Bromma aerodrome, Stockholm (later moving to the nearby Berga heliport) and 2.*Helikopterdivisionen* at Torslanda, near Gothenburg. They were augmented by four Vertol 107-II-17 helicopters (Hkp4B) in 1964 and were replaced in 1973 by a further eight Kawasaki-Vertol KV107-II-16 / Hkp4C variants. Like the Hkp1, the Hkp4 carried an active dipping sonar, but it was also equipped with a search radar fitted on the rear ramp.

Meanwhile, the FRA expanded its fleet of ELINT aircraft with the purchase of two English Electric Canberra B2 (designated Tp52) in 1960. The aircraft were heavily modified, including the fitting a lengthened nose cone to house the same Ericsson PS-431/A radar that was used in the Lansen. The two Canberras were allocated to F8, although when flying ELINT missions over the Baltic Sea the three-man crew included a flight crew member from the FRA. Many of the ELINT missions were tasked directly by the Swedish Armed Forces *Överbefälhavaren* (commander-in-chief – ÖB) and might involve ultra-low-level flying over the sea to penetrate below the cover of long-range search radars in order to 'ambush' shorter range transmitters. The Canberra aircraft were replaced in 1971 by two Sud Aviation Caravelle III (designated Tp85) which were nominally allocated to F13 at Malmen.

Flying the Viggen
Alf Ingesson Thoor • Swedish Air Force Viggen Pilot

What never ceased to amaze me was the Viggen's thrust. In addition to dry power, the aircraft had a three-zone afterburner. When flying in dry power the aircraft was not particularly impressive, perhaps even under-powered. The afterburner zone one was used to retain a speed of M0.9 at low altitude when carrying a heavy load. Zone two was for acceleration and take-off. Zone three was where things began to happen. The word 'accelerate' really is insufficient: with zone three the Viggen simply runs away. When taking off using zone three, the aircraft lifts off after about 400m, with the speed by end of the runway being around 800kph, and M0.8 being reached after about 1km. The pilot's G-load is between four to five G, with the speed increasing to M0.9. The climb angle is now nearly 80 degrees. The time from brakes release to reaching 10,000m is some 1min 50sec. In comparison, this is the same amount of time required for a passenger airliner to get airborne and retract the undercarriage. When flying night sorties against targets in Lake Vättern, firing rockets or dropping bombs, there were occasional opportunities of almost becoming an astronaut. I remember a few such sorties when, having deposited our load on a clear cloud-free and moon-lit night, we had both fuel and time available. More often than not, we were flying in pairs. Increasing the distance to some 500m, flying at an altitude of 200m to 300m above sea level, we received permission from ground control to climb to 12,000m. Flying at speeds of 800kph to 900kph, we lit the zone three, climbing away almost vertically at M0.95. Initially, the jet exhaust of one's wingman was bright yellow and some 15m in length, becoming more faded and blueish at higher altitudes. When passing through 6,000m to 7,000m, each of us rolled slowly, continuing the climb on our backs so to speak and at zero G. At the same time, the earth opened up below us, and as we rolled at 12,000m one had the impression of Gothenburg below on one side, Linköping on the other side, Stockholm a bit further away and the cities of Skåne in the south. Oslo was farther off to one side and Visby (on the island of Gotland in the Baltic Sea) on the other side. The feeling of having ended up in orbit was complete. The entire journey from the dark surface of Lake Vättern to an altitude of 12,000m lasted about 40sec! An enormous starry sky completed the feeling of being in space. After making a couple of half rolls, we quickly arrived back at low level. After landing and taxiing to the tarmac and when walking back to the squadron, one had to smilingly concede that this was a really shitty job, but 'someone has to do it.'

During more than 20 years, I flew some 2,000hr in the Viggen. A nice marriage as long as it lasted.

Like the Canberra, the Caravelle featured a modified nose radome to house the Lansen radar; in addition, their larger size enabled them to carry extra sensors, the aerials for which were located in a ventral radome.

In a re-organization of the *Flygvapnet* command structure in 1966, most of the Air Groups were disbanded and their units became administered directly by the Air Staff (*Flygstaben* – FS); however, the offensive support Air Group E1 was retained, and it was placed under the direct command of the ÖB. The main role of E1 remained that of anti-shipping strikes because of the perceived threat to Sweden of Soviet amphibious forces operating in the Baltic Sea. Beginning in 1971, the obsolescent Lansen was phased out in favour of the SAAB AJ37 Viggen (Thunderbolt). The first Viggen unit was F7 at Såtenäs: F6 and F15 followed suit in subsequent years, but F17 was disbanded, leaving just three wings in the air group. With its double-delta wing and canard, the Viggen had a unique and iconic silhouette, but it also had Mach 2 performance and could be armed with the Rb04, Maverick or RBS-15 ASMs. In 1975 another variant of the Viggen, the SH37, began to replace the S32C reconnaissance variant of the *Lansen*. The 'SH' in the designation stood for *Spaning Havsövervakning* (reconnaissance and maritime surveillance) and the aircraft avionic fit included an improved Ericsson PS-371/A radar which was optimized for maritime surveillance and incorporated a camera to record the radar imagery for post-flight analysis. The aircraft was also typically configured with an external reconnaissance pod containing both optical and infra-red cameras. The SH37 was operated by F13 from Norrköping.

As the 'Catalina Affair' had demonstrated in the 1950s, the military threat to Sweden by the USSR was very real. On 27 October 1981 a Soviet Whiskey-class submarine, the S-363, ran aground near the Swedish naval base at Karlskrona. The crew claimed that it was the result of the failure of the navigation equipment and the Soviet Navy sent a flotilla of ships to recover the vessel without Swedish approval. The Swedish forces stopped the Soviet ships by physically blocking their way and the strike aircraft of E1 were held ready for action if needed. A year later another submarine was detected in the Hårsfjärden, but the subsequent large-scale ASW operation including helicopters failed to locate it or make a positive identification. Soviet fighters also acted aggressively against Swedish aircraft over the Baltic Sea and in 1985 a Sukhoi Su-15TM crashed while trying to follow an SH37 Viggen through its evasive manoeuvres.

Finland

Finland had declared itself neutral in the inter-war years, but the country nevertheless saw almost continuous combat during World War II. During the Winter War of 1939–40, Finland successfully prevented an invasion by the USSR, although in doing so it lost most of the region of Karelia to Russia. The following year after the German invasion of the USSR, the Finns saw an opportunity to regain Karelia and in an alliance with Nazi Germany, they fought the Soviets in the Continuation War of 1941–44. This conflict was concluded in the Moscow Armistice of 1944 which permanently ceded Karelia to Russia and forced Finland to lease the naval installation at Porkkala to the USSR. Subsequently the Finns turned upon their former allies and fought the Germans during the Lapland War of 1944–45.

RIGHT During the 1950s coastal surveillance patrols by the *Ilmavoimat* (Finnish air force) were carried out on an as required basis using whatever aircraft were available at the time, including the Bristol Blenheim. (Laukkanan)

In the post-war years, Finland restated its intention to remain non-aligned and after the experiences of the Winter and Continuation Wars, the USSR was not prepared to intervene militarily as it had done with other neighbouring countries. The Treaty of Friendship, Co-operation and Mutual Assistance (known in Finland as the *Ystävyys-, Yhteistyö- ja Avunantosopimus* or YYA-agreement) signed between the USSR and Finland in 1948 gave some guarantee that neutrality would be respected by the Soviets. However, it did include an article requiring Finland to prevent attacks on the USSR by third parties from its territory. Furthermore, as a former ally of Germany, Finland was bound by the Paris Treaty of 1947, which determined the level of war reparations to be paid by former Axis members to the Allies. It also placed restrictions on the size of post-war armed forces: in the case of Finland, the air force (*Ilmavoimat*) was limited

BELOW The Douglas DC-3 Dakota of the transport squadron was often used for maritime surveillance. The type was also used for ELINT operations until 1985. (Laukkanan)

ABOVE Despite its apparent unsuitability, the Fouga Magister formally took on the maritime role for the *Ilmavoimat* in the late 1950s. Photo reconnaissance was carried out by a crewman using a hand-held camera. (Laukkanan)

to only 60 aircraft, none of which could be an 'aircraft designed primarily as bombers with internal bomb-carrying facilities.'

The basic unit of the *Ilmavoimat* was the air squadron (*Lentolaivue* – LLv). During the 1950s there were five fighter squadrons (*Hävittäjälentolaivue* – abbreviated to HävLLv in 1962) based at Luoenetjärvi (Jyväskylä in central southern Finland), Pori (on the west coast some 70 miles north of Turku) and Utti (some 85 miles northeast of Helsinki). A transport squadron (*Kuljetuslentolaivue*) that operated a mix of aircraft, including Douglas DC-2 and DC-3, was based at Utti and the reconnaissance flight (*Tiedustelulentue* – TieLtue) operated the Bristol Blenheim for photographic surveying from Luoenetjärvi.

The Finnish economy struggled between 1948 and 1952 while the country made every effort to pay off in full the war reparations owed to the USSR, so there was little money to spend on the *Ilmavoimat*, which consequently suffered with poor serviceability and little flying. In the early 1950s occasional sea and ice surveillance flights were carried out by the *Ilmavoimat* using whichever aircraft were available at the time. The maritime role was formalized with the arrival of French-built Fouga Magister in 1958. Despite its limited range and performance, the Magister was used successfully for maritime surveillance and ship identification by HävLLv 13, based at Pori. Two to four sorties a month were flown during open water season either from Pori or Helsinki. The Magister had no reconnaissance fitted, so hand-held cameras were used on all of these flights to photograph ships.

The *Ilmavoimat* acquired three jet-powered Ilyushin Il-28R (Beagle) for reconnaissance in the 1960s and these aircraft proved to be ideally suited to the maritime surveillance task. (Laukkanan)

Maritime surveillance flights became more regular in the 1960s as foreign military naval activity increased in the Gulf of Finland and Baltic Sea and in 1961 the *Kuljetuslentolaivue* acquired a Ilyushin Il-28R for the task. Two more Il-28P Beagles were procured in 1966. Equipped with a PSBN-M radar and fixed reconnaissance cameras, as well as a radar altimeter and reliable autopilot, these aircraft were well suited to descending through cloud to low level to identify and photograph shipping. The Il-28 had a three-hour endurance at most at the economical airspeed of 170kt, making it ideal as an MPA. Interestingly the Soviet PSBN-M radars came without operating manuals, but the Finns discovered that the radar was almost identical to the American AN/APQ-13 that had been used on the Boeing B-29 Superfortress in World War II;

the Soviet radar had been 'reverse engineered' from equipment found on B-29s which had landed in the USSR during the conflict. The Il-28 was initially fitted with Soviet-supplied *Aero Foto Apparat* (AFA – arial photographic apparatus) 33 and AFA 42 cameras installed on pylons in the bomb bay and in the aft fuselage camera compartment. The Soviet-built cameras were replaced in the 1970s by British Vinten G95 Mk2 reconnaissance cameras which had previously been mounted in *Ilmavoimat* Vampires and Gnats.

The *Kuljetuslentolaivue* was responsible for surveillance of a large sea area covering the Gulf of Finland and into the Baltic Sea. The Czechoslovakian Crisis of August 1968 was a particularly busy time as sea traffic in the Gulf of Finland increased to previously unseen levels, with

RIGHT The obsolescent Il-28 were withdrawn in the early 1980s and replaced by two Gates Learjet 35AS multi-role aircraft. Modifications included the incorporation of a Litton APS-504 radar and fitting optical photography windows in the forward fuselage. (Laukkanan)

more than a hundred ships observed in the Gulf. During this period, the Il-28s were held on alert with the crews living in the hangar and one aircraft always at three-minute readiness to launch. In the 1970s a maritime Quick Reaction Alert was established permanently at Utti, with each Il-28 crew taking a 24-hour period to be on 30-minute readiness. As an indication of the Finnish maritime task, the Il-28 squadron completed 177 operational surveillance missions in 1975.

During the Cold War the Baltic Sea was busy with ELINT flights by aircraft of different nationalities flying close to the Finnish borders. These flights were frequently intercepted by *Ilmavoimat* MiG-21 (Fishbed) and *Draken* (Dragon) fighters. However, *Ilmavoimat* also carried out its own ELINT missions over the Gulf of Finland and Baltic Sea from the mid-1970s. Airborne electronic systems named 'Leena' and 'Ursula' were constructed by the intelligence research establishment (*Viestikoelaitos*) and were installed on a DC-3 when required. The missions were flown until 1985 when the DC-3s were withdrawn from service.

The Il-28s were also withdrawn in the early 1980s and replaced by two Gates Learjet 35AS multi-role aircraft. The Learjets were equipped with a Litton APS-504 radar with the antenna mounted in a ventral radome. In addition, a flat optical window was located on each lower side of the front fuselage for photographing vessels. *Ilmavoimat* pilot Jyrki Laukkenan recalled:

Personally, I flew identification flights of foreign ELINT/SIGINT over the Baltic with MiG-21s. The USAF EC-135V was the most

LEFT The Yugoslav JRV was one of the very few operators of the Short Sealand amphibian. Powered by two de Havilland Gipsy Queen 70-3 engines, the Sealand enjoyed a modest performance, but did have an impressive 3½ hour endurance. (Grandolini)

common target. For sea surveillance I also flew a Learjet… I had a special trick when we were flying over the Gulf of Finland and observed a Soviet MiG-23 approaching from behind (our radar warning system activated). I descended down to just 100ft above the sea, took the flaps down and reduced airspeed to 125kt. And then watch the MiG-23 passing by with full forward wings but unable to fly so slowly.

Eire

The Republic of Ireland (Eire) gained independence from the UK in 1922 and has maintained a policy of military neutrality since that date. However, despite this policy, Ireland was consistently sympathetic towards, and helpful to, NATO throughout the Cold War. Although Ireland had its own independent defence forces (*Óglaigh na hÉireann*), which included the Irish Air Corps (*Aer Chór na hÉireann*), the small size of the Irish armed forces, and their lack of ASW or air-defence capabilities, led to a tacit understanding that in the event of major conflict in the

NEXT PAGES During the 1960s, the Irish *Aer Chór na hÉireann* carried out search and rescue missions with three Sud Aviation SA316B Alouette III helicopters. In the 1970s, the operation was expanded with the purchase of eight more helicopters. (*Óglaigh na hÉireann* MA 010 003)

North Atlantic area the defence of the country would be guaranteed by the UK. For most of the Cold War, maritime aviation in Ireland consisted only of coastal SAR missions by the Air Corps Helicopter Flight, which was established at Casement aerodrome, near Baldonnel on the western outskirts of Dublin in 1962. The flight was initially equipped with three Sud Aviation SA316B Alouette III helicopters for search and rescue (SAR) duties. Eight more Alouettes were delivered in 1972 and the unit became the Helicopter Squadron in 1974. After a trial with two SA330J Pumas in the early 1980s, the unit eventually re-equipped in 1986 with five Aerospatiale SA365FI Dauphin, becoming 301 SAR Sqn of the Helicopter Wing.

In 1977/78 two Super King Air 200 were procured for maritime surveillance. From 1980, these aircraft were operated by the maritime squadron from Casement aerodrome. Their role was primarily fishery protection within the Irish exclusive economic zone (EEZ), which extended out to 200 nautical miles from the Irish coast.

Yugoslavia

At the end of World War II, Yugoslavia was one of the closest allies of the USSR. However, over the immediate post-war years, the relationship between Josef Stalin and the Yugoslav leader, Josep Tito, soured and in 1949 Yugoslavia was expelled from the Cominform (Information Bureau of the Communist and Workers' Parties) organization. A communist regime estranged from its ideological partners and with little in common with the NATO membership, Yugoslavia chose to become a leading light for the non-aligned nations of the world. The non-aligned movement (NAM) organization was founded in Yugoslavia in 1956.

BELOW During the 1950s the JRV operated some 80 de Havilland Mosquito FB6 light bombers, some of which were armed with torpedoes. A single de Havilland Mosquito NF38 was equipped with a AN/APS-20 search radar to locate targets for the torpedo carriers. (Grandolini)

ABOVE In 1961, the de Havilland Mosquitoes were replaced by a small number of the indigenous Ikarus 214. The new type was not a success and was withdrawn from service after just three years. (Grandolini)

In 1950, the Yugoslav Air Force (*Jugoslovensko Ratno Vazduhoplovstvo* – JRV) was well-equipped with an inventory that reflected its previous close ties with the USSR. Its basic unit was the aviation regiment (*avijacijske puk*), which comprised three aviation squadrons (*avijacijske eskadrile*). In the early 1950s coastal maritime tasks were carried out by the 21st Mixed Aviation Division (*vazduhoplovstva mesovita divizija*), which had command of the 97th Bomber Aviation Regiment (*bombarderske avijacijske puk* – 97.bap) equipped with the Petlyakov Pe-2 at Zemunik and the 122nd Seaplane Liaison Squadron (*hidroavijacijska eskadrila za vezu*) at Divulja which was equipped with the Short Sealand amphibian and the de Haviland Canada DHC-2 Beaver floatplane. As a non-aligned nation and a former wartime ally, Yugoslavia was able to access more western aircraft in the early 1950s, including nearly 80 de Havilland Mosquito FB6 light bombers and 60 Mosquito NF38 night fighters. As a result, 97.bap was re-equipped with the Mosquito FB6 and from 1954 the aircraft of the second squadron of the regiment were armed with TR45/A torpedoes and were fitted with ASAG mine laying equipment.

In 1956, 21.*divizija* carried out trials of the Short Seamew and Fairey Gannet in the anti-submarine role, but rejected both types as being unsatisfactory. However, the JRV did take an interest in the radar fitted in the Gannet and one set was subsequently delivered to 97.bap. The radar was fitted to a Mosquito NF38 which was used in the anti-shipping role to locate targets for the non-radar equipped Mosquito FB6s to attack. The Mosquitoes were eventually retired in 1961, when they were replaced by the Ikarus 214. An indigenous twin-engined design, the Ikarus 214 was originally conceived as a transport aircraft but was also used for coastal patrols and a small number of aircraft were converted to the Ikarus 214PP (*protivpodmornicki* – anti-submarine) variant. Within the

regiment, now based at Mostar and retitled the 97.ppap (anti-submarine aviation regiment) the Ikarus 214 was operated by 570 and 571.ppae (anti-submarine squadrons) in the maritime patrol and ASW roles until 1964. By then it was apparent that the Ikarus 214, including the upgraded 214AM2 ASW variant, was not a success in the maritime role and it was withdrawn from service. However, the ASW role was continued by the 784th Anti-Submarine Helicopter Squadron (*protivpodmornicka helikopterska eskadrila* – pphe) which was formed in 1961 as part of 97.ppap. The helicopter squadron operated the Westland Whirlwind Mk5 and Mk7, which were equipped with a dipping sonar system and armed with homing torpedoes. In the same year, the 353rd Reconnaissance Aviation Squadron (*izvidačke avijacijske eskadrile* – iae) was formed within 97.ppap with the RF-84G Thunderjet reconnaissance aircraft. This local modification introduced three K-24 cameras fitted in the nose of the aircraft and in each of the wingtip tanks. A limited anti-shipping strike capability was performed by the Republic F-84G Thunderjets of 172nd Fighter-Bomber Aviation Regiment (*lovačko-bombarderski avijacijske puk* – lbap).

After a series of restructures during the mid-1960s, the 97th Regiment was restyled the 97th Naval Support Brigade (*avijacijska brigade za porsku RM*) in 1969. At the same time, it moved to Divulja and was placed under the direct command of the JRV

After the retirement of the F-84F which had carried out the anti-shipping role in the 1960s, another indigenous design, the Soko J-21 Jastreb, took on the role during the 1970s. (Grandolini)

commander-in-chief. Among its constituent regiments was 784.pphe, which had assimilated the seaplanes of 122.esk on the disbandment of that unit and was based with its helicopters and newly-acquired seaplanes at Divulja. The other units in the Brigade were the two Thunderjet squadrons 353.iae with the RF-84G in the maritime reconnaissance role at Mostar and 240.lbae (which had been formed from 172.lbap on the disbandment of that regiment) in the anti-shipping strike role with the F-84G at Zemunika (Zadar). The Whirlwinds of 784.pphe were replaced by the Kamov Ka-25 in 1974, and at the same time the F-84 Thunderjet squadrons re-equipped with the Soko J-21 *Jastreb* (Hawk). Designed and built in Yugoslavia, the *Jastreb* was a single-seat, single-engine strike and reconnaissance aircraft. There were further upgrades in the early 1980s, when the Mil Mi-14PL joined 784.pphe and the *Jastreb* was replaced by the Soko J-22 *Orao* (Eagle). A collaboration with Romania, the two-engine *Orao* was built locally in the Soko factory at Mostar. Whereas the armament of the Thunderjet and *Jastreb* was limited to free-fall bombs or unguided rockets, the *Orao* could be armed with either the TV guided AGM-65 Maverick or the Yugoslav modification of the Soviet Kh-23 *Grom* (AS-7 Kerry) ASM. The aircraft allocated to 353.iae were the early IJ-22 reconnaissance variant that did not have afterburners fitted to its engines. The *Orao* remained in JRV inventory until the end of the Cold War, but the Ka-25 was replaced by the Kamov Ka-28 ASW helicopter in 1988.

BELOW In the early 1980s, the *Jastreb* was replaced by the Yugoslav-Romanian Soko J-22 *Orao* which could be armed with either the TV guided AGM-65 Maverick or the modified Soviet Kh-23 *Grom* (AS-7 Kerry) ASM. However, the maritime role was taken over entirely by helicopters from 1988. (Grandolini)

Albania

An original signatory of the Warsaw Pact, Albania became increasingly estranged from the USSR in the late 1950s as the policies of the Khrushchev administration diverged from the hard-line Stalinist doctrine of the Albanian leadership. Relations between the two countries finally broke down in 1961 when the USSR withdrew its military and economic support for Albania, which became non-aligned. At the time of the diplomatic split, the Albanian Air Force (*Forca Ajrore e Republikës së Shqipërisë* – FAj), which in turn was part of the air-defence command (*Komandës së Mbrojtjes Kundërajrore* – MKA), included two fighter regiments (*Regjimente të Gjuajtës*) equipped with Soviet-supplied aircraft: R 1875 AvG based at Kuçovë with two MiG-15 squadrons (*Skuadrilje*) and R 7594 AvG with one MiG-17F *Skuadril*, one MiG-19PM *Skuadril* and a single Il-28 based at Rinas near Tirana.

China, which was also experiencing a doctrinal shift from the USSR, was quick to fill the void left by the Soviets in Albania and in 1964 the Chinese offered to exchange the 12 MiG-19PM airframes for 80 of the Shenyang J-6 (J – *Jiānjíjī*, fighter) Chinese-built version of the MiG-19S. These aircraft were used to form another *Skuadril* at Rinas and to expand the strength of the other units. Over time, the Soviet-built MiG-17 was also replaced in FAj service by its Chinese equivalent, the Shenyang

BELOW Little is known about the maritime operations conducted by the Albanian FAj, but it seems likely that the Ilyushin Il-28 and later its replacement, a Chinese Harbin H-5, were used for coastal surveillance much in the same way as the Finnish equivalents. (Grandolini)

J-5. Coincident with the departure of the Soviet military assistance, the FAj expanded its role from pure air defence to include ground-attack missions; its regiments therefore became fighter-bomber regiments (*Regjimente të Gjuajtës-Bombardues*).

The single Il-28 was operated by 2 *Skuadrilja,* R 7594 *AvG-B* at Rinas from the late 1950s. Like the Il-28 used by the Finnish *Ilmavoimat*, it was ostensibly used for target-towing, but little is known of its tasking, and it seems likely that, again like the Finnish aircraft, it was also used for coastal surveillance and maritime patrol. It may also have had an ASW role. The Il-28 was replaced by the Chinese-manufactured version, the Harbin H-5, during the early 1970s. This aircraft is known to have been used for ECM and ELINT duties.

Spain

In contrast to Albania, which had started off as a member of an alliance but left it to become non-aligned, Spain entered the Cold War as a non-aligned country and went on later to join NATO. Spain had officially been neutral during World War II, despite having sympathy for the Axis cause, and having dispatched the Blue Division (*División Azul*) to fight against the USSR on the Eastern Front. Because of its connections with Nazi Germany, Spain was ostracized by the victorious Allies in the immediate post-war years, so the country remained non-aligned. However, a rapprochement with the USA in the early 1950s gave Spain access to US arms. Under the terms of the Help Agreement for Mutual Defense, the Economic Assistance Agreement and the Defensive Agreement, all three of which were signed in 1953, the US undertook to provide military aid, including provision of jet aircraft, in exchange for use of the facilities and airbases at Morón, Torrejón, Zaragoza and Rota. So, despite its non-aligned status, Spain hosted USAF and USN combat units which were based permanently in the country, as well as the visiting US aircraft. There was a permanent USN presence at the large naval dockyard at Rota, near Cadiz, where the airfield also served, from 1959, as the home base for USN Fleet Air Reconnaissance Squadron VQ-2, and from 1962 the C-130s of VR-24, naval transport squadron. At Rota, VQ-2 initially flew the Martin P4M-1Q Mercator and Lockheed P2V-5FE Neptune ELINT aircraft, but these types were replaced when the squadron was re-equipped in the early 1960s with the Lockheed EC-121M Constellation.

ABOVE Although it was not a member of NATO, Spain allowed the US to station forces in the country. This Lockheed EP-3B Orion and North American EA-3B Skywarrior, both from VQ-2, are parked on the flight line at Rota, Spain, circa 1976. (NARA)

NEXT PAGES The Dornier Do-24T-3 flying boat was used by the Spanish EdA for search and rescue duties from 1943 until the type was eventually withdrawn in 1971. (Grandolini)

At the beginning of the Cold War the Spanish Air Force (*Ejército del Aire* – EdA) was a large organization, with an inventory of some 1,000 aircraft. However, pure numbers can be misleading: in fact, the EdA had only around 600 serviceable aircraft and of these over 60 per cent were transport or training aircraft. The basic operational unit of the EdA was the air force group (*Grupo de Fuerza Aérea* – GdFFAA), each of which contained two squadrons (*Escuadrones* – Esc). The GdFFAA, which were equipped with offensive support aircraft, were grouped under tactical aviation (*aviacion tactica*) which also had responsibility for supporting naval operations; however with no immediate seaborne threat to Spain, the maritime mission was limited to the SAR role. Routine patrols over the Mediterranean Sea were carried out by *Grupo* 51 from the island of Mallorca. The two squadrons, Esc 52 and 53, operated the Dornier Do-24T-3 flying boat and the Heinkel He-114 seaplane from the aerodrome at Son San Juan near Palma and the flying boat station at Pollensa in the northeast of the island.

A modernization programme for the EdA was initiated in 1952 and from 1955, the GdFFAA structure was progressively replaced by wings (*Alas*) and independent squadrons. The EdA offensive support wings included 21 Light Bomber Wing (*Ala de Bombero Liego* 21) based at

ABOVE Although it was British built, the Hawker Siddeley AV-8S Matador was procured via the USMC due to sensitive relations between the UK and Spain at the time. It was broadly similar to the AV-8A Harrier. (NARA)

Tablada, Ala 26 based at Albacete and Ala 27 based at Malaga. All of these units flew the Casa B.21, a Merlin-powered development of the CASA 2.111, which itself was based on the Heinkel He111. The flying boat and seaplane rescue squadrons (*Escuadrones de Salvamento*) Esc 55, Esc 56, Esc 57 and Esc 58 eventually became, via a series of re-organizations and re-numberings, respectively Esc 801 at Son San Juan, Esc 802 at Gando (Canary Islands) Esc 803 at Getafe (near Madrid) and Esc 804 at Pollensa. Of these units, Esc 801 flew the Do-24T-3 and Esc 804 flew the amphibious Grumman HU-16A Albatross, whereas Esc 802 and Esc 803 operated the Sikorsky H-19B (S-55) Chickasaw helicopter. The Do-24T remained in operational service with the EdA until 1971.

The Spanish Navy (*Armada*) had also noticed the potential of the helicopter and had purchased seven Sikorsky S-55 ASW helicopters in 1957. A more formal organisation was put in place in 1963 with the establishment of the helicopter flotilla (*flotilla de helicópteros*) which comprised two squadrons; one equipped with the Bell 47 and the other with the S-55. There were further expansions in the helicopter fleet and the ASW capability with the formation of the Esc 3 equipped with the AB-204 in 1964 and the Esc 5 flying the SH-3D Sea King in the following year. Meanwhile the EdA had also gained an ASW capability in 1962 with the procurement of Grumman HU-16B Albatross ASW aircraft, which was operated by *Grupo* 61 Esc 601 based at Jerez de la Frontera. After a number of re-organizations, the unit became Ala 22 Esc 206.

In 1967, the *Armada* procured its first aircraft carrier, the *Dédalo* (ex-USS *Cabot* [CVL 28]). At that time the *Armada* was not permitted to operate fixed wing aircraft, so the initial aviation complement was limited to helicopters. These included the SH-3D for ASW and the Bell AH-1G Huey Cobra gunship for supporting coastal operations. However, in 1972 the *Armada* was authorized to form Esc 8 which was equipped with the McDonnell Douglas AV-8S Matador variant of the AV-8A Harrier VTOL strike fighter. In the early 1970s, Esc 6 was formed and equipped with the Hughes 369HM (OH-6 Cayuse) helicopter for ASW operations from Churruca-class destroyers.

In 1970, the ASW capability of the EdA was further enhanced when the Albatross was replaced by the Lockheed P-3A Orion (and the unit renumbered to become Esc 221). Four Deltic variants of the P-3A, incorporating an updated sonar system, were purchased from the USN and a further four were leased from the USN in 1979. The Albatross was also replaced in the SAR role – Esc 801, based on Mallorca, was re-equipped with the CASA 212S Aviocar, and Esc 802, based in Gando, received three Fokker F.27 Friendship MAR fitted, for MPA duties, with a ventrally housed Litton AN/APS-504 search radar.

Spain joined NATO on 30 May 1982.

AFTERWORD

CHANGING IN OUR FAVOUR

'It is with great pleasure that I see the political system of almost every power in Europe changing in our favor since the news of our late successes.'

Captain John Paul Jones, US Navy, *c*.1780.

In the aftermath of the Cold War the countries of central and eastern Europe quickly jettisoned their communist governments and sought to re-establish themselves within a democratic Europe. Over the subsequent 20 years, all of the European membership of the former Warsaw Pact joined both the European Union (EU), to ensure their economic prosperity, and NATO, to secure their new-found democracy from any threat from Russia. As Russia herself struggled with post-communist reforms, her own fighting services swiftly fell into disarray and disrepair. At the same time, NATO switched away from its defensive posture in the North Atlantic region to focus on expeditionary warfare in the Middle East, the Balkans and southwest Asia.

However, under the leadership of Vladimir Putin, Russia began to revitalize its military forces and began to take a confrontational stance against the countries of Europe and North America. In July 2007, Russia suspended its implementation of the Treaty on Conventional Armed Forces in Europe and the following year it invaded Georgia. The Russian annexation of the Crimea in Ukraine in 2014 marked a significantly increased threat to the security of the rest of Europe, which was further increased by the invasion of Ukraine eight years later. The resurgence of the Russian armed forces has coincided with the reduction of NATO forces within the European theatre, but, belatedly, western governments have begun to wake up to the new threat.

OPPOSITE The maiden flight by the first US Navy Lockheed Martin F-35C Lightning II squadron, VFA-101, takes off from Eglin Air Force Base on 14 August 2013. (US Navy)

Political Developments

The communist administrations in eastern Europe were quickly, and in most cases peacefully, replaced by democratically elected governments across the former Warsaw Pact countries. The main exception to this experience was Yugoslavia which was riven by a number of brutal civil wars during the 1990s, causing the country to splinter into seven independent states. The USSR had been almost bankrupted by the cost of maintaining and equipping large military forces: while Western economies suffered a short recession in the early 1990s, the USSR experienced a deep economic crisis. During the 1990s, Russian GDP fell by 50% and inflation was

running at 300%. After an attempted coup against the Soviet leader Mikhail Gorbachev in 1990, the USSR was dissolved in 1991 and Russia became a sovereign state under the leadership of Boris Yeltsin. Russia and most of the former SSRs became members of the Commonwealth of Independent States (CIS), a free trading area similar in concept to the EU. Significantly, the Baltic States chose not to join the CIS. The Tashkent Treaty, which was signed in 1992 by Russia, Armenia, Kazakhstan, Kyrgyzstan, Tajikistan and Uzbekistan, marked the formation of the Collective Security Treaty Organization (*Organizatsiya Dogovora o Kollektivnoy Bezopasnosti* – ODKB). Three more countries, Azerbaijan, Belarus, and Georgia, joined the ODKB at the end of the next year, but in 1999 Azerbaijan, Georgia and Uzbekistan all left the organization.

A Russian AV-MF Tupolev Tu-142MZ (Bear-F) is intercepted by a USAF Boeing F-22 Raptor in the Alaskan air-defense identification zone (ADIZ), 9 March 2020. Incursions into NATO ADIZ by Russian reconnaissance aircraft are becoming more common. (USAF)

Meanwhile NATO instigated the North Atlantic Co-operative Council in 1991 to facilitate dialogue with former Warsaw Pact members. This was followed in 1994 by the Partnership for Peace (PfP) programme, which according to NATO was an opportunity for 'practical bilateral cooperation between individual Euro-Atlantic partner countries and NATO. It allowed partners to build up an individual relationship with NATO, choosing their own priorities for cooperation.' As a result of the PfP initiative Hungary, Poland and the Czech Republic joined NATO in 1999. Russian President Vladimir Putin commented in 2001 that 'NATO was built to counteract the Soviet Union in its day and time. At this point there is no threat coming from the Soviet Union, because there is no Soviet Union anymore. And where there was the Soviet Union once, there is now a number of countries, among them the new and democratic Russia.' However, Bulgaria, Estonia, Latvia, Lithuania, Romania, Slovakia and Slovenia were not persuaded by his argument, and they joined NATO in 2004. They were followed by Albania and Croatia in 2009.

At the same time that NATO expanded its membership into central and eastern Europe, the EU began a similar process. In 2004 ten countries in central Europe joined the organization: Cyprus, the Czech Republic, Estonia, Hungary, Latvia, Lithuania, Malta, Poland, Slovakia and Slovenia. Romania and Bulgaria were granted membership three years later. From the perspective of Russia, it seemed that both NATO and the EU had advanced to the very borders of the former USSR and the east European 'buffer zone' which the Soviets had established to insulate themselves from US and western military forces had disappeared. The Russian President Putin perceived the 'advance' of NATO as a threat to Russia at the same time that Russia was dealing with wars in Chechnya and Georgia, and that it was attempting to influence the political events in an increasingly pro-western Ukraine. From 2008, under the leadership of Putin, Russia began to take a more aggressive and confrontational stance against the West. In 2014 despite being a signatory to the Budapest Memorandum of 1994 in which she undertook to 'refrain from the threat or use of force against the territorial integrity or political independence of the signatories of the memorandum,' Russia annexed the Crimea and began to support separatist factions in the Donbas region of Ukraine. This was followed by a full-scale invasion of Ukraine in 2022. The invasion caused Finland to join NATO in 2023 and Sweden to follow suit the following year. As the former Soviet First Secretary Mikhail Gorbachev observed in 2019, 'we must concede that after the end of the Cold War, new leaders failed to create a modern security architecture, especially in Europe.'

The Russian AV-MF

At the end of the Cold War, the AV-MF was a powerful force whose inventory included some 1,000 fixed-wing aircraft including 130 Tu-22M, 230 Tu-16 and 100 Su-17 and Su-24. At that stage it also possessed the four Kiev-class VTOL aircraft carriers as well as a newer and larger conventional aircraft carrier, *Admiral Kuznetsov*. The latter vessel was equipped with the Sukhoi Su-33 (previously designated Su-27K – Flanker-D) multi-role fighter. However, three of the Kiev-class ships were decommissioned in 1993 and the fourth was sold to India the following year. In practice, the *Kuznetsov* has not proved to be particularly successful: after a cruise in the Mediterranean Sea in 1996 she did not see full service again for eight years until Exercise *Bezopasnost* in 2004. The ship underwent maintenance between 2009 and 2017 when she sailed once more to the Mediterranean Sea. Only a relatively small number of Su-33 fighters can be carried because of the large size of the aircraft and the relatively small size of the ship. In addition, of the 22 Su-33 airframes

A Sukhoi Su-33 (Flanker-D) carrier-borne fighter on the flight deck of the Russian aircraft carrier *Admiral Kuznetsov* in the Mediterranean Sea, 23 February 1996. Only 22 of the type, which was originally designated the Su-27K, were built. (NARA)

PREVIOUS PAGES Under way in the Atlantic Ocean, 19 March 2023: the USS *Gerald R. Ford* (CVN 78) is the first in a new class of USN aircraft carriers and is the largest in the world. The ship has a complement of some 90 aircraft. Two more ships in the class are due to be commissioned over the next five years. (US Navy)

that were built only 17 remain and with little opportunity to practise carrier operations, these aircraft are usually flown from onshore airfields.

The Tu-16 was eventually retired from front line service in 1993 and during post-Cold War reorganizations, the Tu-22M2/3 fleet of the AV-MF was transferred from the Navy to the VVS-DA. Thus, the Su-24M remained as the only anti-shipping strike aircraft available to the Northern Fleet. However, the 45th Army of the Air Force and Air Defence (45 *Armiya VVS i PVO*) which has been responsible for supporting the Northern Fleet since 2015 has begun to replace the Su-24M with the more capable multi-role Sukhoi Su-30SM (Flanker-H). The 45th Air Army also contains one squadron each of Tu-142 and Il-38 MPA/ASW aircraft, but its focus is on the air defence of the northern regions with Sukhoi Su-27 and MiG-31BM (Foxhound) long-range interceptors. The one 'growth area' in the post-Cold War AV-MF is in unmanned combat aerial vehicles (UCAV) which have begun to take over some roles, particularly that of surveillance, from manned aircraft. The 45th Air

Army includes units which operate the 3m wingspan Orlan-10 for reconnaissance and electronic warfare tasks and the larger (8.5m wingspan) *Forpost*-R (Outpost) which can be armed with missiles.

United Strategic Command Northern Fleet (*Obyedinonnoye strategicheskoye komandovaniye - Severnyy flot* – OSK-Sever) was established in December 2014. Based in Arkhangelsk, its role is to control the sea in the inner bastion area of the Barents Sea and Arctic Ocean and to deny the sea to NATO forces in the outer area of the Norwegian Sea. Within the Arctic region the OSK-Sever has deployed multi-layered defences including seaborne, airborne and coastal anti-shipping missile systems and long-range SAM systems, as well as air-defence aircraft. The forces are deployed in three fully autonomous bases in the high north which incorporate airfields, at Nagurskoye on Franz Josef Land, at Rogachevo on Novaya Zemlya and at Kotelny on the main New Siberian Island.

NATO Carrier Aviation

While aircraft carriers proved to be a dead end for the Soviet Navy, those of NATO navies continued to be upgraded in the post-Cold War years. Five more Nimitz-class ships, USS *George Washington* (CVN 73), USS *John C. Stennis* (CVN 74), USS *Harry S. Truman* (CVN 75), USS *Ronald Reagan* (CVN 76) and USS *George H. W. Bush* (CVN 77), were commissioned between 1990 and 2009, and the first of a new class of 100,000-ton carriers, USS *Gerald R. Ford* (CVN 78) was commissioned in 2017. A second ship of the class, USS *John F. Kennedy* (CVN 79), is due to be commissioned in 2025 and a third ship, USS *Enterprise* (CVN 80), will join the fleet in 2028. The Ford-class ships have the electro-magnetic launch system (EMALS) rather than the steam-powered catapults of previous aircraft carriers and can carry up to 90 aircraft, including the F/A-18E/F Super Hornet multi-role fighters, E-2D Advanced Hawkeye AEW aircraft, EA-18G Growler electronic warfare aircraft, MH-60R/S ASW helicopters, and the Lockheed Martin F-35C Lightning II joint strike fighter (JSF). One glaring absence from this list is any fixed-wing ASW aircraft, despite the threat posed to aircraft carriers by submarines armed with long-range anti-ship missiles such as the 3M54-1 Kalibr (SS-N-30A) cruise missiles. The USN currently maintains 11 aircraft carriers in its inventory.

The USN has also carried out trials operating UCAVs from its aircraft carriers. The Boeing MQ-25 Stingray AAR tanker flew from USS *George H. W. Bush* in 2021, proving the concept of autonomous carrier-borne AAR operations. The MQ-25 is due to enter USN service from 2026 and

OPPOSITE A US Navy Boeing F/A-18F Super Hornet from VFA-41 USS *Nimitz* (CVN 68) during a mission over the Persian Gulf in September 2005. The Super Hornet now fulfils all of the roles previously covered by the Tomcat, Intruder and Hornet in a single type. In addition, the F/A-18G Growler variant replaced the EA-6B Prowler.(US Navy)

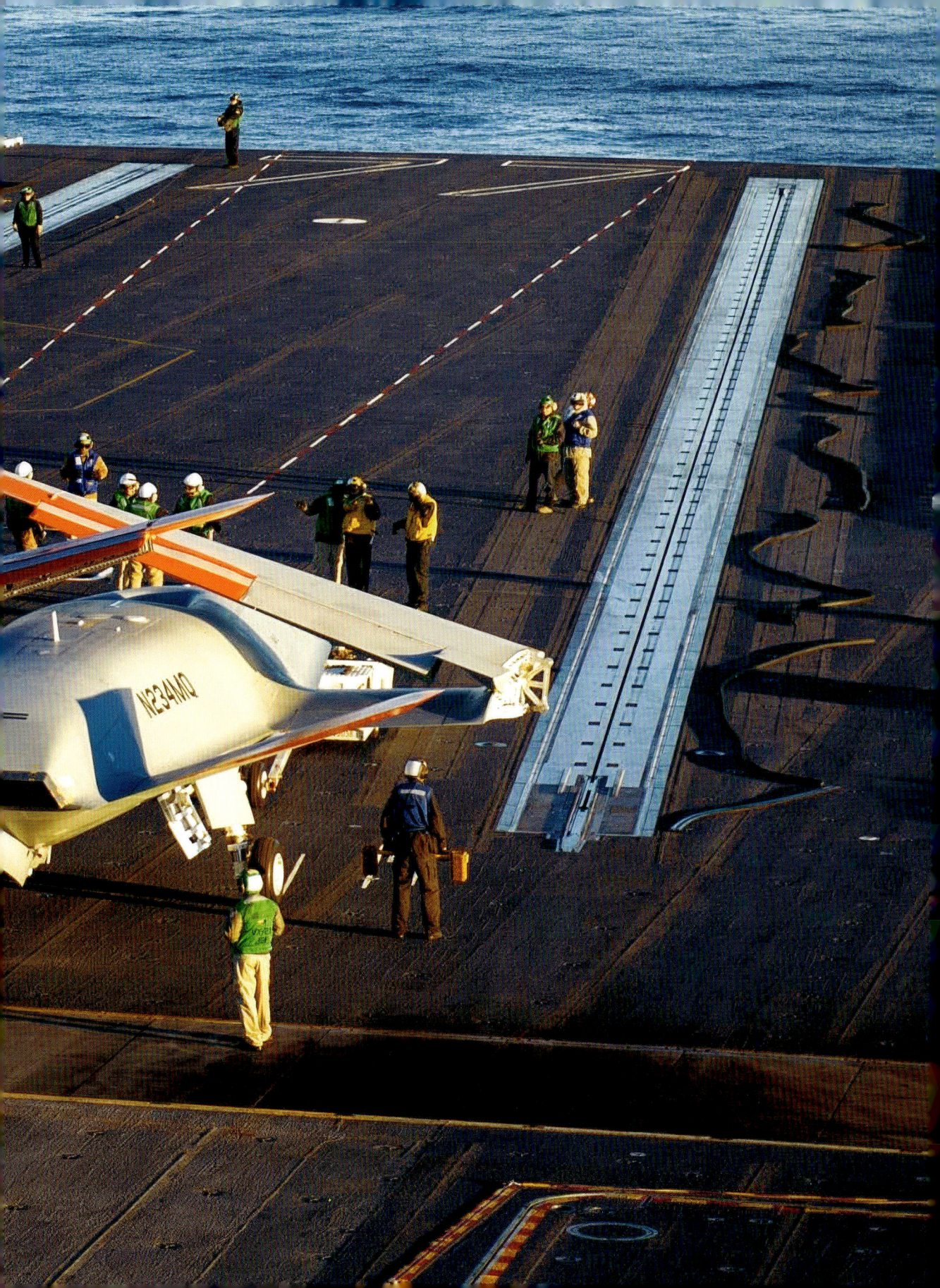

PREVIOUS PAGES A Boeing MQ-25 Stingray unmanned combat air system (UCAS) aboard the aircraft carrier USS *George H. W. Bush* (CVN 77) in December 2021. The Stingray will provide an extremely flexible AAR capability. (US Navy)

OPPOSITE A Northrop-Grumman X-47B UCAS demonstrator conducts a touch and go landing on the flight deck of the USS *George H. W. Bush* in May 2013. The X-47B is a technology demonstrator for the unmanned carrier-launched airborne surveillance and strike (UCLASS) project. (US Navy).

will deliver a significant increase in the range of the F-35C. Experimental trials have also seen the stealth technology Boeing X-45 and Northrop-Grumman X-47 strike drones flying from USN carriers, as well as the Kratos X-58A Valkyrie, a more advanced autonomous strike platform.

After the demise of the Sea Harrier and the Invincible-class carriers in 2010, the RN re-entered aircraft carrier operations in December 2017 with the commissioning of HMS *Queen Elizabeth* (R08) and her sister ship HMS *Prince of Wales* (R09) two years later. The Queen Elizabeth-class ships were designed from the outset around the STOVL concept rather than the more traditional catapult assisted take-off but arrested recovery (CATOBAR) system, thus limiting the ships to the F-35B STOVL variant which has a reduced combat radius of some 25 per cent in comparison to the F-35C as well as a payload nearly 20 per cent lighter than the F-35C. Furthermore, the ships are not compatible with USN aircraft such as the F-35C and F/A-18E/F Super Hornet; they are limited to operating the F-35B, which is only flown by the UK, the USMC and the Italian Navy. The Defence Review of 2010 changed direction: the carriers were now to be built instead as CATOBAR ships and the F-35 order switched to the 'C' variant, but this decision was reversed two years later due to the high cost of amending the design of the ship. The utility of the British carriers, which can carry a routine complement of 24 aircraft (but a maximum of 36 F-35 aircraft), is therefore somewhat limited, especially as by November 2023 the UK had a total of only 24 F-35 Lightnings available to meet the commitment both for the two RN carriers and for land-based tasking for the RAF. During her cruise in 2021 most of the F-35B complement of HMS *Queen Elizabeth* was provided by the USMC. The carriers also operate the AgustaWestland AW101 Merlin HM2 helicopters which are used for ASW as well as for AEW using the Lockheed Martin Crowsnest system. The RN, too, has trialled the operation of UCAVs from its carriers, in this case the General Atomics Mojave, a development of the MQ-1C Gray Eagle. The 52ft wingspan Mojave was flown from HMS *Prince of Wales* during November 2023 and would be used for long endurance surveillance tasking, although it can also be armed for other combat missions.

The French Navy retired the carrier *Clemenceau* in 1997, and *Foch* three years later, but the latter ship was replaced in 2001 by the carrier *Charles de Gaulle* (R91). This nuclear-powered ship has a complement of some 40 aircraft, including the Dassault *Rafale* M multi-role aircraft and the E-2C Hawkeye for AEW. The Hawkeye is due to be replaced by the E-2D Advanced Hawkeye. The Spanish *Armada* also modernized their aircraft carrier, exchanging the elderly *Dédalo* for the modern *Principe de Asturias* (R11) sea control ship in 1988. The new carrier is equipped with 24 EAV-8B Matador II Plus STOVL aircraft as well as SH3D/G Sea King and SH-60B Sea Hawk helicopters. Another operator of the AV-8B Harrier II Plus family is the Italian Navy, which continued to operate the aircraft from the aircraft carrier *Giuseppe Garibaldi* from 1991 and from a second carrier, *Cavour* (C 550), which was commissioned in 2008. The Italian AV-8Bs will be replaced by the F-35B Lightning in 2024/25.

With the reduced threat from Russian surface warships in the immediate post-Cold War years, the German *Marineflieger* disbanded all *Kormoran*-equipped Tornado anti-shipping units in 1994, but the RAF maintained the shore-based anti-shipping strike role, replacing the Buccaneer with Tornado GR1b armed with the Sea Eagle in the same year. However, the UK capability was short-lived, and the Tornado was withdrawn from the role in 2000.

NATO ASW Capabilities

In the first years after the end of the Cold War the submarines of the former Soviet Navy languished in port and fell into disrepair. In 1984 the Soviet Northern Fleet had some 176 submarines in its order of battle, but over three-quarters of them were scrapped during the 1990s. In 1991 Russian nuclear ballistic missile submarines carried out 37 patrols but by 1999 the annual number of patrols had dropped to just seven. The reduction in the threat from Russian submarines led to a reduced response from NATO and what has been described as an atrophy in NATO ASW capabilities: NATO MPA fleets were run down because of the reduced threat and at the same time those MPA that remained in service became more valuable in the intelligence surveillance target acquisition and reconnaissance (ISTAR) tasking in the Middle East and southwest Asia. The NATO ASW command structure was also dissolved in the late 1990s. Another problem was that fewer submarine deployments generated fewer opportunities to gather intelligence about the submarines and to practise tactics against them. In 2016 the NATO Joint Air Power Competence Centre observed that:

Since non-NATO submarine deployments nearly ceased in the mid-1990s, NATO now has a generation of officers and civilian leaders who did not grow up experiencing the 'cat and mouse' environment of submarine warfare which existed during the Cold War. NATO has conducted three major joint operations during since the end of the Cold War. None of these operations were conducted in an area challenged by the presence of an adversary submarine. Just as air chiefs fight the perception NATO will always have air superiority in any campaign, maritime leaders must also engage to challenge the perception that NATO's maritime forces will always have maritime superiority. This perception, coupled with inaccurate beliefs regarding the capability of the Russian Federation's maritime capability, has coloured maritime defence spending for decades. As a result, NATO has ceded much of the advantage it earned at the conclusion of the Cold War.

Since 2008 Russia has resumed a policy of inter-state rivalry and has modernized and expanded its submarine fleet. The construction of two new classes of advanced submarines were started in the 1990s, the Project 885 Yasen (Ash Tree) (Severodvinsk) class nuclear cruise missile and Project 955 Borei (Boreas) (*Dolgorukiy*) class nuclear ballistic missile submarines. Benefitting from modern technology, much of it obtained by espionage, these vessels are far more difficult to detect than the previous classes of Soviet submarines. In 2023 the Northern Fleet had seven SSBN, nine SSN, five SSGN (cruise missile nuclear submarines) and six SSK. The Northern Strategic Bastion in the Barents Sea was formalized in the late 1990s and continues to be the strategic concept adopted by OSK-Sever, which controls some two-thirds of the Russian nuclear strike submarines. Locating Russian submarines in the distant and well-defended waters of the bastion is a significant challenge to NATO ASW forces, especially as the submarines are considerably quieter than their predecessors and the background noise in the ocean is somewhat louder in the early 21st century than it was in the Cold War era. Arctic warming due to global climate changes has also enlarged the area where submarines can patrol, due to the reduction of the Arctic ice sheet. Meanwhile, submarines from the Russian Northern Fleet still carry out occasional patrols into the North Atlantic Ocean and the Mediterranean Sea.

A further challenge to NATO is that of clandestine seabed warfare by Russian forces targeting undersea infrastructure such as communication cables, SOSUS equipment and gas pipelines, under the auspices of the General Directorate of Deep-Sea Research (*Glavnoye Upravleniye Glubokovodnykh Issledovaniy* – GUGI). In 2015 Delta-IV class submarine

NEXT PAGES A Lockheed Martin F-35C Lightning II carrier variant of the joint strike fighter (JSF) on the approach to USS *Nimitz* (CVN 68) in the Pacific Ocean, November 2014. The F-35C will complement the Boeing F/A-18E/F Super Hornet aboard US Navy carriers. (US Navy)

ABOVE The USMC, RN and Italian Navy have selected the Lockheed Martin F-35B VTOL variant of the Lightning II. Here a USMC aircraft, from VMFA-242, turns to land on JS *Izumo*, aircraft carrying destroyer, off the coast of Japan, October 2021. (US Navy)

BS-64 *Podmoskovye* was converted to be an undersea mothership for deep diving mini-submarines and the research ships *Yantar* and *Ladoga* are also equipped with deep diving submersibles. Russian submarines have been tracked along unusual routes which have taken them close to the undersea infrastructure rather than the previously typical patrol routes favoured by strategic submarines. The sabotage of the Nord Stream gas pipelines near Denmark in September 2022 is indicative of the capabilities and possible targets of GUGI operatives.

Although the NATO MPA fleet is considerably smaller than it was during the Cold War, it has recently been re-equipped with very capable aircraft. The USN began to receive the Boeing P-8A Poseidon in 2012 to replace the P-3 Orion. Based on the Boeing 737NG airliner, the Poseidon is equipped with the Raytheon APY-10 radar which is mounted in the enlarged nose radome, and uses a synthetic aperture radar (SAR) mode for detecting ships, and a high-resolution imaging synthetic aperture radar (ISAR) mode for detecting surfaced submarines. The aircraft incorporates a CAE advanced integrated MAD system, and a pneumatic ejection rotary sonobuoy launcher which enables the aircraft to deploy up to 129 sonobuoys for the state-of-the-art acoustic sensor suite. The Northrop-Grumman electronic warfare self-protection suite includes a Terma AN/ALQ-213(V) electronic warfare management system. The Poseidon can be armed with the Raytheon Mk 54 anti-submarine acoustic homing torpedo which can be dropped, if necessary, from high altitude.

The P-8A is also replacing the P-3 Orion in 333 Skv of the RNoAF and MFG 3 of the German *Marineflieger* and the type has been ordered by the RCAF to take over from the CP-140 Aurora in 2026. Almost unbelievably for a maritime nation, the UK completely withdrew from the airborne ASW role on the retirement of the Nimrod MR2 in 2011, and it was forced to call for NATO assistance when unidentified submarines were detected in British waters during 2014 and 2015. However, 120 Sqn and 201 Sqn based at Lossiemouth have recently reformed with the P-8A Poseidon MRA1, restoring a much-needed ASW capacity to the RAF. The French *Aéronavale* is the only remaining operator of the Breguet Atlantique, with some 18 of the modernized Atlantique 2 aircraft which have been systematically upgraded to keep pace with technological advances. The current modification state is Standard 6, which introduces the Thales Searchmaster active electronically scanned array (AESA) radar amongst other updates.

Thus, the NATO ASW force is still able to employ aircraft against the submarine threat in the North Atlantic Ocean and the Norwegian and Barents Seas, while the USN and other allies in the Far East can prosecute Soviet submarines in the Pacific Ocean; but as the NATO joint air power competence centre once described in 2016, the lack of operational experience, the new submarine technology and the pressure on defence budgets all mean that:

BELOW In British service, the Lockheed Martin F-35B Lightnings are shared by the RAF and RN. Here an RAF Lightning recovers to HMS *Queen Elizabeth* (R08) on 9 September 2021, during a cruise of the Far East. (Crown Copyright/MoD)

ABOVE A French *Aéronavale* Dassault *Rafale* M from 11.F launches from the USS *Carl Vinson* (CVN 70) in the Arabian Gulf, 3 March 2015. The *Rafale* has replaced both the F-8E(FN) Crusader and Super Étendard. (US Navy)

The tried-and-true passive detection tactics of the Cold War are no longer viable against modern submarines. Submarines are significantly quieter, the ocean is significantly louder, and the challenge of those two facts would yield an unsustainable sonobuoy utilization rate. Sonobuoy inventory has also affected both the training and proficiency of many NATO MPA and MPH aircrew. It is not uncommon for an inexperienced or less-proficient crew to lose contact on a submarine due to being overly conservative deploying sonobuoys due to national inventory limitations.

In 2018 the Soviet submarine *Severodvinsk* was able to cruise undetected in the North Atlantic for several weeks. Furthermore, the smaller number of aircraft available in the North Atlantic region limits the ability of them to track multiple submarines at the same time. To some extent the lack of MPA numbers can be offset by the use of UCAVs: in the USN the Northrop-Grumman MQ-4C Triton has been operated over the Pacific Ocean from Guam by unmanned patrol squadron (VUP)-19 since January 2020 and has recently also deployed to Mayport, Florida. Based on the RQ-4 Global Hawk, the MQ-4C is capable of taking over maritime surveillance and reconnaissance duties, leaving manned platforms like the P-8 free to concentrate on the more complex ASW role.

LEFT A pair of Spanish Navy McDonnell Douglas AV-8B Harrier II Plus fly over the water after departing Naval Station Rota, Spain, on 15 May 2015. The aircraft operate from the landing helicopter dock Juan Carlos I after the carrier *Príncipe de Asturias* was decommissioned in 2013. (USMC)

NATO also has land-based ASW assets operating over the Baltic and Mediterranean Seas. In this role, the Polish Navy uses the PZL Mielec M28B *Bryza* (Breeze)1RM-bis aircraft, which carries an ARS-800-2 search radar, MAD equipment and a sonobuoy/acoustic sensor suite. In the eastern Mediterranean, the Turkish Navy flies both the CASA/IPTN P-235-100M and ATR 72-600TMPA (P-72) for ASW missions. The MPA fleet is split between 301st Naval Air Squadron (*Deniz Hava Filo*) at Topel Naval Air Station and 302nd *Deniz Hava Filo* at Dalaman, with both units flying both types. The two aircraft are equipped with the Thales airborne maritime situation and control system (AMASCOS)-300 mission system which includes the Ocean Master 400 radar, as well as acoustic sensors, MAD equipment and self-defence systems. They can also be armed with the Mk 54 torpedo. The range of the P-72 is sufficient to allow the Turkish naval aircraft to cover the whole of the eastern Mediterranean, reaching as far west as the Italy-Libya line. For shorter-range ASW missions, the Turkish Navy utilizes the Sikorsky SH-70B Seahawk helicopters which can fly from onshore bases or from frigates. Like the USN, the Turkish Navy has also invested in UCAVs to fulfil surveillance roles and the 312th UAV Squadron (*IHA Filo*) at Dalaman and 313th *IHA Filo* at Çanakkale operate the Anka-B (THS) and Bayraktar TB2 UAV/UCAV Systems. These remotely piloted aircraft can also be armed if necessary.

The ItAF also operates a version of the ATR P-72A, four of which replaced the Atlantique in the joint Italian Navy and air force 41st ASW Wing (41º *Stormo Antisom*); however, the Italian aircraft do not, in fact, have any ASW capability, and are therefore limited in their mission to maritime patrol and surveillance. Greece can also no longer perform long-range ASW tasks, for, having replaced the HU-16B Albatross in 353 MNAS with the P-3B Orion in 1996, the Greek Navy withdrew the Orion in 2009. However, Greece does operate the Sikorsky MH-60R variant of the Seahawk ASW helicopter.

The Future of Naval Aviation

In the first decade after the Cold War, it seemed that the previous 40 years of confrontation with the USSR would be followed by a long period of peaceful co-operation with Russia. However, by the early 2000s Russia had begun a more hostile approach to the West, which seems to have surprised Western governments, who have been slow to react. Indeed the 'cashing in' of the so-called peace dividend in the 1990s and the subsequent cumulative cuts in defence budgets, despite continuous combat operations in Iraq, the Balkans and Afghanistan, have caused an inertia against increased defence spending. Thus, given the head start in re-arming and the technological advances over the last 30 years, Russia has eroded most of the advantages that NATO maritime forces enjoyed during the Cold War.

The question is, therefore, whether the carrier strike group remains an effective means of defending the North Atlantic SLOC and of reinforcing the vulnerable northern flank of NATO. The aircraft carrier has always represented a major target and would be the focus of sustained attacks by Russian surface, submarine and air forces, including active guidance antiship missiles. As a result of space-based reconnaissance systems and long-endurance UCAVs, the ability of the carrier to evade detection is likely to have been degraded since the 1990s and the tactical value of the carrier will depend on its survivability against the improved and restructured Russian defences in the Arctic. It will also have to be able to survive future threats such as attacks by swarms of small UCAVs. In any case, it seems that operations in support of the NATO northern flank are likely to meet with greater force than would have been the case during the Cold War. It may also be that littoral strikes could be prosecuted more effectively by weapons such as the submarine-launched cruise missile such as the Tomahawk.

The Lockheed Martin F-35B Lightning II will replace the McDonnell Douglas AV-8B Harrier on the Italian Navy aircraft carrier *Cavour*. Here the Harriers are participating in NATO Exercise *Neptune Strike* in late January 2022. (US Navy)

ABOVE A Russian Navy Kilo-class attack submarine photographed in the English Channel in October 2018. Armed with Novator 3M54-1 Kalibr (SS-N-27 Sizzler) cruise missiles, these 1980s-vintage diesel-electric submarines still represent a significant threat. (Crown Copyright/MoD)

According to a report by the RAND corporation in 2017:

the threats are beginning to demand longer standoff ranges and potentially a longer period in which to establish air and sea dominance. Integrated air wings remain capable of operating in this environment, but the evolving threat will likely require a change in concepts of operation and might also affect the required capability for the supporting aircraft carrier… Long-range strikes carried out by stealth aircraft will also be paramount. Combining the F-35's long combat radius of over

600nm with carrier-launched unmanned air-to-air refuelling aircraft, the aircraft carrier would be able to perform long-range strike missions with a range up to 1,000nm. Additionally, F-35s have the ability to obtain target locations of key A2/AD nodes while operating inside threat envelopes, then pass them to systems operating outside threat envelopes that can engage the targets.

However, the unique flexibility, speed and reach of naval tactical air power mean that it remains a vital part of NATO strategy. Indeed, the USN maintains a fleet of 11 Nimitz-class and Ford-class ships with modernized air components as instruments of US foreign and defence policy, while other NATO allies, the UK, France, Italy and Spain, also have a more limited, but nonetheless credible, capabilities for carrier-borne operations.

The UCAV offers a less expensive complement to manned aircraft, filling roles that can be taken easily from manned platforms, enabling the crews of conventional aircraft to concentrate on the more demanding

BELOW After a ten-year hiatus, the RAF once again has an MPA/ASW capability with the procurement of the Boeing P-8A. This Poseidon, from 120 Sqn, is dropping a Mark 54 Lightweight Torpedo training round in July 2021. As well as US and UK forces, the P-8A will also equip many NATO maritime air forces, including those of Canada, Norway and Germany. (Crown Copyright/MoD)

missions without being distracted or overloaded by simpler but time-consuming tasks. The use of the MQ-25 Stingray unmanned AAR tanker is a good example of the useful substitution of unmanned systems for manned aircraft. The UCAV is also well-suited to long endurance tasks such as maritime surveillance and it may be possible that UCAV operations could also be augmented by the use of artificial intelligence (AI) in the future. Data fusion from multiple sources, enabled by datalink, acts as a force multiplier by ensuring that all platforms are used as efficiently as possible. Thus, it seems most likely that a partnership of manned aircraft and UCAVs will operate both from aircraft carriers and also from onshore bases in the future.

The ASW role has probably become the most challenging for NATO maritime air power since the end of the Cold War. This is partly because of the nature of modern Russian low-noise submarines and partly because of the lack of exposure by aircraft crews to ASW operations. The shorter detection ranges of newer submarines lead in turn to higher sonobuoy usage, which has a direct monetary cost at a time when budgets are already stretched. However, the increased threat from Russian submarines may in turn be countered by advances in detection technology. Nevertheless, the sheer distance of the Soviet bastion from NATO airfields and the formidable nature of the bastion defences will make ASW operations over the Norwegian and Barents Seas very challenging. Perhaps this is another mission that would be best accomplished by a fusion of manned and unmanned systems. In any case it seems likely that for the foreseeable future, the manned aircraft will remain the best weapon for combating the submarine at long range.

BELOW Like the US Navy, the RN is looking into applications for UCAVS. This General Atomics Mojave reconnaissance vehicle launched from and recovered to HMS *Prince of Wales* (R09) on 15 November 2023. (Crown Copyright/MoD)

ABOVE In 2023, the USMC evaluated the Kratos XQ-58A Valkyrie UCAV for its penetrating affordable autonomous collaborative killer – portfolio (PAACK-P) programme. (USAF)

In August 2023 the Soviet business newspaper *Vzglyad* wrote: 'the Arctic is becoming one of the most important regions for the Russian Armed Forces… Geography dictates the nature of threats to Russia in this region. From the point of view of Naval Aviation of the Russian Navy, this means that 99 per cent of all combat missions of the MA will be carried out in the western direction – in the Norwegian and Barents Seas.'

The remoteness of the Arctic lends itself to unmanned solutions and it would seem that a mix of UCAV and space-borne reconnaissance and targeting systems could potentially replace long-range aircraft in the AV-MF. This would be particularly attractive at a time when the economic and military powers of Russia are waning. Indeed, at Severomorsk, the 216th Independent UAV Squadron *(bespilotnykh letatel'nykh apparatov eskadril'ya* – BPLAE) already operates the Orlan and Forpost UCAVs, as well as the newer 30m wingspan Kronstadt *Inokhodets-RU* Sirius UCAV, a medium altitude long endurance (MALE) system which is intended to patrol the Soviet EEZ in the Arctic.

With no credible aircraft carrier, for the *Admiral Kuznetsov* must be regarded as seriously compromised, there seems little need for the AV-MF to operate fighter aircraft, since the air force and air-defence force is ultimately responsible for air defence in the Arctic regions. Again unmanned (missile) weapons systems would seem to be best suited to air

ABOVE Designed for high altitude long endurance surveillance tasks, the Northrop-Grumman MQ-4C Triton UCAV has been acquired by the US Navy. Initial deployment has been in the Pacific region. (US Navy)

defence in the remote Arctic region. The future of the AV-MF as an operator of manned fixed-wing aircraft must therefore hang in the balance: it would seem to be more efficient for the Soviet Navy to concentrate on ship-borne helicopters for short-range ASW tasks and UCAVs for longer-range surveillance and target acquisition missions. This may be especially true as climate change continues to warm the Arctic Ocean and melt the Arctic ice sheet, because that will increase, almost exponentially, the area of open ocean and length of coastline to be patrolled. Unmanned air platforms may be the only economically viable way to patrol these huge and remote areas.

In summary, the future of naval and maritime aviation in both NATO and Russia will increasingly depend on the UCAV. However, manned aircraft will still have their place for complex roles such as ASW or strike missions. The helicopter, which has proved to be particularly well suited to naval operations, will continue to be an important part of naval aviation. Finally, the aircraft carrier will continue to have relevance in the NATO theatre, even though its prime role has become one of global power projection, rather than a weapons system with specific application in the North Atlantic.

ABOVE Despite the proliferation of UCAVs, the days of the manned aeroplane are far from over. For the foreseeable future the US Navy aircraft fleet will include the Lockheed Martin F-35C Lightning IIs and Boeing F/A-18E/F Super Hornets, seen here in a mixed formation over the Naval Air Station Fallon (NASF) Range Training Complex in September 2015. (US Navy)

APPENDIX 1
Abbreviations and Acronyms

AAM	Air-to-Air Missile
AAR	Air-to-Air Refuelling
ABM	Anti-Ballistic Missile
ACE	(NATO) Allied Command Europe
ACLANT	(NATO) Allied Command Atlantic
ADIZ	Air Defence Indentification Zone
AEW	Airborne Early Warning
AFCENT	(NATO) Allied Forces Central Europe
AFMED	(NATO) Allied Forces Mediterranean
AFSOUTH	(NATO) Allied Forces South
AMF	(NATO) ACE Mobile Force
ARIES	Airborne Reconnaissance Integrated Electronic System
ARM	Anti-Radiation Missile
ASM	Air-to-Surface Missile
ASuW	Anti-Surface Warfare
ASV	Air-to-Surface Vessel radar
ASW	Anti-Submarine Warfare
AV-MF	*Aviatsiya Voyenno-Morskogo Flota* (Soviet Naval Aviation)
BALTAP	(NATO) Baltic Approaches region
BARLANT	Atlantic Barrier patrol
BARPAC	Pacific Barrier patrol
BDR	*Bundesrepublik Deutschland* (West Germany)
BLC	Boundary Layer Control
BMEWS	Ballistic Missile Early Warning System
CAF	Canadian Armed Forces (post-1968)
CAP	Combat Air Patrol
CATOBAR	Catapult Assisted Take-Off But Arrested Recovery
CIA	(US) Central Intelligence Agency
CNO	(USN) Chief of Naval Operations
COD	Carrier Onboard Delivery
COMNON	(NATO) Commander North Norway
CONAD	USAF Continental Air Defense Command

CSCE	Conference on Security and Cooperation in Europe
DDR	*Deutsche Demokratische Republik* (East Germany)
DEW	Distant Early Warning
DIFAR	Directional Frequency Analysis and Recording (passive acoustic sonobuoy)
ECM	Electronic Countermeasures
EdA	*Ejercito del Aire* (Spanish Air Force)
ELINT	Electronic Intelligence gathering
EMALS	Electro-Magnetic Launch System
Esk	*Eskadrille* (RDAF squadron)
ESM	Electronic Support Measures
EU	European Union
FAA	(British) Fleet Air Arm
FAP	*Força Aérea Portuguesa* (Portuguese Air Force)
FLIR	Forward Looking Infra-Red
GIUK Gap	Greenland-Iceland-United Kingdom Gap
GUGI	*Glavnoye Upravleniye Glubokovodnykh Issledovaniy* (General Directorate of Deep Sea Research)
HARM	High speed Anti-Radiation Missile
HMCS	Her/His Majesty's Canadian Ship
HMS	Her/His Majesty's Ship
ISAR	Imaging Synthetic Aperture Radar
ISTAR	Intelligence Surveillance Target Acquisition and Reconnaissance
ItAF	Italian Air Force
JATO	Jet Assisted Take-Off
JRV	*Jugoslovensko Ratno Vazduhoplovstvo* (Yugoslav Air Force)
LOFAR	Low Frequency Analysis and Recording (passive acoustic sonobuoy)
MAD	Magnetic Anomaly Detector
MARAIRMED	(NATO) Maritime Air Mediterranean command
MARPAT	(Netherlands) Maritime Patrol group
MBFR	Mutually and Balanced Force Reduction negotiations
MDAP	Mutual Defense Assistance Program
MEZ	Missile Engagement Zone
MFG	*Marinefliegergeschwader* (German Naval Air Wing)
MLD	*Marine Luchtvaart Dienst* (Netherlands Naval Air Service)
MNAS	*Moíra Naftikís Synergasías* (Greek Naval Cooperation Squadron)

MNF	Multi-National Force
MPA	Maritime Patrol Aircraft
MRAP	*Morskoy Raketonosnyy Aviatsionnyy Polk* (Soviet Naval Missile Aviation Regiment)
MRR	Maritime Radar Reconnaissance
NAM	Non-Aligned Movement
NAS	1) (British) Naval Air Squadron or 2) (US) Naval Air Station
NATO	North Atlantic Treaty Organization
NORAD	Joint USAF/RCAF North American Air Defence Command
NTDS	Naval Tactical Data System
OCU	(RAF) Operational Conversion Unit
ODKB	*Organizatsiya Dogovora o Kollektivnoy Bezopasnosti* (Collective Security Treaty Organization)
OPLAP DD	*Otdel'naya Protivolodochnaya Aviatsionnaya Polk Dal'nego Deystviya* (Soviet independent long range anti-submarine aviation regiment)
PDC	Practice Depth Charge
PfP	Partnership for Peace
PL MW	*Pułk Lotnictwa Marynarki Wojenne* (Polish Naval Aviation Regiment)
QRA	Quick Reaction Alert
RADAF	Royal Danish Air Force (*Flyvevåbnet*)
RAF	(British) Royal Air Force
RCAF	Royal Canadian Air Force (pre-1968)
RCN	Royal Canadian Navy (pre-1968)
RN	(British) Royal Navy
RNoAF	Royal Norwegian Air Force (*Luftforsvaret*)
SACEUR	(NATO) Supreme Allied Comander Europe
SACLANT	(NATO) Supreme Allied Commander Atlantic
SAG	Surface Action Group
SALT	Strategic Arms Limitation Talks
SAM	Surface-to-Air Missile
SAR	1) Search And Rescue or 2) Synthetic Aperture Radar
SIGINT	Signals Intelligence gathering
Skv	*Skvadron* (RNoAF squadron)
SLOC	Sea Lines of Communication
SOSUS	Sound Surveillance System
Sqn	Squadron
SSB	Fleet ballistic missile submarine

SSBN	Fleet ballistic missile submarine (nuclear powered)
SSG	Guided missile submarine
SSGN	Guided missile submarine (nuclear powered)
SSK	Attack submarine
SSN	Submarine (nuclear powered)
SSR	Soviet Socialist Republic
STOVL	Short Take-Off Vertical Landing
STRKFLTLANT	(NATO) Strike Fleet Atlantic
TACCO	(US Navy) Tactical Coordinator
TARPS	Tactical Airbone Reconnaissance Pod System
TRAM	Target Recognition Multi-sensor
UAR	United Arab Republic
UCAV	Unmanned Combat Air Vehicles
UKADR	United Kingdom Air Defence Region
USAF	United States Air Force
USMC	United States Marine Corps
USN	United States Navy
USS	United States Ship
USSR	Union of Soviet Socialist Republics
VTOL	Vertical Take-Off and Landing
VVS	*Voenno-Vozdushnye Sily* (Soviet Air Force)
VVS-DA	*Voenno-Vozdushnye Sily- Dal'naya Aviatsiya* (Soviet Air Force Long-Range Aviation)
WEU	Western European Union
YEMPA	Yankee East Pacific Missile Patrol Area

APPENDIX 2
Special Arms Systems

Nomenclature of Naval and Maritime Air Units and Systems

'The seas and oceans have for long been a specific area of rivalry and armed conflict, entailing the creation of special arms systems and the birth of forces subsumed under the term "navy".'
            Admiral Sergei Gorshkov, Soviet Navy, 1979

Aviation is a technical subject and it has its own technical language…

US Naval Aircraft
Prior to 1962, US naval aircraft were known by an alpha-numeric designation indicating: [Role] [Manufacturer Sequence Number] [Manufacturer] - [Mark or Variant] 'Aircraft Name'.

Thus, for example, the F3H-2 Demon was a fighter (F), the third type produced by the manufacturer (3), McDonnell (H), Mark 2 (-2). The most common role designators were F for Fighter, A for Attack and P for Patrol; some of the most common manufacturer designation letters were D for Douglas, F for Grumman, H for McDonnell, J for North American and U for Vought. Further suffix letters could be used to indicate specialized sub-types or roles; for example in the Grumman TBM-3W Avenger, the 'W' indicated that the aircraft variant was configured for the early warning role (note – in this particular case the 'M' in TBM denotes that the airframes were manufactured by General Motors).

From 1962 the US Navy adopted the same designation system as the USAF, namely: [Role] - [Role Sequence Number] [Mark or Variant] 'Aircraft Name'.

Thus, for example, the F-4C Phantom was a fighter (F), the fourth fighter type in service (-4), Mark 3 (C). The role designations F, A and P remained as per the previous system. The designations of all aircraft in service with the USN were converted to the new system, so for example the F3H-2 Demon became the F-3B Demon; however, in some cases the manufacturer sequence number was simply used as the role sequence number to simplify the conversion, so for example the F8U-2 Crusader became the F-8B Crusader.

US Naval Aviation Units

The letter 'V' was used by the US Navy to indicate heavier-than-air machines and the letter 'Z' to designate craft that were lighter-than-air. USN squadrons were designated by (V or Z) then [Role Designator] - [Unit Number], using the same role designators as above. Thus, VF-14 indicated the 14th Heavier-than-air fighter squadron. Most US Navy squadrons also have unit nicknames, for example VF-14 are colloquially known as the 'Tophatters'.

US Navy Carrier Air Groups (CVG) were redesignated as Carrier Air Wings (CVW) in 1963.

US Aircraft Carriers

US Navy ships were allocated a hull classification code, giving each vessel a unique identification. This is particularly useful in differentiating ships which share the same name. The classification codes pertaining to aircraft carriers were as follows:

CV	Fleet Carrier
CVA	Fleet Attack Carrier
CVAN	Nuclear-powered Attack Carrier (CVN from 1975)
CVS	Anti-Submarine Carrier

These were followed by a two-digit pennant number for each ship, so, for example the attack carrier USS *Forrestal* had the hull classification code CVA 59.

British Aircraft

Unlike US aircraft, British aircraft were not defined by an alpha-numeric designation but were known by the name bestowed by the manufacturer, followed by an alpha-numeric which indicated role and mark. Thus, for example, the de Havilland Sea Vixen FAW2 indicated that the aircraft was the Mk 2 version of the Sea Vixen fighter, all-weather (FAW). The most common role designators were F for fighter, S for strike and AS for anti-submarine. The designations for French aircraft followed a similar pattern.

Canada used its own designation which was similar format to the post 1962 US Navy system but sometimes differed from it in role sequence number and name. For example, the P-3 Orion was known in Canadian service as the CP-140 Aurora.

British and NATO Aviation Units

British naval aviation units were known as Naval Air Squadrons (NAS) and were designated by a number; for example, 892 NAS operated the Phantom FG1 from HMS *Ark Royal* during the 1970s. German Navy units were *Marinefliegergeschwader* (MFG) and Italian Navy units were *Gruppi*. French naval units were *Flottilles* and designated by an 'F', for example: 21F was a Neptune unit in the 1960s.

British (RAF), Norwegian (RNoAF), Danish (RDAF) and Dutch (RNLAF) units were, respectively Squadron (Sqn), *Skvadron* (Skv), *Eskadrille* (Esk) and Squadron (Sqn).

The Royal Canadian Navy initially reflected the British pattern but adopted a similar system to the US Navy in the early-1950s, while the RCAF used the RAF system throughout.

British and NATO Aircraft Carriers

Royal Navy ships carried a unique pennant number, which was similar in concept to the US hull classification code. The letter 'R' denoted an aircraft carrier. Once again, this is useful in differentiating ships which share the same name: for example, the aircraft carrier HMS *Ark Royal* (1955–79) had the pennant number R09 whereas HMS *Ark Royal* (1985–2011) had the pennant number R07.

The Canadian, Dutch and French navies all used a similar pennant number system to the British.

Soviet Naval Aviation Units

Soviet Naval Aviation (AV-MF – *Aviatsiya Voyenno-Morskogo Flota*) was divided between the Northern, Baltic, Black Sea and Pacific Fleets (*Severnyy, Baltiyskiy, Chernomorskiy* and *Tikhookeanskiy Floty*). Within each Fleet, the air forces were divided into aviation divisions (*aviatsionnyye divizii* – AD) which were subdivided into (typically three) aviation regiments (*aviatsionnyye polki* – AP). Each regiment comprised three aviation squadrons (*aviatsionnyye eskadril'i* – AE), which were broadly similar in size to NATO flying squadrons. Some AV-MF units were also independent (*otdelnyy* – O) of the divisional structure and came under direct command of the respective fleet. Under the Soviet military system, units that had a distinguished service record during World War II were granted the honorary title of Guards (*gvardeyskiy* – Gv) which entitled them to preferential treatment in terms of equipment and support. The titles of AV-MF units reflected the role and type of the formation, for example:

Mine Laying and Torpedo	*minno-torpednyy* (MT)
Reconnaissance	*razvedyvatelnyy* (R)
Naval Missile	*morskoy raketonosnyy* (MR)
Anti-Submarine	*protivolodochnyy* (P)
Maritime Assault	*morskoy shturmovoy* (MSh)
Long Range	*dal'nego deystviya*

For example:

- 5th Naval Missile Aviation Division (*Morskoy Raketonosnyy Aviatsionnyy Diviziya*) was designated the 5-ya MRAD
- 24th Independent Long-Range Anti-Submarine Aviation Regiment (*Otdel'naya Protivolodochnaya Aviatsionnaya Polk Dal'nego Deystviya*) was designated the 24-ye OPLAP DD
- 846th Independent Guards Maritime Assault Aviation Regiment (*Otdel'nyy Gvardeyskiy Morskoy Shturmovoy Aviatsionnyy Polk*) was designated the 846-y OGvMShAP

Soviet Equipment – General

Most Soviet weapons systems were designated within the USSR by Project numbers and were sometimes also given names. However, to ease the identification reporting of Soviet equipment, NATO allocated designations and reporting names to each vessel, or missile or aircraft type.

Soviet Aircraft – NATO codenames

Soviet aircraft were denoted by: [Manufacturer] - [Manufacturer's Sequence Number] [Role or Variant Designation]. For example, the Tu-95RTs was the 95th design (-95) by the Tupolev design bureau (Tu) and was a *Razvedchik-Tseleookazatel* (RTs) reconnaissance target-designator aircraft. The NATO reporting names consisted of a name beginning with 'F' for a fighter type, 'B' for a bomber type, 'H' for a helicopter or 'M' for miscellaneous. A single syllable name denoted a propeller-driven type, while a two-syllable name denoted a jet-powered aircraft; sub variants were designated by a suffix letter. Thus, the NATO reporting name for the Tu-95ST was Bear-D. The main Soviet aircraft types involved in maritime operations during the Cold War were:

SOVIET DESIGNATION	NATO REPORTING NAME	ROLE
Be-12	Mail	MPA/ASW
Be-6	Madge	MPA/ASW
Il-28	Beagle	ASW
Il-38	May	MPA/ASW
Ka-15	Hen	ASW
Ka-25	Hormone	ASW
Ka-27	Helix	ASW
Mil-14	Haze	ASW
Su-17M2	Fitter-D	ASW
Su-22M4	Fitter-K	ASW
Tu-14T	Bosun	ASW
Tu-16	Badger	ASW
Tu-22M	Backfire	ASW
Tu-22R	Blinder-C	ASW
Tu-95	Bear	ASW/Recce
Tu-142	Bear-F	MPA/ASW
Yak-38	Forger	Shipboard Fighter

Soviet Aircraft Carriers

Soviet aircraft carriers carried three-digit pennant numbers, but unlike the fixed system used by NATO, the Soviets periodically changed the pennant numbers for the ships. For example, at different times the aircraft carrier *Minsk* carried numbers 011 and 015, while *Novorossiysk* carried 018 and 137.

Soviet Submarines – NATO codenames

In the NATO nomenclature, Soviet submarines were divided into classes, of which the major Soviet submarine types during the Cold war were:

SOVIET DESIGNATION	NATO REPORTING NAME	TYPE
Project 611	Zulu-class	SSK
Project 613	Whiskey-class	SSK
Project 627	November-class	SSN
Project 629	Golf-class	SSB
Project 633	Romeo-class	SSK
Project 641	Foxtrot-class	SSK
Project 650	Echo I- class	SSGN

Project 651	Juliett-class	SSG
Project 667A	Yankee-class	SSBN
Project 667B	Delta-class	SSBN
Project 671	Victor-class	SSN
Project 675	Echo II-class	SSGN
Project 941	Typhoon-class	SSBN
Project 949	Oscar I-class	SSGN

Appendix 3
A Culture of Innovation And Creativity

Complement of the USS *Forrestal* (CV 59) Over Four Decades

'We must foster a culture of innovation and creativity to stay competitive in a rapidly changing world.'

James V. Forrestal, United States Secretary of State for the Navy, 1944–47.

These four 'snapshots' of the air complement of the USS *Forrestal* show how the equipment of the USN altered and matured over four decades.

RIGHT USS Forrestal in the Mediterranean Sea during the Jordanian Crisis of 1957. The A3D-1 Skywarriors of VAH-1 dominate the aft deck, while FJ-3M Furies of VF-84 prepare to launch from the waist catapults. (US Navy)

ABOVE USS *Forrestal* underway in the Atlantic Ocean on 12 August 1967, just a month after the ship was damaged by a serious fire while operating off the Vietnamese coast. F-4B Phantoms, A-4E Skyhawks, A-6A Intruders, E-2A Hawkeyes, UH-2A Seasprites and an RA-5 Vigilante are all visible on deck. (NARA)

January–July 1957 (Mediterranean Sea)

CVG-1

UNIT	NICKNAME	AIRCRAFT TYPE
VF-14	'Tophatters'	F3H-2N Demon
VF-84	'Vagabonds'	FJ-3M Fury
VA-76	'Spirits'	F9F-8 Cougar
VA-15	'Valions'	AD-6 Skyraider
VAW-12	'Bats'	AD-5W Skyraider
VA(AW)-33	'Nighthawks'	AD-5N Skyraider
VAH-1	'Smokin' Tigers'	A3D-1 Skywarrior
VFP-62	'Fightin' Photos'	F2H-2P Banshee
HU-2	'Fleet Angels'	HUP-2 Retriever

June–September 1967 (Vietnam War)

CVW-17		
UNIT	**NICKNAME**	**AIRCRAFT TYPE**
VF-11	'Red Rippers'	F-4B Phantom II
VF-74	'Be-Devilers'	F-4B Phantom II
VA-46	'Clansmen'	A-4E Skyhawk
VA-106	'Gladiators'	A-4E Skyhawk
VA-65	'Tigers'	A-6A Intruder
RVAH-11	'Checkertails'	RA-5C Vigilante
VAW-123	'Screwtops'	E-2A Hawkeye
VAH-10	'Vikings'	KA-3B Skywarrior
VAW-33	'Knighthawks'	EA-1F Skyraider
HC-2	'Fleet Angels'	UH-2A Seasprite

March–September 1975 (Mediterranean)

CVW-17		
UNIT	**NICKNAME**	**AIRCRAFT TYPE**
VF-11	'Red Rippers'	F-4J Phantom II
VF-74	'Be-Devilers'	F-4J Phantom II
VA-81	'Sunliners'	A-7E Corsair II
VA-83	'Rampagers'	A-7E Corsair II
VA-85	'Black Falcons'	A-6E, KA-6D Intruder
RVAH-7	'Peacemakers of the Fleet'	RA-5C Vigilante
VAQ-134	'Garudas'	EA-6B Prowler
VAW-111	'Gray Berets'	E-2B Hawkeye
HS-3	'Tridents'	SH-3D Sea King

RIGHT USS *Forrestal* in the Mediterranean Sea on 7 August 1975. The aircraft complement looks little different from that of eight years previously, although the F-4J Phantoms and A-6E Intruders are later models than those of 1967. (US Navy)

April–October 1988 (Mediterranean Sea, Indian Ocean)

CVW-6		
UNIT	NICKNAME	AIRCRAFT TYPE
VF-11	'Red Rippers'	F-14A Tomcat
VF-31	'Tomcatters'	F-14A Tomcat
VA-37	'Bulls'	A-7E Corsair II
VA-105	'Gunslingers'	A-7E Corsair II
VA-176	'Thunderbolts'	A-6E, KA-6D Intruder
VAW-122	'Steeljaws'	E-2C Hawkeye
VAQ-132	'Scorpions'	EA-6B Prowler
HS-15	'Red Lions'	SH-3H Sea King
VS-28	'Gamblers'	S-3A Viking

BELOW USS *Forrestal* replenishing in the Mediterranean Sea on 16 June 1988. The typical complement of the 1980s can be seen on deck, including F-14A Tomcats, A-7E Corsairs and A-6E Intruders. A C-2A Greyhound Carrier Onboard Delivery aircraft is parked amidships. (NARA)

BIBLIOGRAPHY

Books

Grossnick, Roy A., *Dictionary of American Naval Aviation Squadrons Volume I, The History of VA, VAH, VAK, VAL, VAP and VFA Squadrons*, Naval Historical Center, 1995

Polmar, Norman, *Aircraft Carriers – A History of Carrier Aviation and its Influence on World Events, Vol II 1946–2006*, Potomac Books, 2008

Roberts, Michael D., *Dictionary of American Naval Aviation Squadrons Volume II, The History of VP, VPB, VP(HL) and VP(AM) Squadrons*, Naval Historical Center, 2000

Spink, Tom, *Pacific Patrol, A History of Patrol Aviation During the Cold War in the Pacific*, Kindle Publishing, 2020

Swanborough, Gordon & Bowes, Peter M., *United State Navy Aircraft since 1911*, Putnam, 1983

Thetford, Owen, *Aircraft of the Royal Air Force since 1918*, Putnam, 1979

Thetford, Owen, *British Naval Aircraft since 1912*, Putnam, 1982

Articles/Papers

Agle, D. C., 'The Gutless Cutlass', *Smithsonian Air & Space Magazine*, August 2012

Allen, R. A., Department of the Navy Carrier Airborne Early Warning Squadron One Hundred and Twenty Three, forwarding of (OPNAVINST 5750.12A) Command History for calendar year 1976, May 1977

Anon, '130,000 Sq Miles Radar-Swept in 1 Hour – by 1 Vector Air Clues', *Royal Air Force Magazine*, Vol 20, No 10, Royal Air Force, July 1966

Anon, 'Delivering Carrier Strike', House of Commons Committee of Public Accounts, January 2018

Anon, 'Exercise Fish Play IV', NATO, September 1959

Anon, 'Kormoran and Penguin Weapon Systems', *Proceedings*, Vol 103/8/894, US Naval Institute, August 1977

Anon, 'Navy Estimates, 1950–51', *Navy Supplementary Estimate, 1949–50*, Volume 472: debated on Wednesday 22 March 1950, Hansard, 1950

Anon, *Navy News*, No 10, March 1955

Anon, *Navy News*, No 172, October 1968

Anon, 'Noi Degli Antisom La Nostra Storia', *Club Degli Antisom*, No 7, 2019

Anon, 'On Thin Ice: UK Defence in the Arctic', House of Commons Defence Select Committee, Hansard, August 2018

Anon, Post War Naval Aviation', Ministero della Difesa, 2018

Anon, 'Proceedings, Twenty-Second Ordinary Session, Second Part, November 1976', Western European Union, 1976

Anon, 'Recent Developments in Soviet Amphibious Forces: An Intelligence Assessment', US Central Intelligence Agency, September 1985

Anon, 'Report by the Standing Group to the North Atlantic Military Council on NATO Exercises 1955', NATO May 1956

Anon, 'Soviet and East European General Purpose Forces Part I – Naval Forces', US Central Intelligence Agency, August 1969

Anon, 'Soviet Antisubmarine Warfare: Current Capabilities and Priorities', US Central Intelligence Agency, September 1972

Anon, 'Soviet Capabilities to Counter US Aircraft Carriers', US Central Intelligence Agency, May 1972

Anon, 'Soviet Military Power, Department of Defense, May 1981

Anon, 'Soviet Navy – Intelligence and Analysis During the Cold War', US Central Intelligence Agency, 2004

Anon, 'Sweden National Intelligence Survey', US NIS Committee, May 1973

Anon, 'The Crowsnest', *The Royal Canadian Navy's Magazine*, Vol 6, No 2, December 1953

Anon, 'The Role of Interdiction at Sea in Soviet Naval Strategy and Operations', US Central Intelligence Agency, February 1978

Anon, 'The Soviet Attack Submarine Force: Evolution and Operations', US Central Intelligence Agency, September 1971

Anon, 'Warsaw Pact Forces Opposite NATO Volume II – The Estimate', US Central Intelligence Agency, January 1979

Arnold, Lt Cdr David R., 'Conflict with Libya: Operational Art In The War On Terrorism', Naval War College, November 1993

Barker, Cdr Edward L., 'Soviet Naval Aviation', *Proceedings*, Vol 87/1/695, US Naval Institute, January 1961

Barlow, Jeffrey G., 'Answering the Call: Carriers in Crises Response Since World War II', *Naval Aviation News*, February 1997

Benbow, Tim, 'British Uses of Aircraft Carriers and Amphibious Ships: 1945–2010', *Corbet Paper No 9*, Kings College London, March 2012

Birkeland, John Olav, 'Maritime airborne intelligence, surveillance and reconnaissance in the High North – The role of anti-submarine warfare – 1945 to the present', University of Glasgow, June 2020

Blanchard, Cdr Ralph W., 'Maritime Air Forces Mediterranean', *Proceedings*, Vol 96/1/803, US Naval Institute, January 1970

Blanchfield, Maj Jody L., 'Bombs Away: A Strategic Analysis of Air Power in a Limited Conflict', United States Army Command and General Staff College, May 2000

Bonnar, Capt Todd (ed.), 'Cutting the Bow Wave: Combined Joint Operations From The Sea Centre Of Excellence', CJOS COE, April 2019

Børresen, Jacob, 'Alliance Naval Strategies and Norway in the Final Years of the Cold War', *Naval War College Review*, Vol. 64: No. 2, Article 7, 2011

Borst, Marco P. J., 'Orions of Spain', *Lockheed Airborne Log Magazine*, Spring 1994

Borst, Marco P. J., 'Preparing for the Future: The Royal Netherlands Navy's Maritime Patrol Group', *VP International Maritime Patrol Aviation Magazine*, April 2001

Borst, Marco P. J., 'The Watching Wolves of Portugal', *VP International Maritime Patrol Aviation Magazine*, June 2000

Broder, John M., 'U.S. Shoots Down 2 Libya Jets; Kadafi Vows to Seek Revenge: F-14s Fired in Self-Defense, Carlucci Says', *Los Angeles Times*, January 1989

Burr, William & Blanton, Thomas S. (ed.), 'The Submarines of October, US and Soviet Naval Encounters During the Cuban Missile Crisis', *National Security Archive Electronic Briefing Book*, No 75, October 2002

Buss, L. H. et al, 'Continental Air Defense Command and North American Air Defense Command, Historical Summary July–December 1957', Directorate of Command History HQ NORAD, April 1958

Campbell-Baldwin, Lt Cdr J., 'Baltops: An Exercise in Alliance Cohesion, Capability, Transparency And Partnership', NATO, July 2021

Campbell, Isabel, 'Canadian Insights into NATO Maritime Strategy, 1949–70: The Role of National and Service Interests', *The Northern Mariner/Le marin du nord*, XXV, No. 3 239–264, July 2015

Campbell, Isabel, 'A Brave New World (1945–1960)', Royal Canadian Navy, March 2018

Childs, Nick, 'Gauging the Gap: The Greenland–Iceland–United Kingdom Gap – A Strategic Assessment', International Institute for Strategic Studies, April 2022

Clarke, J., Davies, D. E. N. & Radford, M. F., 'Review of United Kingdom Radar', *IEEE Transactions on Aerospace and Electronic Systems*, Vol AES-20 No5, September 1984

de Roij, Ronald, 'Service history of the Lockheed P-3C Orion with the MLD', Ronald's Photo Site, undated

Drent, Jan, 'Confrontation in the Sargasso Sea: Soviet Submarines During the Cuban Missile Crisis', *The Northern Mariner/Le marin du nord*, XIII, No. 3, 1–19, July 2003

Dyndal, Gjert Lage, 'Land Based Air Power or Aircraft Carriers? The British debate about Maritime Air Power in the 1960s', University of Glasgow Department of History, 2009

Elliott, Flt Sgt R. W., '543 Squadron History', 543 Squadron, 1964

Ellner, A., 'Carrier Airpower in the Royal Navy during the Cold War: The International Strategic Context', *Defense and Security Analysis*, 22(1), 23–44, 2006

Endicott, Judy G,. 'Raid on Libya: Operation Eldorado Canyon', *Short of War – Major USAF Contingency Operations 1947–1997*, Air University Press, 2000

Garrett, Sara Anne, 'Beyond Submarines: Development and Use of CTOL Aircraft Carriers in the Soviet Union and Russian Federation, 1945-present', Ohio State University, 2011

Garrett, William B., 'The U.S. Navy's Role in the 1956 Suez Crisis', *Naval War College Review*, March 1970, Vol. 22, No. 7, pp. 66-78, March 1970

Getler, Michael, 'US Navy Fighters Shoot Down 2 Libyan Jets', *Washington Post*, August 1981

Goldstein, Lyle J. & Zhukov, Yuri M., 'A Tale of Two Fleets – A Russian Perspective on the 1973 Naval Standoff in the Mediterranean', *Naval War College Review*, Vol. 57: No.2, Article 4, 2004

Gordon, Doug, 'Naval Starfighters – Prowling the Baltic', *Aviation News Incorporating Jets*, August 2016

Grisell, Bengt et al, 'The DC-3 A KTH Project', KTH Department of Underwater Technology Royal Institute of Technology, Stockholm, 2007

Grossnick, Roy A., *Kite Balloons to Airships… The Navy's Lighter-Than-Air Experience*, Documents Government Printing Office, Washington, DC, 1986

Herrick, R. W., 'The Evolution of Soviet Naval Strategy and the Effect of the Revolution in Military Affairs', *US Naval War College Review*, December 1964, Vol. 17, No. 4, pp. 1-52, December 1964

Holler, Roger A., 'The Evolution of the Sonobuoy from World War II to The Cold War', *US Navy Journal of Underwater Acoustics*, January 2014

Jefford, C. G. (Ed), *Royal Air Force Historical Society Journal 33*, RAFHS, 2005

Jorgensen, Lt Cdr Jason T., *The United States Navy's Ability to Counter The Diesel And Nuclear Submarine Threat With Long-Range Antisubmarine Warfare Aircraft*, US Army Command and General Staff College, May 2002

Kassing, David, 'Changes in Soviet Naval Forces', Center for Naval Analyses, November 1976

Kealy, J. D. F. & Russel, E. C., *A History of Canadian Naval Aviation 1918–1962*, The Naval Historical Section Canadian Forces Headquarters Department of National Defence Ottawa, 1965

Keys, James E. Jr, 'Sweden: NATO's Silent Partner', Naval Postgraduate School, December 1984

Kilby, K. T., 'Department of the Navy Fighter Squadron Eleven, Command History for 1978: forwarding of (OPNAV Report 5750-1)', March 1979

Kissinger, Henry A., 'Soviet Naval Threat in the Baltic and North Sea', The White House, November 1971

Kreitler, Walter M., 'The Close Aboard Bastion: A Soviet Ballistic Missile Submarine Development Strategy', Naval Postgraduate School, September 1988

Lee, Vice Adm J. M., 'North Atlantic Military Committee Press Release IMSWM-4-68', January 1968

Magnuson, Warren G. (Chair), 'Soviet Oceans Development', Committee on Commerce and National Ocean Policy Study, US Government, October 1976

Mahon, Michel Kevin, 'Defending Norway and the Northern Flank: Analysis of NATO's Strategic Options', US Naval Postgraduate School, December 1985

Mayne, Richard, 'Cinderella's Star: The CP 140 Aurora and the Evolution of the Royal Canadian Air Force's Modern Long Range Patrol Capability, 1939–2015', *Canadian Military History* Vol 30, Issue 1, 2021

McCormick, Gordon H., 'Stranger than Fiction: Soviet Submarine Operations in Swedish Waters', RAND Corporation, January 1990

McCormick, Gordon H., 'The Soviet Presence in the Mediterranean', RAND Corporation, October 1987

McDonald, Adm David L., 'Carrier Employment Since 1950', *Proceedings*, Vol 90/11/741, US Naval Institute, November 1964

Mosier, Melvin M., 'Soviet Naval Aviation: Its Changing Roles', Defense Intelligence College, August 1985

Mustin, Vice Adm Henry C., 'Maritime Strategy from the Deckplates', *Proceedings*, Vol 112/9/1,003, US Naval Institute, September 1986

Newlin, John, 'Eye to Eye with a Bear', *Smithsonian Air & Space Magazine*, undated

Perkins, Cdr William, 'Alliance Airborne Anti-Submarine Warfare: A Forecast for Maritime Air ASW in the Future Operational Environment', The Joint Air Power Competence Centre, June 2016

Pommer, Cdr E. P., 'Analysis of Soviet Command and Control', US Naval War College, September 1976

Ruiz Palmer, Diego A., 'The Cold War's Long Haul (1949–1989) – A Strategic Odyssey: Constancy of Purpose and Strategy-Making in NATO, 1949–2019', NATO Defense College, 2019

Ruiz Palmer, Diego A., 'A Strategic Odyssey: Constancy of Purpose and Strategy-Making in NATO, 1949–2019', *NATO Defense College Paper 03*, June 2019

Rysworth, Michael, 'The British Fleet Air Arm, 1958', *Proceedings*, Vol 85/3/673, US Naval Institute, March 1959

Say, Cdr Harold Bradley, 'Mainbrace – A Potential Becomes Reality', *Proceedings*, Vol 79/1/599, US Naval Institute, January 1953

Schindler, John R., 'A Dangerous Business: The US Navy and National Reconnaissance During the Cold War – Commemorating Silent Sacrifices', National Security Agency, undated

Shlapak, David A., Gardiner, Samuel & Simons, William, 'Sample Campaign Plans and Staff assessments for NATO's Southern Region', RAND Corporation, August 1989

Sokolsky, Joel J., 'Soviet Naval Aviation and the Northern Flank: Its Military and Political Implications', *US Naval War College Review*, January–February 1981, Vol. 34, No. 1 pp. 34–45, February 1981

Stanton, Don, 'Looking Back at The Cold War And P-3c Anti-Submarine Warfare (ASW) 40 Years Ago', *Przegląd Nauk o Obronności*, 2017

Stöhs, Jeremy, 'Into the Abyss? European Naval Power in the Post-Cold War Era', *Naval War College Review*, Vol. 71 : No. 3 , Article 4, 2018

Struckmann, Capt A., 'North Atlantic Military Committee Press Release MCM-86-66', June 1966

Sünnetçi, Ibrahim, 'Naval Air Command', *Defence Turkey*, Vol 15, Issue 107, 2021

Swartz, Peter M., 'The U.S. Navy in the World (1970-–980): Context for U.S. Navy Capstone Strategies and Concepts', Center for Naval Analyses, December 2011

Tossini, J. Vitor, 'The Chokepoint in Britain's Backyard', *UK Defence Journal*, January 2023

Utz, Curtis A., *Cordon of Steel: the U.S. Navy and the Cuban Missile Crisis*, Naval Historical Center, Department of the Navy, 1993

Vallee, Col G., 'North Atlantic Military Committee Press Release MCM-94-64', Augst 1964

Veitch, Kim W., 'The Warsaw Pact Baltic Fleet', Naval Postgraduate School, September 1984

Watson, Lt Cdr B. W. & Walton, Lt Cdr M. A., 'Okean-1975', *Proceedings*, Vol 102/7/88, US Naval Institute, July 1976

Wettern, Desmond, 'NATO's Northern Flank', *Proceedings*, Vol. 95/7/797, US Naval Institute, January 1970

Whitby, Michael, 'Exceptional Circumstances: Canada's Maritime Response to the Cuban Missile Crisis October-November 1962', Canadian Armed Forces, Directory of History and Heritage, 2022

Whitby, Michael, 'A New Look at Cold War Maritime Defense – The Royal Canadian Navy's Seaward Defence Report and the Threat of the Missile-Firing Submarine, 1955,' *Naval War College Review*, Vol. 73: No. 4, Article 8, 2020

Whiting, Kenneth R., 'Soviet Air Power 1917–1976', Air University, August 1976

Williamson, Corbin, 'We Are Still One Fleet: U.S. Navy Relations with the British, Canadian, and Australian Navies, 1945–1953', Ohio State University, 2015

TNA Files

ADM 239/536, Soviet Naval Air Force 1959
ADM 239/574, Soviet and European Satellite Navies: Order of Battle 1963
AIR 15/952, Soviet Naval Exercise 1962
DEFE 63/12, Soviet Naval Air Force 1964
FCO 46/3973, Soviet Naval Exercises 1984

Websites

https://fas.org/nuke/guide/russia/bomber/tu-95.htm
https://www.scramble.nl/planning/orbats/poland

Index

Page numbers in **bold** refer to illustrations and their captions.

Abraham Lincoln, USS 212
Admiral Kuznetsov (Soviet later Russian aircraft carrier) 206, 265, **265**, 287
Aerospatiale SA365FI Dauphin 248
Afghanistan, Soviet invasion of 177, 178
aircraft carriers 13, 27, 288; *see also* individual navies; individual vessels
airships **51**, 53, 79–80, **84**
air-to-air refuelling **23**, 25, **43**, 45, **160**
Albania 44, 45, 253–254, **253**
Albion, HMS 55, 62, 80, 172
Alekseev A-90 *Orlyonok* (Eaglet) 209
Alekseev Project 903 Lun (Duck) **208**, 209, 212
Allied Command Europe (ACE) Mobile Force (AMF) 120, 121
America, USS 106, **106**, 107, 159–160, 161, **189**, **190**, **191**, **203**, **204**, **210–211**, 213–214, 215–216, **217**, 225, 226–227, **230–231**
Antietam, USS 18, 27
Apollo missions 100
Arab-Israeli War, October 1973: 135
Arctic, the 287, 287–288
Ark Royal, HMS 54, 56, 64, 80, 81, 82, 112, **114–115**, **122**, 134, **134**, 137, **148**, **169**, 172, 174, 193, 220, 227
bombs 15
Arromanches, (French aircraft carrier) 38, 59–60, **59**, 62
artificial intelligence 286
Atlantic Ocean 12, 14
Avro Lancaster 35, 38, **41**
Avro Shackleton 35, **57**, 57–58, 84, 93, **98**, **116–117**, **196**

Badoeng Strait USS **11**

Baku (Soviet aircraft carrier) 205–206
Baltic Sea 19, **42–43**, 114–115, 129–130, 134, 167, 175, 233, 234, 238, 242, 244, 282
Bennington, USS **28**, 40
Beriev Be-6 (Madge) 17
Beriev Be-12 Chayka (seagull) **70**, 71, **184**
Berlin, blockade of 10
Berlin Wall, fall of 231
Blackburn Buccaneer S1: 81, **84**, **85**
Blackburn Firebrand **32**, **32**, 33
Boeing B-17 Fortress **12**, 19
Boeing F-22 Raptor **262–263**
Boeing F/A-18E/F Super Hornet **268**, **289**
Boeing MQ-25 Stingray 269, **270–271**, 286
Boeing P-8A Poseidon 278–279, **284–285**
Boeing PB-1 Fortress 35
Boeing-Vertol UH-46D Sea Knight **216**
Bois de Belleau, (French aircraft carrier) 38
Bon Homme, USS 18
Bonaventure, HMCS **58**, 59, 85, 99, 109, 120, 140
Boxer, USS 18, 79
Breguet BR 1150 Atlantique 115, **119**, **141**, 198, 221, 279
Brezhnev (Soviet aircraft carrier) 206
Brezhnev, Leonid 177–178
Bristol Blenheim **240**
British Aerospace Sea Harrier FRS1: 192–193, **192**, **218–219**, 226
Bulgaria 45, 46, 106, 204
Bulwark, HMS 55, 62, 64, 80, 193

Canadair CF-104 Starfighter **144**, 167
Canadair CP-107 Argus **90**, **101**, **140**, 149, 167, 196
Canadian Armed Forces (CAF) 140, **140**, **144**, 167, 196, 220, 295
Carl Vinson, USS 185
carrier onboard delivery (COD) **205**
Catalina Affair 236, 239
Cavour (Italian aircraft carrier) 274, **283**
Centaur, HMS 55, 80, 112, 118
China 253
Clemenceau, (French aircraft carrier) 87, 118, 160, 167, 199, 221, 274
Cod War 139, 161, 163, **168**, 227, 230–231
Cold War 177–178, 282–283
　aftermath 261–264
　end of 231
　origins and early years 9–13
Commander, Submarine Forces, US Atlantic Fleet (COMSUBLANT) 199
Commander Task Force (CTF) 84, North Atlantic Treaty Organization (NATO) 199
Conference on Security and Co-operation in Europe (CSCE) 123
Consolidated PB4Y Privateer **11**, 19, 38
Consolidated PBY Catalina 16–17, 38, **42–43**, **234**, 236
Constellation, USS 72, 100, 134, **186–187**, 188
Convair P3Y Tradewind 54
Coordinated Air Defense in Mutual Support (CADIMS) concept 203
Coral Sea, USS 17, **80**, 188, 213, 215, 215–216, **225**
Crimea, annexation of 261, 264
Cuban Missile Crisis 95–99, **99**, **101**, **102**
Curtiss SB2C Helldiver 38
Cyprus 166
Czechoslovakian Crisis 243–244

Dassault Étendard IVM 87, **172–173**
Dassault Étendard IVP **93**, **94**, **96**, 199
Dassault *Rafale* 221, 274, **280**
Dassault Super Étendard 167, 169, 199, **200**, **201**
de Havilland Mosquito **248**, 249
de Havilland Sea Hornet 32, **33**

de Havilland Sea Venom 33, **34**, 35, 61
de Havilland Sea Vixen **52–53**, 55, 56
de Havilland Vampire 234
Dédalo (Spanish aircraft carrier) **222–223**, 224
distant early warning (DEW) line 53–54
Dornier Do-24T-3 flying boat 254, **256–257**, 258
Douglas A-3 Sky Warrior 48, **65,** 107–108
Douglas A4 Skyhawk 48, **106**
Douglas AD Skyraider **21**, 22–23, 32, **34**, 76
Douglas DC-3 Dakota **240**, 241
Douglas EA-3B Skywarrior **160**, 216, **217**, 225
Douglas F3D-2 Skyknight 22
Douglas F4D Skyray 48–49, **65**
Douglas F-6A Skyray **100**
Douglas KA-3B Skywarrior AAR tanker **82–83**
Douglas SB2C-5 Helldiver 39
Douglas TA-4J Skyhawk **160**
Dwight D. Eisenhower, USS **129**, **130**, **158–159**, 159, **176**, **181**, 191–192, **218–219**

Eagle, HMS **28,** 29, 32, 39–40, 54, 62, 64, 80, 112, 120, **135**, 137
East Germany (Deutsche Demokratische Republik – DDR) 45, 46, 106, 204
Eire (Republic of Ireland) 245, **246–247**, 248
ekroplans **208**, 209, 212
English Electric Canberra B2: 237
Enterprise, USS 72, 96, 159, 185
Essex, USS 18, 62, 64, 79, 95, 97, 98
Exercise *Baltops* 134
Exercise *Bezopasnost* 265
Exercise *Cold Road* 93
Exercise *Dawn Breeze VII* 118
Exercise *Dawn Patrol* 119, 137, 160, 167, 174
Exercise *Deep Furrow* 119
Exercise *Display Determination* 174, 216
Exercise *Distant Drum* **200**
Exercise *Fairwind VII* 118
Exercise *Fishplay* 64
Exercise *Fishplay VII* 118–119
Exercise *Lime Jug* 137, **138**

Exercise *Mainbrace* 39–40
Exercise *Mariner* 40–41
Exercise *Neptune Journey* 92–93
Exercise *Neptune Strike* **283**
Exercise *Northern Wedding* 172, 207, 224–225
Exercise *Northern Wedding* 86: **206**, 227
Exercise *Ocean Safari* 172, **190**, 202–203, **205**, 224–227, **230–231**
Exercise *Ocean Venture* **210–211**
Exercise *Okean* 174
Exercise *Okean-70* (Ocean-70) 124–125
Exercise *Okean-75*: 154–156
Exercise *Royal Knight* 134
Exercise *Silver Tower* 119–120
Exercise *Strong Express* 172
Exercise *Summerex* 208, 230–231
Exercise *Team Sprit* 207
Exercise *Teamwork* 119–120, 161, 172, 174, **214–215**, **216**, 224–225
Exercise *West Wind* 88: **213**
Exercise *Zapad-81*: 185

Fairey Firefly 29, **30–31**, 32, 37
Fairey Gannet **55**, 56, 82, 84, **88–89**, 249
Falkland War 178, 193–194
Finland 239–245, **240**, **241**, **242–243**, **244**, 264
Fleet Air Arm (FAA)
    800 NAS 81–82, **84**, **218–219**
    801 NAS 81, **85**
    803 NAS 55
    809 NAS **148**
    813 NAS 32, 33
    815 NAS 82
    824 NAS 56, 194
    826 NAS 56
    827 NAS 32
    849 NAS 84, **88–89**, 194
    890 NAS 56
    892 NAS 112
    899 NAS **87**
    early 1950s 29, 32–33, 35
    early 1960s 81–82, 84
    early 1970s 137–139
    mid–late 1950s 55–57
    mid–late 1960s 112–114
    mid–late 1970s 164, 166
    unit designations 296

see also individual aircraft
Foch (French aircraft carrier) 87, 199, **200**, **201**, 216, 221, 227, 274
Forrestal, USS **6**, **26**, **46**, 47, 64, **73**, **77**, 101, 130–131, 172, 190–191, **205**, **213**, **214–215**, 216, **216**, 225, 227, 300–303, **300**, **301**, **302**, **303**
forward operations 202–203, 230–231
Fouga Magister 241, **241**
Franklin D. Roosevelt, USS **15**, 17, **17**, 40, 64, 119, 135, **162–163**
French naval air service (*Aéronavale*) 38, **41**, 59–60, **59**, **60**, **61**, **63**, 87, 88, **93**, **94**, **96**, 109, 115–116, 116, **119**, 121, 167, 169, **170–171**, **172–173**, 199, **200**, **201**, **202**, 221, 274, 279, **280**, 285, 296

Gates Learjet 35AS 244–245, **244**
Gemini missions 100
General Dynamics F-16A 197, **197**, 220
George H. W. Bush, USS 269, **270–271**
Gerald R. Ford, USS **266–267**, 269
Germany 231, 279
Giuseppe Garibaldi (Italian aircraft carrier) 224, 274
Glory, HMS 27
Goodyear ZPG-3W airship **84**
Goodyear ZS2G-1 airship **51**, 53
Gorbachev, Mikhail 177–178
Gorshkov, Admiral Sergey G. 44
Greenland-Iceland-UK Gap (GIUK Gap) 50–51, 127, 133, 203, 208
Greenland-Iceland-United Kingdom Early Warning Barrier 80
Grumman A6 Intruder 76–77, **77**, 79, 107–108, **162–163**
Grumman A-6E Intruder **130**, 132, **166**, 188, **191**, **217**, **228–229**
Grumman AF Guardian **11**, 19
Grumman C-2A Greyhound **205**
Grumman CS2F Tracker 86
Grumman E-2 Hawkeye 79, **80**, **204**
Grumman EA-6B Prowler **165**, 188
Grumman F6F Hellcat 38
Grumman F9F Panther **17**, 21–22
Grumman F9F-8 Cougar **24–25**, 25
Grumman F11F Tiger 49, **49**
Grumman F-14A Tomcat **146**, 175, **176**, **181**, 190, **190**, 191–192,

201–202, **203**, **210–211**, 213, 217, **217**
Grumman HU-16 Albatross 92, **97**, 258, 259
Grumman S-2 Tracker 50, **81**, 87, **132**
Grumman TBM-3E Avenger 35, 37, **37**, **39**
Grumman TBM-3S Avenger **8**, 19, 59
Grumman TBM-3S2 Avenger 92
Grumman TBM-3W Avenger **8**, **10**, 19, 59, **63**, 92

Hancock, USS 101, 130, 159
Handley Page Hastings T5: 161, 163, **168**
Handley Page Victor 114
Harbin H-5: **253**
Hawker Sea Fury 29, **29**, 32, 37
Hawker Sea Hawk **8**, 33, 35, **36**, 59, **63**, **91**
Hawker Siddeley AV-8S Matador **222–223**, 224, **258**, 259
Hawker Siddeley Buccaneer S2: 112, 113, 114, **135**, 137, **138**, **139**, **148**, 153–154, 164, 196
Hawker Siddeley Nimrod MR1: **116–117**, 138–139, **139**
Hawker Siddeley Nimrod MR2: 164, 166, **194**, 195, 220, 279
Hawker Siddeley Sea Vixen 82, **87**, 137
helicopters *see* individual navies: individual types
Hellenic Air Force 141, 142, 169, 199, 224, 282
Hellenic Navy 199
Hermes, HMS 55, 80, 112, **135**, 164, 166, **192**, 193, 220, 225

Ikarus 214: 249, **249**, 251
Illustrious, HMS 27, 40
Illustrious, HMS (ASW carrier) 193, **218–219**, 227
Ilyushin Il-10 Sturmovik 47
Ilyushin Il-28 (Beagle) 15, 242–243, **242–243**, 244, **253**
Ilyushin Il-38 (May) 104, **104–105**, 151, **151**, 156, 158, 174, **184**, 185
Implacable, HMS 27
Independence, USS 47, 96, 120, 130–131, 134, 135, 159, 172, 191–192, 225
Indomitable, HMS 27, 32
Intrepid, USS **24–25**, 64, 100, 130, 134
Invincible, HMS 192, 193
Italy 39, 61, 94, 116, 140–141, 169, 199, 224, 274, 282, **283**, 285, 296

Jet Assisted Take Off (JATO) rockets 25
John F. Kennedy, USS 107, **107**, **131**, 135, **146**, 159, 161, 172, 174, 191–192, 216, 217

Kaman H-2 Seasprite 79
Kamov Ka-15 (Hen) 45
Kamov Ka-25 (Hormone) 103–104, **103, 152, 155**, 157
Kamov Ka-27PL (Helix-A) 179, **180**, 205
Kamov Ka-28: 252
Karel Doorman, HMNLS **8**, 37, 59, 87, **91**, **92**, 116
Kawasaki-Vertol KV107-II-16: 237
Kearsarge, USS 18, 100
Khrushchev, Nikita S. 42, 95, 98
Kiev (Soviet aircraft carrier) **153**, 156–158, 174–175, **174**, 185, 208
Kissinger, Henry 129
Kitty Hawk, USS 72
Korean War 15, 16, **17**, 18, **18**, 21–22, 23, 29, **29**, 32
Kratos XQ-58A Valkyrie **287**
Kuznetsov, Admiral Nikolay G. 14, 42, 44

La Fayette, (French aircraft carrier) 38, 62, 87
Lake Champlain, USS 18, 64, 100
Lebanon 191–192, 199
Leyte, USS 17
Libya **166**, 178, 190–191, **204**, 213–216, 217, **225**
Lim-5P interceptor 106–107
Lim-6bis 106–107, 130, 204
Ling-Temco-Vought (LTV) A-7 Corsair II 108, **110–111**, **129**, 132, **158–159**, 188, **189**
Lockheed CP-140 Aurora 196
Lockheed EP-3B Orion **255**
Lockheed F-104 Starfighter 91, 142, 143, 167, **197**

Lockheed Martin F-35 Lightning **260**, 269, **276–277**, **278**, **279**, **283**, **289**
Lockheed P2 Neptune **15**, 19–20, 25, 35, 38, **38**, 50–51, 59, 94, 95, 108, 141–142, 169, 198
Lockheed P-3 Orion 80, **102**, 108, 115, 133, **133**, 142, **152**, 167, 175, 197, **198**, 220, 221, 224, 259, 279
Lockheed P-3C Orion **145**, 147, 148, 149, 149–151, **212**, 220
Lockheed PV-2 Harpoon 37, 39, **41**
Lockheed S-3A Viking **132**, 133, **213**, 217
Lockheed SP-2H Neptune 87, 90, **93**, **98**, **103**, **142**
Lockheed WV-121 Warning Star 54

McCormick, Admiral Lynde D. 12
McDonnell FH-1 Phantom **16**, 21, 107–108
McDonnell Douglas A-4 Skyhawk **66**, **126**, **128**
McDonnell Douglas AV-8B Harrier **281**, **283**
McDonnell Douglas AV-8S Matador 224, **258**, 259
McDonnell Douglas F-4 Phantom 76, 79, **107**, 112, 114, **114–115**, **134**, **162–163**, **166**, 188
McDonnell Douglas F-4B Phantom **74–75**, **128**
McDonnell Douglas F-4J Phantom 132, 132–133, **188**
McDonnell Douglas F/A-18A Hornet **186–187**, 188
McDonnell Douglas FG1 Phantom **122**, 136, 137, **138**
McDonnell F2H Banshee **18**, 21–22, **58**
McDonnell F3H Demon **47**, 48, **65**, **101**
Magnificent, HMCS 37, 40, 59
Martin AM Mauler 20, **20**, 22–23
Martin P4M Mercator **14**, 19–20
Martin P5M Marlin **16**, 20
Mediterranean Sea 12, 14, 44, 94, 105, 116, 121, 130–131, 133, 142, 148, 159–160, 166, 174, 175, 181, 188, **191**, 199, **200**, 282, **300**, 301, 302, **302**, 303, **303**
Mercury missions 100

Mid-Canada Line 53–54
Midway, USS 17, 40, **151**
Mikoyan MiG-15 (Fagot) 16
Mikoyan-Gurevich MiG-17 (Fresco) 45, 95
Mikoyan-Gurevich MiG-19 (Farmer) 45
Mikoyan-Gurevich MiG-21 (Fishbed) 244
Mikoyan-Gurevich MiG-23 (Flogger) 217
Mikoyan-Gurevich MiG-31BM (Foxhound) 268
Mil Mi-2RM (Hoplite) 130
Mil Mi-4MT (Hound) 46
Mil Mi-14 (Haze) 157, 204, **205**
mines 15
Minsk (Soviet aircraft carrier) 156, **178**
Montreux Convention 44, 105
Moskva, (Soviet helicopter cruiser) 103–104, **103**, **152**
Mutual and Balanced Force Reduction (MBFR) talks 123
Mutual Defense Assistance Program (MDAP) 32, 35

naval aviation, future of 282–288
Nimitz, USS 130, 159, 160, 190–191, 216, 227, **228–229**, 268, **276–277**
North American A-5 Vigilante 73, **73**, 76, 79, 107–108
North American Air Defence Command (NORAD) 54
North American AJ Savage **23**, 25
North American EA-3B Skywarrior **255**
North American F2H-3 Banshee **46**
North American F-100D Super Sabre 92, 167, **169**, 197
North American FJ-2: 25–26
North American FJ-3 Fury 25–26, **46**
North American FJ-4B Fury 48, **48**
North American RA-5C Vigilante **156–157**
North Atlantic Co-operative Council 264
North Atlantic Treaty Organization (NATO) 103, 175, 177, 227, 230, 261
  aircraft carriers 269, 272, 274, 296
  air-defence management system 201–203, 203

air-defence tactics 201–203
anti-submarine tactics 143–151, 175, 199, 201
ASW capabilities 274–275, 278–280, 282
command control 199
Commander Task Force (CTF) 84: 201
commands 12
exercises *see* individual exercises
expansion 264
formation of 10–11
forward operations 202–203, 230–231
Maritime Air Mediterranean command (MARAIRMED) 116
mid–late 1960s 107–109, 112–116
mid–late 1980s 220–221, 224
North Atlantic Co-operative Council 264
Soviet aircraft codenames 297–298
Soviet submarine codenames 298–299
strength 67
unit designations 296
Northrop F-5A **144**
Northrop-Grumman MQ-4C Triton 280, **288**
Northrop-Grumman X-47B UCAS 272, **272–273**
Novorossiysk (Soviet aircraft carrier) **178**, 179
nuclear weapons 9, 13, 48, 55, 73, 76, **76**, 95, 102–103, 120, 206–207

Ocean, HMS 27
Operation *Anadyr* 95
Operation *Aport* 208–209, 227
Operation *Atrina* 208–209, 227
Operation *Attain Document* 213–214
Operation *Blue Bat* 62
Operation *Blue Moon* 95–99, **99**
Operation *Chainsaw* 202
Operation *Deep Water* 64
Operation *El Dorado Canyon* 215–216
Operation *Market* 101
Operation *Neptune Journey* 51
Operation *Prairie Fire* 214–215
Operation *Strikeback* 64, **65**
Operation *Tank Saw* 202
Oriskany, USS 18, 130

Panavia Tornado 197–198, 221, **221**
Philippine Sea, USS 18
Piasecki HUP Retriever **44**
Pittsburgh, USS **44**
Poland 45, 46–47, 106–107, 130, 178, 185, 204, **205**, 231, 282
Portugal 39, 141–142, 169, 221
Prince of Wales, HMS 272, **274**, **286**
Princeton, USS 18, 79
Putin, Vladimir 261, 264

Queen Elizabeth, HMS 272, **279**

Randolph, USS 97, 100
Ranger, USS 47
Reagan, Ronald 178
Republic F-84G Thunderjets 251, 252
Reykjavik Summit, 1986: 178
Richard, USS 18
Romania 45–46, 106, 204
Royal Air Force (RAF) 136, 161, 166, 193, 195–196, 201
  12 Sqn 112, 196
  43 Sqn 112, 137
  120 Sqn **284–285**
  208 Sqn 196
  543 Sqn 114
  anti-surface warfare tactics 153–154
  Coastal Command 35, 57–58, **57**, 84
  see also individual aircraft
Royal Canadian Air Force (RCAF) 85–86, **90**, 279
  Maritime Group 35, 37, **41**
Royal Canadian Maritime Air Command 109
Royal Canadian Navy (RCN) 9, **29**, 37, **58**, 59, 85, **101**, 121, 296
Royal Danish Air Force 38, **42–43**, 92, 114, 167, **169**, 197, **197**, 296
Royal Navy 12, 13, 142, 175, 279
  aircraft carriers 27, 29, 33, 54–55, 80, 112, 137, 164, 192–193, 220, 272, **274**, 284–285, 296
  aircraft designations 295
  commands 27
  doctrine 13
  early 1950s 27, 29, 32–33, 35
  early 1960s 80–82, 84
  early 1970s 137–139
  early 1980s 192–194

Far East Squadron 27
helicopters 56–57, 80, 82, **86**, 164, 166, 193–194, **194**, 220
Home Fleet 27
Mediterranean Fleet 27
mid–late 1950s 54–57
mid–late 1970s 161, 164, 166
UCAVs **286**
unit designations 296
see also individual aircraft; individual vessels
Royal Netherlands Navy **8**, **29**, 37, **41**, 87, **91**, **92**, **93**, 116, 121, 140, **141**, **142**, 167, 198, **198**, 220
Royal Norwegian Air Force 38, 92–93, 114–115, 142, 143, **144**, 149, 167, 197, **197**, 201, 296
Russia 261–264, 283, 287
    aircraft carriers 287
    annexation of Crimea 261, 264
    AV-MF **262**–**263**, 265, **265**, 268–269, 287–288
    invasion of Ukraine 264
    Northern Fleet 275
    Northern Strategic Bastion 275
    submarine force 274–275, 278, 279–280, **284**
    UCAVs 287
    United Strategic Command Northern Fleet 269

SAAB 37 Viggen **232**, **237**, 238, 238–239
SAAB A32A Lansen 234, 235, 236, **236**, **237**, 239
SAAB B-18: 234, **235**
Saratoga, USS 47, **47**, 49, 62, 64, **65**, 99, **114–115**, 131, 159–160, 213, 214
Sea King Improvement Program (SKIP) 140
sea lines of communication (SLOC) 14
Shangri-La, USS **109**
Short Sealand **239**, 249
Short Seamew **56**, 249
Sicily 94
Sikorsky CH-124 Sea King 140, 167, 196
Sikorsky H-3 Sea King 79
Sikorsky HAS1 Sea King 137, 164
Sikorsky HSS-1 Seabat 50, **78**, 79

Sikorsky S-55: 258
Sikorsky SH-3D Sea King **83**, 131, 224, 258–259
Sikorsky SH-3H Sea King ASW **214**–**215**
Sikorsky SH-34J Sea Bat 87
Sikorsky SH-60B Seahawk 190
Sikorsky SH-70B Seahawk 282
Sikorsky Super King Air 200: 248
Soko J-21 Jastreb **250**–**251**, 252
Soko J-22 *Orao* 252, **252**
sonobuoys 143–148, 164, 195, 196
sound surveillance system (SOSUS) sensors 147
Soviet Air Force 15, 68, 70–71; *see also* individual aircraft
Soviet Air Force Long Range Aviation 184–185
Soviet aircraft codenames 297–298
Soviet Navy
    air arm 13, 15, 181, 184–185
    aircraft carriers **153**, 156–158, 174–175, **178**, 179, **179**, 205–206, 298
    anti-submarine tactics 151–152
    anti-surface warfare tactics 152–153
    Baltic Fleet 13, 105, 127, 129, 158–159, 175, 185, 208
    bastion strategy 230, 286
    Black Sea Fleet 13, 15, 104, 127, 129, 156, 174–175, 185, 208
    early 1950s 13–17
    early 1960s 68, 70–72
    early 1970s 124–130, 135
    early 1980s 179–181, 184–185
    enlargement 14–15
    equipment designations 297
    exercises 124–125, 128, 135, 154–156, 174, 208, 230–231
    helicopters 103–104, **103**, 130, **152**, **155**, 157, 179, **180**, 205
    mid–late 1950s 42, 44–45
    mid–late 1960s 102–107
    mid–late 1970s 154–159
    mid–late 1980s 205–209, 212
    Northern Fleet 72, 81, 92, 104, 128, 158, 181, 206–207, 208
    organisation 13
    Pacific Fleet 13, 127, 156, 158, **178**, 179, 181, 184, 207

strength 12, 13, 65, 67, 121, 179–180
submarine force 14, 44, 58, 65, 68, 92, 102–103, 120–121, 127, 149, 180, 207, 208–209, 227, 274, 286, 298–299
threat perception 13–14
threat to Sweden 236, 239
unit designations 296–297
wing in ground effect vehicles **208**, 209, 212
see also individual aircraft
Soviet submarine codenames 298–299
space 100
space-based reconnaissance systems 283, 287
Spain **222–223**, 224, 233, 254–255, **256–257**, 258–259, **258**, 274, **281**, 285
Strategic Arms Limitation Talks (SALT) and treaties 123–124
Sud Aviation Caravelle III 237–238
Sud Aviation SA 321G Super Frelon 116
Sud Aviation SA316B Alouette III **246–247**, 248
Suez Crisis 33, **34**, **60**, 62
Sukhoi Su-15TM (Flagon-F) 207
Sukhoi Su-17M2 (Fitter-D) 159
Sukhoi Su-22M4 (Fitter-K) 204
Sukhoi Su-24M 268
Sukhoi Su-27 (Flanker) 206, 220, 268
Sukhoi Su-33 (Flanker-D) 265, **265**, 268
Super Frelon 169, 199
Supermarine Attacker **28**, 29
Supermarine Scimitar 33, **51,** 55–56
Supermarine Seafire 29, 32
Sweden
Sweden and the Swedish Air Force 232, 233–239, **234**, **235**, **236**, 237, **237,** 264

tactics
  air-defence 201–203
  anti-submarine 143–152, 175, 199, 201
  anti-surface warfare 152–154
Tarawa, USS **22**, 64
Tblisi (Soviet aircraft carrier) 206
Theodore Roosevelt, USS 212, **216**, 227
Theseus, HMS 27, 40

Ticonderoga, USS 100, 213
Triumph, HMS 29
Tupolev Tu-2 (Bat) 15
Tupolev Tu-4 (Bull) 16
Tupolev Tu-14T (Bosun) 15
Tupolev Tu-16 (Badger) **43**, 45, 156, 268
Tupolev Tu-16R (Badger-E) 45, **124**
Tupolev Tu-16K-10 (Badger-C) 71, **72–73**, 127, 185
Tupolev Tu-16KSR (Badger-G) 126–127
Tupolev Tu-16RM (Badger-E) 106, **206**
Tupolev Tu-16RM-2 (Badger-F) **182–183**
Tupolev Tu-22 (Blinder) **166**
Tupolev Tu-22M2 (Backfire-B) **155,** 156, 158, 181, 184, 201–202, 230, 268
Tupolev Tu-22M3 (Backfire-C) 206–207
Tupolev Tu-95: 125, 174
Tupolev Tu-95K (Bear-B) 70–71, 106, 155–156
Tupolev Tu-95K22 (Bear-G) 184–185
Tupolev Tu-95MR (Bear-E) 70
Tupolev Tu-95RT (Bear- D) 68, 70, **70, 146,** 158, **181,** 207
Tupolev Tu-142 (Bear-F) **126,** 151–152, 158, 174, 184–185, **262–263**
Turkish Naval Air Command 141, 142, 169, 199, 224, 282

UCAVs 272, **272–273**, 280, 282, 283, **286, 286,** 287, **287,** 288, **288**
UK Air Defence Region (UKADR) 137
Ukraine, Russian invasion of 264
undersea infrastructure 278
United Arab Republic (UAR) 62
United States of America 9
  air defence identification zone (ADIZ) 207
  nuclear weapons 9, 13, 73, 76, **76,** 102–103
US Marine Corps **17**, 22, 23, 26, **48,** 62, 191, **278**
US Navy 12, 13, 64, 94, 254
  aircraft carrier hull classification code 294–295
  aircraft carriers 13, 17–19, 21, 27, 47–48, 49–50, 72–73, 79, 100, 107–108, 121, 130–131, 159, 175,

185, 212, **266–267**, 269, 273, 284–285
aircraft designations 294–295
airships **51**, 53, 79–80, **84**
casualties and losses 19, 161, 191–192, 216, 225
doctrine 13, 121
early 1950s 17–23, 25–27
early 1960s 72–73, 76–77, 79–80
early 1970s 130–136
early 1980s 185, 188, 190–192
helicopters 50, **78**, 79, **83**, 131, 190, **214–215**, **216**
mid–late 1950s 47–51, 53–54
mid–late 1960s 107–108
mid–late 1970s 159–161
mid–late 1980s 212–217, 220
strength 17–18
submarine force 102
UCAVs 272, **272–273**, **287**, **288**
unit designations 294–295
Update II programme 188, 190
see also individual aircraft; individual vessels
US Navy units
  2nd Fleet 17
  6th Fleet 12, 15, 17, 62, 109, 135, 142, 174, 190–191
  7th Fleet 17
  Airship Early Warning Squadron (ZW-1) 53
USAF, Continental Air Defense Command (CONAD) 53–54
USSR 9–10
  change of leadership, 1980s 177–178
  collapse of 231, 262–263
  invasion of Afghanistan 177, 178
  military power 12
  nuclear weapons 95, 102–103, 206–207
  threat to Finland 239

Valley Forge, USS 18, 79
Vector Logic 201–202
Vengeance HMS 29, 32
Vertol 44A 237
Vertol 107-II-17: 237
Victorious, HMS 27, 54–55, 55, 80, 112, 118
Vietnam War 23, **66**, 100–101, 108, 130, 207, 302
Vought F4U Corsair **22,** 23, **60**
Vought F6U Pirate 21
Vought F7U-3 Cutlass 26, **26**
Vought F-8 Crusader 49, 87, 88, 95–96, **99**, **109**, **131**, **170–171**, 199, **202**, 221

Warrior, HMCS 37
Warsaw Pact 178
  1950s 45–47
  1980s 204
  dissolution 231
  exercises 185
Wasp, USS 18, 40, 62, 64, 99, 100, 120
West Germany 9–10, 60–61, **63**, 90–91, 115–116, **119**, 167, 197–198, 221, **221**
Western European Union (WEU) 149
Westland Lynx 164, 166, 221
Westland Sea King 194, **194,** 220
Westland Wasp 82
Westland Wessex 80, **86**
Westland Whirlwind 56–57, 80, 82, 251, 252
Westland Wyvern 32, 33, **36**

Yakovlev Yak-38 (Forger) **153**, 156–157, **174**, 175, **178**, **179**, 185, 193, 205–206
Yugoslavia **239**, 248–249, **248**, **249**, **250–251**, 251–252, **252**, 262

Acknowledgements

I'm very grateful to Helge Andreassen, Mike Blissett, Chris Bolton, Tim Eastaugh, Norton Hatfield, Jyrki Laukkanen, Tom Spink and Don Stanton for their stories which appear in the book, and which give colour and context to the technical details. Also, my sincere thanks to Eric Bannwarth, Gillian Cooke, Albert Grandolini, Jyrki Laukkanen (again), Phil Jarrett, Tobias Jensen and Stian Roen of the Royal Danish Air Force, Morten Hoel Johansen of the Royal Norwegian Air Force, Sven-Erik Jönsson from FlygHistoria and Graham Pitchfork for providing some wonderful imagery.

A Fairey Gannet AEW3 flies past HMS *Victorious* (R38) in 1967, before the ship was decommissioned that year. The complement of Wessex helicopters, Buccaneers and Sea Vixens are visible on the flight deck. (Pitchfork)